Creative Cash

How To Sell Your Crafts,
Needlework, Designs & Know-How

By Barbara Brabec

Illustrated by Alice Bidwell

Countryside
Books

D1208265

Photo by Carolyn Lane

About the author...

Barbara Brabec, former editor of *Artisan Crafts* magazine, is a free-lance writer whose columns appear regularly in *Crafts* and *Creative Crafts* magazines. Her articles have sold to *Better Homes and Gardens, Needlecraft for Today,* and other consumer publications. She also sells her original needlework and craft designs.

Barbara's interest in crafts, which began as a hobby, eventually led her and her husband to start *Artisan Crafts,* a venture that kept her very busy for five years. During this period she compiled two editions of a national crafts directory called *Guide to the Craft World,* and created *Craftspirit '76,* a special Bicentennial series that received official recognition from the Bicentennial Administration.

Barbara has been married since 1961 to Harry Brabec, a professional musician and crafts show producer whose work has taken them all over America and Europe. Her favorite leisure-time activities include reading, needlework, Maori handweaving and ethnic cooking.

Cover needlework designed and stitched by the author.

Cover created by Samata Design Group, Ltd.

Library of Congress Data
Brabec, Barbara
    Creative Cash: How to Sell
    Your Crafts, Needlework, Designs & Know-how.
    1. Crafts — How to sell 2. Income opportunities —
      Small business
    I. Title
      LC No. 79-64792
ISBN 0-88453-017-5

Countryside Books

A. B. Morse Company
200 James Street
Barrington, Illinois 60010

This book is for my mother, Marcella Schaumburg,
who convinced me many years ago that
I could do anything I really wanted to do;
And for my husband, Harry,
who inspired this dedication when he said,
"Behind most successful women you'll find
an encouraging mother and an amazed husband."

Acknowledgements

Perhaps the only people who read the acknowledgement page of a book are the ones who hope to find their name mentioned there with flowery thanks.

It is impossible, of course, to name everyone who shared precious time, helpful information, and wise advice, but their valuable contribution to *Creative Cash* has at least been acknowledged in the text and, in most cases, the Resource Chapter as well. Thank you, everyone! My special thanks to Marilyn Heise, editor of *The Working Craftsman,* who recommended me to the publisher who wanted this book written.

I am especially grateful to my husband, who offered encouragement and advice, yet never tried to influence the direction or content of this book. In fact, right from the start, Harry nicknamed me ''Agatha'' (after the great mystery writer, of course), and then went about with a grin telling everyone that what I was writing was a mystery to him.

Contents

Introduction

As a word, "creative" is *in* these days, but like many homemakers, it's a bit overworked.

For example, we speak of creative cooking, creative living, creative gardening, and creative crafts — things that are possible only because we have creative minds. Now, at the risk of exhausting a word that is already tired, I give you "creative cash," a new phrase coined for the special kind of money you can make by utilizing two of your most natural resources: your designing mind and talented hands.

Of course you have a designing mind! All women do. And no woman could run an efficient home, raise children, or hold down a job unless she possessed gifted hands. I suppose there will always be women who claim they have no real talent for anything, but just for the record, I didn't write this book for them. I wrote it for YOU and everyone like you who KNOWS she has a special talent or ability — but DOESN'T KNOW how to use it to make money.

This book tells you how to earn your share of today's "creative cash market," simply by doing things you enjoy most, and may already do best. It's filled with inspiring success stories about real people who have generously shared (without thought of monetary gain) their secrets for success, their expert advice, their best how-to-sell techniques and ideas. Perhaps you will find your counterpart somewhere in the pages of this book, perhaps not, but you will surely find valuable information, usable ideas, and a host of reasons why you should do something about your long-dreamed-of ideas.

Although this manual has been written with homemakers in mind, it is *not* for women only. In fact, any man with an artistic ability or serious hobbycraft interest would do well to read it. In an age when men are needlepointing and women are blacksmithing, who among us would dare to hang masculine or feminine tags on things like talent, ingenuity and creativity? Harry and I are only one of perhaps thousands of husband-and-wife teams who have recently been caught up in America's growing crafts movement, and whether you realize it or not, you may already be one-half of a potential home business just waiting to be born.

Of course, you don't have to be married in order to make money from your arts and crafts, nor do you have to be a certain age, or live in any particular part of the country. If you have a good product, a market awaits it somewhere. This book shows you how to find it.

One of the most important features of *Creative Cash* is its resource chapter, the last one in the book. A quick look at it will reveal the names and addresses of many interesting art and craft periodicals and organizations, plus sources for numerous craft-related publications, services, and products. In addition, the complete address is given for all government agencies, publishers, manufacturers, and other businesses mentioned in the book's text. But perhaps the best listing of all is the one that gives the addresses of the many individuals who contributed to the text of *Creative Cash*. They have been included to facilitate an easy exchange of correspondence between creative people with similar interests.

In all, there are more than 300 listings to explore in the Resource Chapter, a fact that makes *Creative Cash* not just a good marketing manual, but also an invaluable directory of information sources previously unknown to the average crafts-person or needleworker.

After you have put some of the information and ideas in this book to work for you, I hope you will write to me in care of the publisher, and tell me about your accomplishments in the field of arts and crafts, as well as any unusual problems you may have encountered along the way. Although I could not answer every letter received, I would read each of them with all the eagerness of a child at Christmas. Nothing pleases me as much as an interesting letter, and with enough mail from the readers of *Creative Cash,* I'd soon have sufficient material for a sequel to this book — which would benefit you, please me and my publisher, and further amaze my husband.

Behind the Scenes

When I first sat down to write this book, my husband offered encouragement and a little wise (though unsolicited) guidance.

"Just remember," he warned in his best advice-giving voice, "you're not writing for yourself, you're writing for your readers."

He was tactfully trying to tell me that most people aren't like me, don't think like me, and are certainly not going to see everything my way. True, I am too competitive, I hate to lose, and I always want the last word, and, admittedly, that kind of attitude could certainly bias a book if not held in check. So, with Harry's remark ringing in my ears, I laid the framework for this book by writing dozens of letters to special contacts in the crafts field, determined to reflect not just my ideas and opinions, but the combined knowledge and experience of many talented and imaginative people in America today.

10 I asked for comments from individuals both famous and little known; sought advice from professionals and amateurs alike; and queried homemakers, craftspeople, artists, hobbyists, designers, teachers, writers, shop owners, magazine editors, store buyers, craft suppliers, manufacturers, publishers, and others whose categories escape me now. For days and days my typewriter clattered like a machine gun gone berserk, and for weeks thereafter my mailbox spilled over with some of the most fascinating mail it has ever yielded.

What did all this typewriting accomplish? You could say that I've let my fingers do the walking for you. By sharing the enlightening answers I received to questions both brilliant and stupid, I've saved you a lot of time and legwork.

I hasten to add, however, that this book is built on much more than just a few dozen letters written over a period of several weeks. Success, especially in the field of crafts, doesn't come overnight in a gift-wrapped package, and comprehensive books aren't written overnight either.

This one is the result of almost ten years of diligent work and concentrated effort on my part, and an unimaginable amount of patience on the part of my husband. For five years Harry and I published a quarterly magazine called *Artisan Crafts,* whose presence in our home not only disrupted normal day-to-day living, but eventually came to dominate our lives. It was, sad to say, rather like inviting to dinner a friend who refused to leave when the evening was over. We ceased publication in late 1976, having learned by then what it really means to have a full-time publishing business in one's home, and how difficult it can sometimes be to realize a true profit from one's productive efforts. These days we are quite content to let *Artisan Crafts* rest on its reprints while we pursue other avenues of endeavor.

As regards Harry's patience, let me say that not only did he have to live through the five-year period mentioned above — which meant putting up with an ill-kept house and hastily prepared meals, to say nothing of an often nervous, over-worked, and disheveled wife — but he also had to go through what countless husbands everywhere are no doubt just encountering: his wife's search for something special to do with her free time.

Looking back, I now see that while I was happily experimenting with first one craft and then another in an attempt to develop new abilities, Harry was patiently tolerating such aggravations as glitter in his soup, yarn clippings in bed, and ceramic chips in the shag rug — the latter often discovered at midnight by surprised bare feet, on what might otherwise have been a silent run to the refrigerator. At one time or another in recent years, he has also been assaulted with the bad smell of lacquer thinner still in the air at mealtime, zonked on the nose by flying wood chips, and virtually overwhelmed by thirty-foot macrame cords being flung in frenzy. Now you know why he encouraged me to write this book. He knew it would keep me out of mischief for months.

The point of my story is simply this: Most people who are totally involved in crafts today, on either a part- or full-time basis, did not start out with that thought in mind. Like me, many began as hobbyists, looking for something special to do in their spare time, and one thing just led to another. As you will soon see from the interesting success stories herein of other men and women in America, this kind of natural progression from hobby to profession is a commonplace occurrence today. In fact, where crafts are concerned, one thing always leads to another, and, although there is always a beginning to everyone's craft life, those of us who are seriously involved with crafts can see no end in sight to the things we want to do in the future. And that is precisely why the word "crafts" means excitement to so many people today, young and old alike!

Each person has some unique talent or ability that makes him special, including YOU. A serious involvement in some creative endeavor could bring wonderful and surprising changes into your life, but you will never know where your talent and ideas might take you if you don't give them a chance to grow and develop.

Don't you agree the possibilities ought to be explored?

*Arts and crafts have not only become household words in recent years,
but in many cases have actually taken over entire houses in the process.
Activities such as those depicted in our imaginary cutaway house often
generate a considerable amount of extra income for a family.*

1

So Many Crafts, So Many Possibilities

Have you ever thought about the amazing variety of art and craft activities that take place daily in every room of the American home? More important, have you considered the amount of money such activities are generating for some people?

Today, in living rooms that share space with spinning wheels and looms, yarns are spun and weavings are done for sale through galleries and shops. In the corners of rooms once used only for dining will now be found cozy little offices where creative souls are writing, designing, and developing all kinds of crafty ideas for the marketplace. People everywhere are no longer just sleeping in bedrooms, but sewing, quilting, and needlepointing as well.

Recreation rooms used to be a place where Dad disappeared to shoot pool, or the kids went to play ping pong. Now, the whole family is apt to go there after dinner to make handcrafts that will be sold at craft fairs, through a mail order catalog, or perhaps in a home-based studio-workshop. And do you realize how many cars in America are without a roof over their hoods because their garages have been converted into workshops for crafts like ceramics, woodworking, metalworking, or stained glass?

And the kitchen? Ah yes, the kitchen. Granted, there's no time left to cook anymore, what with all this craft busyness going on, but all manner of magical things are likely to emerge from this room to end up for sale at church bazaars or local shops. It's hard to believe the number of ordinary kitchen products that are currently being used as raw materials for arts and crafts projects. Take salt and flour, for example. Once sifted to make cakes, these ingredients are now mixed to make ornaments for the Christmas tree. And bread dough isn't something you bake and eat, it's something you shape and paint in pretty colors to hang on the wall. Macaroni that once stuck in the pan now sticks to a variety of box tops and containers. Apples are carved into dolls, seeds are dried to make beads, and eggs have become a favorite craft medium for thousands of devoted "eggers." Once served sunny-side up to contented husbands everywhere, eggs are often served scrambled these days because that's the only way to keep the shell intact for decorating.

Finally we come to the smallest room in the house, only to discover that even the bathroom does double duty as a workroom from time to time. I'll bet more than one person goes to the bathroom daily to dye yarn or dip batik, and it's anybody's guess as to where the finished products go.

That leaves us with the back yard and it, too, has become a working area for many people who use the sun as a tool to dry driftwood and weeds for decorative wall plaques, flowers for sachet packets, or herbs for gourmet cooking. Still others make sun prints or "weather" their growing collection of barn siding.

What does all this light-hearted patter prove? Simply that "arts and crafts" have not only become household words in recent years, but in many cases have actually taken over entire houses in the process. Don't you agree that anything that takes control of one's home at least ought to contribute to its support? But how? Wouldn't it be wonderful if you could wave a wand over your home and magically transform all its *busyness* into *business*?

Perhaps this kind of magic isn't as impossible as it seems. Although I'm no magician, I've certainly pulled more than one trick out of my sleeve in the past, and I'll bet you have, too. In effect, this book is your trick-up-the-sleeve, your key to success in the marketing world of arts and crafts. Once you've read it, I predict you'll be so inspired about your ideas and the possibilities that exist for bringing them to fruition that you won't want to sleep for weeks, let alone cook or clean house. Until now you may have lacked the incentive or know-how to get your ideas off the ground, but no more. *Creative Cash* shows you how others have achieved success in arts and crafts businesses, and it will convince you that your dreams can be realized too.

Your "Ladder of Success"

Have you ever wondered where you stand in today's art/craft world, as compared to others? If so, you might try thinking about your position in terms of standing on a ladder. Imagine that the first rung is for all the beginners in this field. (And for now, let's think of "beginners" as being only those who are nonsellers, since they may already be professionals when talent and ability are considered.)

The top rung of our make-believe ladder would naturally represent the full-time professional sellers — the artists, craftsmen, designers, teachers, writers, shopowners, and others who have become successful in their chosen fields — those who have "made it to the top of the ladder."

Between the top and bottom rungs, then, are the many different steps to be taken on the way up. You and only you know where you stand right now, and where you would eventually like to be. The real purpose of this book is to get you moving toward the goal you want to reach, whether it's halfway up the ladder or all the way to the top. Once you have started the climb it will be up to you to find the rung that's right for you and your individual lifestyle.

As you begin, let me remind you of two things. First, anything worth doing is worth doing well. (Yes, it's an old saying, but it's still a good one.) Second, it always pays to be professional in your approach to anything, especially selling. If you get started on the right foot, it will be easy to keep moving forward in a professional manner, and soon you will find yourself reaching for new heights on your own ladder of success.

Who Are You and What Do You Do?

If someone were to ask you that question, what would you say? Before you can properly promote or advertise yourself or your products, you must know the answer to this question. You should be able to sum it up in a few words, such as: "I am a designer who creates patterns for toymakers," or, "I am an artist who specializes in miniature paintings," or, "I am a woodworker who designs and makes decorative objects," etc. Once you have decided who and what you are, it will be easier to explain it to others, and especially useful when you sit down to write your first classified ad, press release, or copy for your brochure or catalog.

In writing this book, I tried to visualize its readers and the thousands of things they were making and hoping to sell. I finally gave up, of course, because that is as impossible as trying to define the words "artist" or "craftsman."

My husband once said that the definition of a craftsman cannot be put down as simply as you would the 12 points of the Scout law (a scout is trustworthy, loyal, helpful, etc.) and he was right. Still, many people take delight in trying to define the word, such as Raymond Martell, a jeweler-

craftsman from New Jersey who once said, "If a person thinks of himself as a craftsman, then he or she *is* a craftsman." Someone else remarked that a craftsman is someone who loves to talk to you with his hands, and another observed that a craftsman is someone who wouldn't sell an elegant hand-woven wall hanging for less than $500, but would give it to a friend without hesitation.

If you prefer to be more technical, you can consider the following broad categories that define individuals who pursue crafts on a vocational basis. These definitions emerged from a recent planning study sponsored by the National Endowment for the Arts:

15

ARTIST CRAFTSMAN — A craftsman who works to his own design concept and makes one-of-a-kind objects.

DESIGNER CRAFTSMAN — A craftsman who works to his own design concept and makes prototypes for small and large industry.

PRODUCTION CRAFTSMAN — A craftsman who works to his own design concept, or to the design concept of another individual, period, or group, and who makes multiples of an object.

ARTISAN — A craftsman who works to the design concept of another individual, period, or group, and who makes one-of-a-kind, prototype, or multiple objects.

Further classifications were also made by the study group, based on the style of design a craftsman uses — contemporary, ethnic/folk, traditional, restoration crafts, and crafts made in industry.

In this book, I have generally used the term "craftsmen" when speaking about men and women who have made crafts a part- or full-time profession, and "craftspeople" when referring to a group of people whose interests and approaches to crafts may be quite varied. Those who read art and craft periodicals will note that the terms "artists" and "artisans" are often used as substitutes for "craftsmen" and "craftspeople"; thus, my use of the word "artist" does not necessarily mean one who paints, any more than the word "artisan" suggests a lack of artistic ability (as implied by the NEA planning study above).

While I have always thought of myself as a craftsman, I realize that many women cannot abide the word. Once, when this topic was being discussed at length in *Artisan Crafts,* a Tennessee toymaker offered a perfect solution to the whole problem. In a charming two-line poem submitted for publication, Jude Martin said, simply, *"I is... a CraftsMs."*

If you occasionally feel left out of a discussion when I use certain terms to describe a group of creative men and women, please forgive me and try to remember that it is often difficult for today's writers and magazine editors to find the one word that will properly describe everyone, without offending or excluding anyone. As I said before, there are so many crafts and so many possibilities.

Enough chatter! Let's get down to work. If you have already begun to sell your crafts or needlework, the next chapter will help you gain perspective on the manner in which you first entered the marketplace, and point out a few things you may have overlooked in the beginning. If you are not yet selling your work, perhaps you have reached the stage where you are beginning to wonder what you're going to do with everything you're making. If so, you may soon have to make a decision: either stop producing, or start selling!

2

Stop Producing Or Start Selling!

If you're a prolific producer who hasn't yet begun to sell, you'll know exactly what I mean when I say that my mother's home is decorated in "early Barbara." And many of my friends have things made in that period before I began to sell, just as your friends probably have your handmade gifts in their homes. Isn't it logical to start selling when you're producing so much you can't give it all away? It seemed that way to me several years ago when I was going through this phase.

Although the idea of earning extra money was appealing to me, my real motivation to sell came when I looked around, saw all the stuff piling up, and heard my husband say, "It's nice, but what do you plan to do with all of it?" Like so many people before and after me, I had reached the "crafts saturation point." I simply had to stop producing or start selling. Of course, stopping was out of the question because I was having too much fun. Thus I began to sell in order to make room for all the new things coming, and also to earn enough money to buy the supplies and materials needed to make them. (Does this story sound familiar?)

Like all beginners, I soon learned that making things and selling things are two different things entirely. It's rather like the fisherman who, when asked if the fishin' was good, replied: "Oh, the fishin' is easy, it's the *catchin'* that's hard."

Is there some special secret to selling? Rosemaler Carolyn Handy of Illinois has an answer to that question. She thinks selling is "nothing more than having a product that is attractive, well executed, priced right, available, and presided over by the craftsman who is happy to serve the customer." But she also says it is amazing how many people, trying to sell, fail to observe any of the above. "The creative person, if he is to find homes for his creations, must meet the consumer halfway. As in any new area of endeavor, the early days of selling a craft can be trying, and it does take time to find the best places to sell, learn what the public wants, and decide who and what your customer is."

Another woman wrote, "Selling one's work is a natural step in looking for a response to one's creative efforts." She also told me she entered her first craft show a good distance from home because she "sure didn't want to take a chance locally where those I knew could see me fail." Of course, she didn't fail, but this lack of confidence on the part of beginning sellers is easy to understand. For every person who has immediate success with selling, there are surely hundreds of others who have to struggle for it on a trial-and-error basis.

The Importance of Quality

This is as good a time as any to begin harping on something that is always going to be important to your selling success, whether you are trying to

17

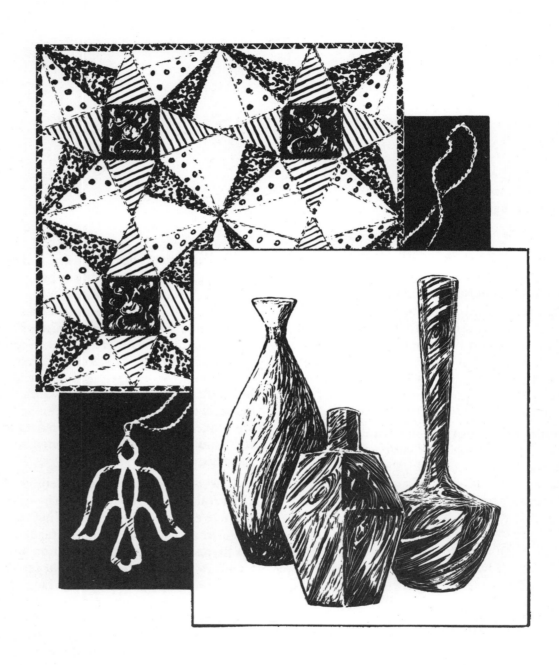

18

market handcrafts, needlework, designs, publications, services, or know-how. That something is QUALITY. Remember when I said that if you had a good product, there was a market for it somewhere? The key word, of course, is "good."

What constitutes quality in crafts and needlework? You'll get varying answers from different people, just as you would if you were to ask them if something was expensive. That which seems expensive to me might be cheap at half the price to you, or vice versa. Thus, the word "quality" will mean one thing to a New York gallery owner who features designer crafts, and something else entirely to a small town shop owner who sells a variety of local handmades. My dictionary defines quality as "a peculiar and essential character; an inherent feature; superiority in kind; a distinguishing attribute," and these are certainly good thoughts to keep in mind when you are creating anything for sale.

If you have any doubts about the quality or salability of your work, look around and see how it compares to the work of others. Visit craft shows, browse in fine gift and craft shops, and make a study of mail-order catalogs. By all means, read several books and magazines pertaining to your field of interest, giving special attention to the advertisements and photographs. Soon you will begin to understand what the word "quality" means to various buyers, and in the process gain a better idea as to where your particular products belong in today's marketplace.

I must inject something at this point. I respect all forms of creativity, whether they are called art, craft, handicraft, hobby, or profession, and I would never deliberately imply that what one person does is any less important or special than what another might do, since anyone who has discovered the pleasure of working with his hands is a very special person indeed. However — and this is a big however — there are certain handmade products that have little, if any, commerical value, regardless of how well they are made. If you are currently making things from kits, or creating scrap crafts and other items that might be described by some as "artsy-craftsy," don't be surprised to find there are few markets for them outside the range of church bazaars, home boutiques, and homemaker fairs.

But look at it this way: If you are clever enough to create charming handmades out of scraps or hobbycraft materials, then it follows that you are also clever enough to make some real, honest-to-goodness handcrafts from more durable materials. And the list of acceptable materials is endless, as anyone can see by noting the wide variety of items for sale at any quality craft shop or fair.

Needleworkers should also realize that no commercial market exists for finished needlework made from a kit. I'm not downgrading needlework kits by any means — merely stating that today's sophisticated shop owners have no desire to purchase *for resale* any item that is not originally designed, and this applies to both needlework and crafts. But this does not mean that needleworkers have no markets for their work, only *different* ones. In a letter, Connie A. Stano, owner of The Greenfield Needlewomen in Greenfield, Indiana, stated, "A woman can, indeed, make a career from needlework, but it takes great motivation, not to mention experience and some creative ability. If the needlewoman is willing to work by herself in her own community, it would be possible to be very busy today merely by running an ad in her local paper offering to finish kits, or frame or design custom pieces."

Your work (needlework or crafts) may be the best of its kind, or it may be not nearly as good as you have been led to believe. While it is great to receive compliments from friends and relatives, their praise is only an indication that your work will sell, not a guarantee. Always remember that the marketplace is the only place to test the quality and salability of your work. If it's good and you are reaching the right market, your work will sell. It's as simple as that. Not so simple, however, is the task of finding the right market for your product and the best way to sell it. This is what is known as "market research," and every successful seller understands its importance.

Market Research

Doing market research is rather like being a

19

detective, in that you must turn up a few clues in order to solve the mystery. To take some of the mystery out of selling, you must first discover who your potential customers are, and how large your potential market is. While doing this you should also be considering the various selling methods open to you (direct selling at shows or by mail order, indirect selling in shops or through a sales representative, etc.) and whether, in fact, you have a salable product at all.

To begin, ask yourself a few questions. For instance, do people really need what you're making? If so, how many people? What kind of people? Where do they live? Can they easily get what you make from someone else, perhaps at a lower price than what you would have to charge to make a profit? Or, if people don't really need your product, do you think they might simply want it? For example, no one really needs another ceramic coffee mug, more handwoven place mats, or three more pictures for the wall, but there will always be people who want such things. In fact, most people today buy crafts not because they need them, but simply because they want them, and prefer them to mass-produced merchandise.

Once you have determined who your customers will be, you must tailor your marketing appeal and your product to that group. It will always be the market itself that determines your product, and nothing will kill the success of a product faster than its being the wrong product for the intended audience. Your success in selling — and thus your profit — will largely depend on how well you have done your market research. Having the best product in the world is useless unless you also have an interested market for it, *and* a way to reach that market.

Most craftspeople make a habit of producing what they want to produce; then, when it's finished, they try to find a buyer for it. That's backward thinking, especially if you really want to make money. First, you should find out what the marketplace wants or needs; then, try to produce it. Otherwise, you'll have to create your own market, and sometimes that can be very difficult.

After you have decided which products you are going to sell, and to whom, you must give serious thought to the production methods you will use and be prepared to handle a large order if it comes your way. Will you be specializing in one-of-a-kind creations, making multiples of one or more items, or working as a small manufacturer using assembly-line techniques? If you will be a small manufacturer, will you plan to do everyting yourself or hire outside help?

Qualities Needed for Success

It's true that market research is not required if you only want to make what *you* want to make, and sell just for the fun of selling. But if you're serious about selling — and making a profit — you should make every effort to enter the crafts marketplace in as professional a manner as possible. Why? Because there is a great deal of competition in this field, and to succeed you must know what you're doing. Besides, there are already too many amateurs trying to sell these days, and too many truly talented people who will not succeed in their attempt at business simply because they failed to grasp the importance of such things as market research, record keeping, and the promotion of one's business. Colette Wolff, a successful New York toy designer, agrees.

"The craft field doesn't need any more amateurs," she says. "Granted, everyone has to start somewhere, and everyone is an amateur at the beginning. But to become a craft professional, in the best sense, with something to contribute and with something to express — that's for the FEW, not the many. There's a big difference between the hobbyist and the professional. It's an attitude, it's intention, it's point of view, it's the ability to conceptualize, it's the grasp of techniques required to produce, and it's the ability to organize and understand business practices. It's also a level of understanding about aesthetic values. To be a professional, a person has to be a self-starter. Disciplined. Industrious. I would never encourage anyone to become a craftsman just because he's creative."

True, creativity alone is not enough to insure success in business, but it's a good place to start. "Creativity and enthusiasm," says Sybil Harp,

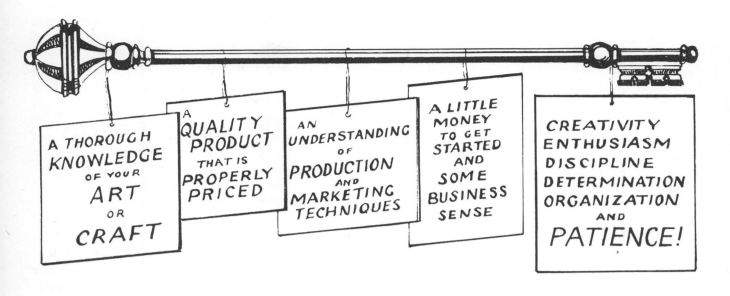

A THOROUGH KNOWLEDGE OF YOUR ART OR CRAFT

A QUALITY PRODUCT THAT IS PROPERLY PRICED

AN UNDERSTANDING OF PRODUCTION AND MARKETING TECHNIQUES

A LITTLE MONEY TO GET STARTED AND SOME BUSINESS SENSE

CREATIVITY ENTHUSIASM DISCIPLINE DETERMINATION ORGANIZATION AND PATIENCE!

WHAT YOU NEED TO MAKE THE PROGRESSION
FROM HOBBY TO PROFESSION

editor of *Creative Crafts* magazine, "are two absolutely essential qualities that one must possess to be successful in the craft field. But they are not enough. Since crafts are also a business, some business sense, or at least an understanding of basic business principles, is essential, as is the know-how to translate all that creativity and enthusiasm for crafts into services that will be marketable to craft manufacturers, merchandisers, publishers, organizations, educators, and others commercially involved in crafts."

Sybil also points out that the craft industry is full of individuals whose interest in crafts has advanced from hobby to career status. "My own observations over the past ten years have convinced me that the most effective and successful people in crafts today are those who began as hobbyists," she says. "They are the people with originality and enthusiasm who love the field more for itself than for its lucrative possibilities."

By heeding the words of experts such as Sybil Harp and Colette Wolff, and following the professional guidelines offered by others in this book,

you will automatically place yourself several jumps ahead of many so-called professionals today. Not only will you increase your chances for success, but you will greatly enhance the possibilities of *making a profit* from your art or craft business.

Blending Business into Your Lifestyle

Most people think in terms of making a profit when they start selling their artwork, needlework, or crafts, but not everyone sells just for the money. The need for extra income is only part of the picture for many women today who are simply searching for something special to do that will make them feel more satisfied as individuals. In fact, my conversations and correspondence with married women, particularly those between the ages of 40 and 50, often revealed restless feelings about this.

Most women agreed there should be more to life than just having a nice husband, home, and family. They thought there ought to be something special just for them, something that would let them have a private and fulfilling life of their own — within the confines of marriage, of course. Using their artistic talents and creative abilities seemed the most natural way for them to go, because an involvement in this field could easily be worked into their normal day-to-day routine of homemaking and family responsibilities. But these same women were quick to point out that they didn't want to do anything that would seriously disrupt normal family living, or create unnecessary problems for, or with, their husbands. They just wanted to do something creative that would prove satisfying and perhaps profitable as well, reasoning that this would make them better people/wives/mothers. I couldn't agree more.

It was sheer boredom that sparked the creative streak in Joni DeBus of Riverside, California. When she was about 40, she suddenly realized she was a very bored housewife. "Our children were getting older and would soon be finished with school," Joni remembers, "and when I looked at my friends whose children were already gone, I saw the void in their lives." It was a void Joni planned to AVOID in her own life.

Handthrown pottery was something she had always wanted to do, so she signed up for a class at a local art center. That did it. That class changed her whole life. Today Joni is selling 800 to 1200 wind chimes a month and turning away new accounts because she can't produce enough to keep up with the demand for her work — even with the help of four or five part-time workers.

Of course, the development of Joni's business wasn't as easy as that sentence makes it sound, although it did grow right from the start. The hard times were in the beginning when Joni was learning her craft, had to cash in her savings bonds to get the money to buy her potter's wheel, and then had to save all her craft income for months in order to get the down payment for the $3000 kiln she "just had to have." She had it completely paid for three months after she brought it home, however, and perhaps the most traumatic thing about this purchase was the effect it had on her husband. "When the kiln was delivered," says Joni, "my husband almost passed out. He had

never seen one before, and he wasn't all that excited about it (to put it mildly)."

Blending several tons of kiln into the DeBus lifestyle surely took considerable effort on the part of everyone in the family, but today Joni says she and her husband "really have it made." She does add, however, that she would not suggest her business for anyone without "nerves of steel, a back like a horse, and a good business head." Joni's husband, Bill, recently retired after 25 years with the police department and has gone into full-time work as a manufacturing jeweler, a craft he apprenticed for many years ago. For 25 years he worked at it part time, and now both he and Joni have workshops in their home and love it, although they do tend to work too many hours.

"Working at home isn't always as good as it's cracked up to be," warns Joni. "You spend half, or perhaps three-quarters, of your life (or 99%?) in jeans and sweatshirt, and you tend to work on weekends, nights, and holidays to get orders out. You have very little contact with the outside world. My days are not eight-hour days; more like fourteen or eighteen."

It does take a lot of time to operate a home business, and for those who happen to have children and too little time to operate even a part-time business, Ruby Tobey, a Kansas artist, offers this practical advice: "Keep working a little whenever you can and the ideas and abilities will develop, and soon the day will come when you will have more time. Just don't quit completely and let your craft or ability get rusty. One day the kids will be a little older, or the other job less demanding. Or, you might be like me and just learn to work your craft around the other things in your life."

Ruby has three children between the ages of 9 and 18, and she says they grew up in the middle of her artwork and have always accepted it as a part of her life, just as she does. But she is quick to add, "Serving God and raising my family will always be first, so I have to fit my work around that."

Carol Bernier of Wentworth, New Hampshire, has three children (aged 4 to 11) and a retail shop in her home. She told me that her children have an active part in the goings-on of their household. "Their chores make them aware that they belong and are important to the functioning of this house and family," she writes. "They have a pride in our property and business because they work within it. We have made them aware that the little they do is vital." Carol also emphasizes the importance of keeping the business (shop or office) apart from the living quarters because children need to play and fight and can't lead a sterile life because a customer or client may come through the door at any minute. And she adds that a husband who can't feel free to put his feet up or have a beer when he wants to will soon come to resent the business that is interfering with his happy home life.

Incidentally, if you, as a wife, are seriously thinking about starting a home business in partnership with your husband, think twice. As another woman reminded me, "Being in love with a man who goes away from the house eight to ten hours a day is a lot different from loving and liking one who is home twenty-four hours a day."

There must be thousands of women in America today who have sorted their priorities, set their values, and managed to pursue a career successfully without abandoning children or alienating husbands. How *do* they do it?

That question so intrigued Jean Ray Laury that she wrote a whole book on the topic and called it *The Creative Woman's Getting-It-All-Together-At-Home Book.* Published by Van Nostrand Reinhold in late 1977, it tells how women everywhere are attempting, with varying degrees of success, to combine the roles of creative artist, mother, homemaker, and wife. Jean, one of America's most beloved craft and needlework authors, is a delightful example of an all-together woman whose multifaceted career of writing, designing, lecturing, and teaching has been a natural outgrowth of her many artistic interests and skills. Her book, based on letters from fiber artists all over the country, sparkles with excitement and offers help and encouragement to women everywhere who want desperately to "do something," yet have too little time and not enough space in which to work. Reading Jean's book is like being part of one of the greatest women's meetings in the world, in which everyone is sounding off for the first time in her life to someone who really understands what she is saying.

Maintaining your home, caring for a husband or family, and running a business as well, can be a real challenge, and not every woman can — or should try to — cope with such stress. For those who feel up to it, however, the possibilities are exhilarating and practically unlimited.

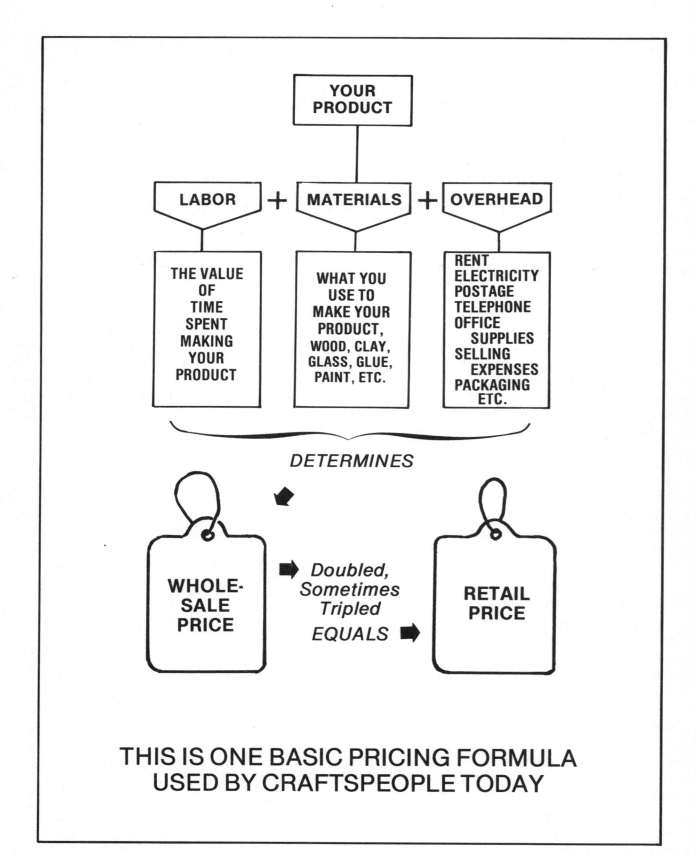

**THIS IS ONE BASIC PRICING FORMULA
USED BY CRAFTSPEOPLE TODAY**

3

Pricing Is Everybody's Problem

Arts and crafts have become such an important part of my life that if someone asked me to visualize the proverbial pot of gold, I'd probably see in my mind's eye a ceramic pot sitting on a handwoven rug with a rainbow of batik spilling into it. However, I do tend to get practical when I think about what's in that pot: MONEY MONEY MONEY — and I don't mean golden guldens. GREEN is my color, and lots is the quantity I prefer. But alas, in order to make lots of money, I must first have "lots of something" to sell. Having that, my problems won't be over, because I will still have to *price my products to sell.*

Basic Pricing Formulas

Putting just any price on something is easy, but determining the right selling price is not so simple, as most craftspeople will agree. The *right selling price* must be high enough to cover your costs and allow you to make a profit, yet low enough to attract customers. Some people just use common sense when it comes to pricing their work; others use a basic pricing formula, such as this: Labor + Materials + Overhead = Wholesale Price. Wholesale price doubled (sometimes tripled) = Retail Price.

For the benefit of those who do not understand the various elements in this formula, let me explain them briefly. *Labor* represents the value

placed on the time you, or someone else, spends in making the article. (See "A Matter of Values" later in this chapter.) The *materials* figure should include the cost of all raw materials used to make what you sell. *Overhead* includes all operating costs not directly related to the production of what you make, such as rent, utilities, telephone, transportation, freight charges, office supplies, selling expenses, and so on. *Wholesale price* is the price at which you will sell your products to someone else who intends to resell them, such as a shop owner. *Retail price,* as you know, is the price eventually paid by the customer who takes your product home.

Understanding the individual elements in various pricing formulas is one thing, but understanding how craftspeople use specific formulas to establish prices is another thing entirely. Here, then, are some examples of how certain artists and craftsmen set prices on handmade articles.

Lois Moyer is a creative homemaker-turned-kit-manufacturer whose basic pricing formula would be helpful to anyone who wants to produce an item in quantity for sale at wholesale prices. She simply calculates her actual costs for each item and multiplies that amount by at least two, and sometimes three, to arrive at her suggested retail price. Then she uses her common sense to decide if the item will sell at that price, making any necessary adjustments. Her wholesale price is generally half the retail price, and there is a sufficient amount built into this price to allow for a 10 percent commission to sales representatives, and an additional 10 percent for volume discounts if necessary.

In applying this formula to your business, it's important to remember that actual costs include not only materials and labor, but overhead and selling expenses as well. Although Lois started her business less than three years ago with just one basic kit idea, she has since developed a complete line of kits now being sold by eleven manufacturer's representative organizations. This kind of growth would have been impossible if Lois had not made allowances for all her costs from the very beginning.

Author Merle Dowd explains it another way in his book, *How To Earn More Money from Your Crafts*. After discussing all the elements involved in pricing, he warns: "Unless you consider these elements in your pricing, you will experience problems in attempting to move from minor selling on your own to a larger volume distributed through the mail, a retail shop, or on consignment. But if you consider all of these elements, you can operate flexibly and share earnings according to the marketing functions you perform."*

The Common-Sense Factor

Here's another formula used by a successful jeweler-craftsman who wholesales a line of silver rings. Ray Martell of Little Falls, New Jersey, begins with the cost of materials and adds labor costs calculated at the rate he would have to pay someone else to replace him at the bench. Then he adds 40 percent of the labor-plus-materials figure for overhead, and doubles the whole thing for retail price. "Then," quips Ray, "I throw the whole thing out and figure what I can get!"

Once again, we have run into the "common-sense factor" that is so important to the pricing of any handmade article. Craftsmen aren't born with common sense when it comes to pricing; they have to acquire it much as they acquire their craft skill.

Ray adds to his knowledge in this area by keeping loose-leaf folders into which he pastes, by category, advertisements of local jewelers and department stores, etc. "Whenever I am pricing," he says, "I look through the ads in the category and my prices go up!"

If you do not produce in great quantity, nor sell at wholesale, the above pricing methods may seem unsuitable for you, or just too complicated. In that case, you might consider this common pricing formula, which is used by many craftspeople today: Cost of Materials x 3 = Retail Price. Ruby Tobey, the Kansas artist you met in the previous chapter, says this is a good rule-of-thumb method for her, although it doesn't always work. She explains: "On some items the cost is low for materials, but the time involved is high, so I must price according to that. On other items I am lucky to get three times the cost of materials." Because Ruby has a realistic view of both pricing and selling, she makes a lot of "bread and butter" items, (items one can easily produce at low cost and sell just as easily at a good profit). "When I try something new," Ruby continues, "I try to find a way to make it as cheaply as possible and still have a quality item. Otherwise, I just forget about making it for sale. If I want to keep selling and working, I have to think at least part of the time in terms of what will sell and not just what is art."

Some artisans who are timid about pricing may seek advice from shop owners. While some shops do not want the responsibility of pricing a craftsman's work, others will offer advice when asked. As a former co-owner of The Fringe & Frame, Inc. in Pittsburgh, Pennsylvania, Bucky King was often called upon for advice in pricing, and, as a professional textile craftsman, she certainly understood the problems of the beginning sellers who came into the shop. Often, Bucky told me, if they were young and without a known reputation, she advised them to price their articles at half of what they felt they were worth. "In this way," she explained, "their work was usually sold, and their personal morale was encouraged. As their rate of sales increased, we advised a price increase in accordance with sales, perhaps making suggestions as to what we felt would sell best in color, pattern, and design." Bucky said they did not use pricing formulas as such, but always treated each craftsperson as an individual, using their combined common sense in arriving at a price for each item.

Ayn Chase, who owns a seasonal craft shop in Oak Bluffs, Massachusetts, is an enterprising artist-craftswoman who produces a variety of items for sale to the tourists who throng to Martha's Vineyard each summer. Primarily a weaver, she brings her common-sense judgment into play when she prices her own work because she is used to hearing such remarks as, "How can you sell these at such low prices?" and, conversely, "Your things are lovely, but I can't afford them." With these comments in mind, Ayn says she often tries to imagine herself in the buyer's shoes, "to see if my prices are too high for me if I were to buy the same item."

Another craftsman and shop owner I once knew in the Ozarks operated in much the same way, except that she used "plain horse sense" to figure out a price. "Regardless of the cost of materials and time," she said, "if the item is priced so high it will not sell, then it should not be made for sale or bought for resale."

A Matter of Values

Everyone who sells is aware that the cost of materials must be carefully considered when pricing, but often it is the labor factor that determines the selling price of a handmade item. Have you ever wondered why the same type of handmade article sells for one price here, and another price there?

This confusion is easily explained when you consider that no two people picked at random will ever place the same value on their time. The decision as to what your time is worth is a very personal one, and it may be influenced by any number of factors, such as your education or degree of skill, your age, your reputaton (if any), your previous salaried job experience (if any), the area in which you live, the demand in your area for what you make or do, and your need for money. Finally, there is the matter of *ego*. Bucky King notes: "As age and reputation increase, the

tendency to placate the ego rears its ugly head, and one's prices seem to soar along with ego. Flexibility is very important here, because inflated self-esteem can put a mighty big hole in your balloon."

Who and what you are will always affect the prices you charge for your work, just as it will affect the prices you are willing to pay for the hand-work of others. If you are married, I wouldn't be at all surprised to hear that your husband doesn't agree with you on the topic of what your time is worth. This is particularly true concerning the pricing of handmade articles. A man will always argue on the basis of his working experience and salary, and a homemaker will naturally tend to think in terms of what she would ordinarily be doing with her spare time if she weren't making something for sale — such as keeping an eye on the baby, watching television, reading, puttering with a hobby, or simply waiting for the casserole to come out of the oven.

While this kind of logic is immediately understood by women everywhere — and is okay for those who just want to earn a little pin money — it's not at all practical for professionals, or those who aspire to be professional in their approach to selling. Time is a very precious commodity that should never be given away carelessly. Thus it is important for all serious sellers to set some sort of value on their time — even if it's only a couple of dollars an hour — and try to work out prices accordingly.

Incidentally, if you think $2 per hour seems low, consider that professional artists and craftsmen often have difficulty in getting even this small amount for their time. Bucky King, who now lives and works on a ranch in Sheridan, Wyoming, writes: "You never get the value of your time for your work. The minimum wage is going to be $3.50 per hour before long, but just imagine anyone paying me $350 for 100 hours of work! As a fiber artist I am expected to receive only $2 per hour because, even though I have just as much ability as any ditch digger, cab driver, or salesman, the public does not pay for art by the hour."

Bucky also reminded me that there is another factor to be considered when crafts and

27

needlework are being priced for sale: *the love factor*. As she explains, "Most of us would continue to produce if we never sold another piece, simply because we love what we do. I use no formula to price what I make because *love* goes into my work. It is design and pattern, informed with sensitivity. But, I am not a dreamer either, so I put realistic prices on items that are for sale." As an exhibitor in numerous nationally recognized exhibitions, Bucky's prices are usually established by what other professional textile craftsmen charge. "Most of us are fortunate to get $200 to $400 for a medium-sized wall hanging," she says. "As spinners, even if we get $1.50 for an ounce of handspun wool or silk, we are underpaid for our efforts in shearing, washing, carding, spinning, and dyeing the thread — but we had the love of doing. We don't get paid for love."

A decorative painter wrote, "I love to paint and I'd rather paint and sell it than paint and look at it. My husband and I both figure our costs by time and material and take that into consideration when pricing our merchandise. We have been told time and again that our prices are too low, but we are getting a fair return and we are selling."

It's certainly true that if you are doing what you want to do, on a schedule of your own making, you will be content to accept a lower hourly rate of pay than you might demand if you were working for someone else. As another woman put it, "You don't punch a time clock in this kind of work, so I don't think time should be counted."

Needleworkers, perhaps more than others, realize that time cannot be considered in terms of so many dollars for so many hours spent. As a needleworker myself, I work primarily at two times: when I'm "watching" television, or when I'm traveling. To my way of thinking, the hours spent in these activities would normally be time wasted, so when I eventually complete a piece of needlework in the process, I always feel I've gained, not lost, something in the bargain. Thus, to needleworkers everywhere who take great pride in doing quality work, the hours spent are not important. If a great deal of needlework can be turned out in a year during spare time hours, that's a bonus, indeed. And if it can also be sold at reasonable prices to appreciative buyers, so much the better.

The Psychology of Pricing

The selling artisan should understand that all buyers have preconceived notions as to what any item should cost. When you take this fact into consideration, you are applying psychology, as well as common sense, to your pricing formula. Perhaps one of the first things any producing craftsman learns is that certain items must be priced to compensate for others. Quite often an item that takes a lesser amount of time and effort to produce can be priced higher than something that may have been twice as difficult to make and took three times as long besides. Always try to find out what "the going prices" are for items similar to those you produce, and never feel guilty about taking a larger profit on something you have produced easily and quickly, because sooner or later you will have to take a loss on something that should be priced higher, but cannot be, for one reason or another.

You should also realize that certain prices — such as $2.29, $4.88, and $7.98 — are just plain bad for handcrafts. That's because they sound like amounts one might expect to pay for items in a discount house. This is a good example of the "psychology of pricing." It's difficult to explain, but after you have sold many things, you will begin to notice that items with a certain price sell better than others. If you will look closely at the price tag on handcrafts the next time you go to a large, professional show, you will probably note an interesting pattern emerging — a pattern that will offer a reliable guideline for pricing your own products.

Guidelines are important, but in the long run, you must not forget that *the customer is King*. He is not concerned with how long it takes to create an item, nor what it costs to make. His decision to buy, or not to buy, is based simply on what he is willing to pay to own the item. If he wants it badly enough, he will find the money to buy it.

Buying Supplies Wholesale

The price you pay for materials can greatly affect the selling price of your products, so it's only

28

To make the job of finding supplies easier, read one or more craft periodicals regularly, and gradually acquire a well-rounded library of supply catalogs and directories. Membership in a local craft organization might also be helpful, inasmuch as organizations can buy at quantity discounts and pass savings along to their members.

natural for you to ask, "Where can I get it wholesale?" Many of you have already discovered one thing: The fact that you can use craft or needlework supplies in quantity does not necessarily entitle you to buy them at wholesale prices. You may have discovered, too, that the solution does not always lie in merely obtaining a resale tax number. (See Chapter 14.) Most manufacturers and wholesalers do not wish to sell to individuals because it is too expensive for them to handle small orders, and they also want to protect their "legitimate dealers" — those who own retail establishments. Their point is well taken if you consider the situation from the dealer's viewpoint. How would you feel if you were a struggling craft supply shop owner who learned that an individual working out of her home was able to buy the same supplies at wholesale that you were selling in your shop? You, as a retailer, would have enormous overhead costs to contend with, while the individual would not. To shop owners, this does not seem fair at all.

From the craftsman's viewpoint, however, I know how frustrating it is to have to buy materials at retail prices when it also means the price of your finished products must be raised to compensate for the higher cost of materials. Often this will make craftwork too expensive to be readily salable, if salable at all. Thus it is that many individuals soon discover they cannot afford to produce certain objects for sale.

Although no one seems to have all the answers on the problem of how and where to buy materials wholesale, here are a few guidelines that may prove helpful to you. First, you must learn who sells what you need. *Profitable Crafts Merchandising*, a trade journal for the crafts industry, will direct you to wholesalers and manufacturers in this field, or you can track them down by reading consumer craft magazines such as *Creative Crafts, Decorating & Craft Ideas,* or *Crafts,* all of which are available on newsstands. The major craft suppliers advertise in these magazines, and in addition, readers often share information on sources for hard-to-find items.

When responding to advertisements in consumer magazines, remember that all advertisers will be promoting their retail catalogs since they are expecting to sell to individual buyers. Thus, you will have to specifically request their wholesale price list or catalog when it is not mentioned in an ad. But, before you do, remember my earlier advice about being professional in your approach. Naturally, you should be using printed letterheads, and you should be prepared to provide your resale tax number if and when it is required. Type your letters to suppliers whenever possible, but if you have no typewriter, at least write neatly and legibly. Do not hastily scrawl a hand-written note on yellow tablet paper and expect a supplier to believe you are a likely prospect for a good order.

Once you have your collection of catalogs and price lists, you will probably discover that some minimum order requirements are too large for you to handle. In that case, you may have to write and ask for the name of a distributor or jobber in your area who might sell to you in lesser quantities. If your business is just too small to meet everyone's minimum requirements, ask your local craft or needlework supply shop if it can offer any kind of discount, should you decide to buy in quantity.

When it comes to buying supplies, it may pay you to belong to a local art, craft, or needlework guild, since membership in such organizations often provides special opportunities for obtaining supplies and materials at wholesale or discounted prices. If there are no organizations like this in your area, you might give some thought to forming a special cooperative organizaton in order to buy materials in bulk. (See Chapter 15.)

In addition to the above suggestions, you might want to explore a craft supply directory such as the biennial *Contemporary Crafts Marketplace.* Compiled by the American Crafts Council, it lists supplies classified by item within special categories of clay, fiber, glass, metal, wood, etc. Another directory, *National Guide to Craft Supplies* (published by Van Nostrand Reinhold), offers a complete mail-order shopping guide to more than 600 sources of supply, and each entry includes information about the cost of catalogs, as well as the company's minimum order and wholesale purchase requirements — a great help, indeed. (Incidentally, the term "crafts" is used loosely here to cover sewing and needlework supplies as well as craft materials.)

Tracking down suppliers who will sell to individual artisans, even those with legitimate home businesses, is one of the most frustrating jobs you will have once you decide to become a serious seller, but you can do it. All it takes is time, patience, and an unending supply of stamps. (See the resource chapter for information about other directories that may be helpful to you.)

4

What To Do When Your Work Won't Sell

"What do you do when your work is good, and still won't sell?" a beginning seller asked me one day. The question was not new to me, so I naturally had a few answers ready and waiting:

1. Make something else, or
2. Change your prices, or
3. Change the function of your product, or
4. Change the materials being used, or
5. Change your colors or designs, or
6. Change the name of your product.

Make Some Changes

Let's discuss the above suggestions one by one, as I did in my meeting with Pamela Milroy, owner of Global Designs. Our conversation, summarized below, may give you a few ideas that can be applied to your own selling problem, if indeed you have one at all.

First, let me describe Pamela's product. She makes beautiful Christmas ornaments using styrofoam balls, stainless steel pins, high quality glass beads, sequins, and velvet trims. She creates her own designs, which are basically geometric. In the beginning she was making huge ornaments the size of basketballs, reasoning that they would be great for display purposes in department stores, restaurants, and fancy shops. When Pam's grandmother saw them, however, she told her they wouldn't sell, and she was right. Says Pam, "I

have to sell them for $75 each wholesale, and I realize now that no matter how much I enjoy making them, no one's going to pay that much for them."

When I suggested she make something else, Pam explained that simply wasn't the solution for her. She happens to like making this type of ornament and doesn't want to make anything else. (She is fascinated by spherical shapes and enjoys working with the many beautiful beads and trims she uses.)

We agreed that her pricing was correct, so we proceeded to talk about the idea of making decorative home accessories (global-shaped, of course) that would be suitable for display all year long, instead of just during the holiday season. For example, not Christmas tree ornaments, but small sculptures perhaps, with her ornamented balls "speared" with a stainless steel rod and mounted on an appropriate base.

"But who would want glass-beaded ornaments with velvet ribbons sitting on their coffee table all year?" Pam asked, adding that they would certainly be great dust catchers.

"Right," I agreed, "so why not think about changing your materials? Instead of glass beads, you could experiment with handmade ceramic beads or metal beads; instead of velvet ribbons, try metallic trims."

I also suggested that Pam give some thought

to changing her colors and making her designs less Christmassy — perhaps more ethnic, since anything ethnic now seems to be in vogue. Then we talked about how to create such designs when one is not an artist. (See end of this chapter.)

Finally, Pam and I discussed how a change of name can affect an item's salability. For example, you can only get so much money for a Christmas ornament, yet if you make something ornamental and call it *sculpture*, people are automatically willing to pay more for it. And, sometimes, what you call *yourself* can affect the salability of your work. Or, as E.J. Tangerman, a well-known woodcarver, once said: "If you're a 'primitive' carver, you can charge three times what you would if you just admitted you are crude."

My interview with Pam ended on a high note. She had gained new perspective on her particular selling problem, and I had gained a new idea for my book. Pam is now making regular-sized ornaments, and trying to find a few wholesale outlets for them. She is also working on the idea of making mobiles from her smaller ornaments, a possibility that presented itself during our conversation.

Improve Your Marketing Strategy

If you have a selling problem, it may be necessary to change not only your product, but your marketing strategy. Perhaps you can learn from the experience of a woodcarver friend of mine.

In the early days of editing *Artisan Crafts* magazine, I was doing some whittling on the side and became acquainted with Dave Leitem, a fellow woodcarver from Butler, Pennsylvania. He really had selling problems. Like Pamela, Dave had great confidence in his craftsmanship, but was frustrated by his lack of ability to sell what he was making. We corresponded for some time and it became something of a personal challenge to resolve Dave's marketing problem.

Because he was so emotionally involved with his work, Dave couldn't see certain things that were evident to me, so I offered some suggestions that he considered, tried, and eventually profited from. Some craftsmen go through life with their heads stuck in the sand, unable or unwilling to change anything, but not Dave. He experimented with different types of ads, wrote and rewrote price lists and brochures, and kept trying new techniques of selling at craft shows and approaching buyers. Eventually he achieved the success he so desired.

A recent newspaper article about Dave's latest accomplishments accompanied his last letter to me. His now-successful woodcarving business has been expanded to include the carving of candles, and his whole family works with him on this, much to his delight. With an annual income from crafts now substantial enough to support his family, Dave's greatest problem is not in selling, but in trying to fill the many orders he's receiving. Now that's a problem any craftsman welcomes, and one he can solve for himself.

32

The right solution to a selling problem may be difficult to find. In addition to some of the things already discussed, you might consider changing your marketing outlet. If you are selling in shops, perhaps your product is better suited to sell at craft fairs, or vice versa. Or maybe you have a perfect mail-order product and just don't know it. Have you ever wondered why you can't buy the same things in a Sears store that you can buy in the catalog? Sears must have a good reason for selling certain items by mail and others by sight and sound and touch. Try to relate that reasoning to your product and see what happens.

Let me regress for a moment and return to a point I made earlier; namely, "make something else." Do you realize that the item most in vogue at the time is the one that is going to be hardest to sell? That is, if decoupage or macrame or small hand weavings are currently the most popular items being produced by hobbyists, you will probably have difficulty selling such crafts unless you are doing something entirely different from everyone else. If your aunt or your neighbor can make the same things you are making, why would they, or anyone else, need to buy them from you? Or, as one macrame artist puts it, "The secret to marketing any craft is constructing an item that few other people are willing to attempt."

Get a Good Gimmick

If you insist on making what everyone else is making, then, to sell, you must at least *do something different* with your craft to make it stand out from the crowd. In that case, perhaps a good gimmick will solve your selling problem.

A gimmick, according to Webster, is "an important feature that is not immediately apparent," or "a new and ingenious scheme or angle." Every successful seller has a good gimmick, and it need not be cheap, faddish, scheming, deceitful, or tricky, as the word sometimes implies. One weaver I know has a clever gimmick that illustrates this point.

Bonny Cook Lowry used to have trouble selling her work, until she accidentally discovered *fur weaving*. When she found out that this type of weaving required nothing more than an ordinary loom and a second-hand fur coat, she decided to try it. Recalls Bonny, "I was happily surprised that my very first pieces were salable and did sell immediately. Suddenly, I was being asked to demonstrate at craft fairs and to enter craft shows and special exhibitions. Then came the one-man shows."

Why? Because, quite accidentally, Bonny had developed a *good gimmick*. "When ecology became the resounding cry across the country," she said, "I thought sure the demand for articles woven of fur was doomed. But, quite the contrary. Because I primarily use second-hand fur, people considered that I was recycling. Another unexpected gimmick." Bonny went on to write a book titled *Weaving with Antique (Second-Hand) Fur*, illustrating once again how one craft thing always leads to another.

Gimmicks come in all forms, and Ruby Tobey recently discovered one that has increased her sales considerably. She calls her china painting "Kansas Delft" because she lives in Kansas and paints American scenes in blue. The name has caught on and she can't keep enough painted because many people who collect genuine Delft or the Copenhagen Blue now buy her things to add to their collections. She is currently in the process of registering the trademark for both "Kansas Delft" and another kind of Delft she is doing called "Dirt Farmer's Delft," done in browns. As Ruby says, "It's coming across new ideas like these that makes working fun." (And it's gimmicks like this that put additional cash into one's pocket.)

Sandy Mooney of Flint, Michigan, accidentally discovered her gimmick while demonstrating batik at a local fair. One customer, amused by her colorful display of life-sized stuffed batik character dolls remarked, "They're great, but you should make some of them into hookers." Sandy thought that sounded like fun, so she made one a few weeks later. "For some reason," she said, "she looked like the great-grandmother of all the madams instead of the beautiful sexy gal that I had in mind. Someone bought her (perhaps as a gift for a grandfather) and after several more tries I finally came up with a good-looking sexy lady."

33

Sandy still makes her charming character dolls, along with pillows, scarves, aprons, and "whatever else I think up that can be translated into batik," but realizes it is her unusual "Ladies of the Evening" who are attracting the most attention. With this thought in mind she has recently begun to include several "naughty ladies" in her slide presentations for fair jurying, and no doubt they are already playing an important role in helping Sandy gain national recognition as a selling craftswoman.

One of Sandy Mooney's "Ladies of the Evening".

The unique gimmick used by tinsmith Horman Foose of Fleetwood, Pennsylvania, illustrates the old saying, "Necessity is the mother of invention." The Pennsylvania Dutch have a wonderful taste treat called funnel cakes, a fried pastry sprinkled with powdered sugar. To make it, a special batter is poured into a funnel while the bottom is kept closed with one finger. Then, placing the filled funnel over a skillet of hot oil, the batter is quickly released and spiraled outward from the center to form a flat, circular cake that's served hot. But, just any old funnel won't do — the hole must be a particular size, and a handle on the funnel is also required for efficiency. And Horman Foose makes and sells that special funnel, including the recipe for funnel cakes along with it. Of course, the funnel is just one of dozens of items in his line, but it is his gimmick nonetheless. Whenever possible, Horman and his wife, Maria, demonstrate two crafts at once: She makes and sells the cakes, and he makes and sells the funnels. (And to taste a hot funnel cake is to want the recipe and the special handcrafted utensil it requires.)

Action is often the most important quality of a clever gimmick, and a good "spiel" delivered with flourish will often sell more crafts than superb craftsmanship. Remember, in order to sell, one must first capture the attention of the buyer. Blacksmith Harry Houpt certainly knows how to do that. A regular demonstrator at the annual Kutztown Folk Festival in Pennsylvania, he always draws large crowds with his rhythmic "musical anvil," which he plays with a hammer before fanning the forge and demonstrating his blacksmithing skills. As he makes a miniature horseshoe (a good gimmick in itself), he talks about life and the lessons it holds for all of us. Everyone listens, especially the children, one of whom will be the lucky recipient of the newly-created horseshoe.

A quiet-spoken fellow named Bill Reed, from Parkersburg, West Virginia, has built a successful woodcarving business by developing a delightful line of rocking horses. Actually, they aren't horses at all, but fanciful mules, cows, buffaloes, giraffes, and other critters such as a rocking duck and a "log hog." Because they are cleverly displayed in a rail-fence corral, these handcarved

When Sybil Harp, editor of Creative Crafts, saw Bill Reed's giant rocking horse at a crafts fair, she decided to accept his invitation to "mount up" and have her photograph taken. This is the artist's version of that photograph.

animals always draw a great deal of attention at a show. But an even greater number of prospective buyers are lured to Bill's stand whenever he brings his "big beast" to the show with him. He's a wonderful rocking mule that stands almost six feet tall, and anyone who thinks he can mount this magnificent monster is cordially invited to climb aboard and have his picture taken. True, people may leave Bill's exhibit empty-handed, since not everyone has a need for a rocking animal, but they will always take with them a vivid memory that will certainly be shared with friends, thus providing splendid word-of-mouth advertising for a modest woodcarver who seldom toots his own horn.

As Bonny Lowry reminds us, "Gimmicks are great for publicity. They stir the imagination of the customer. Just as fingerprints set each individual apart, but do not make the person, gimmicks set apart similar crafts, but do not make the craft. It still takes the craftsman."

Naturally, gimmicks will never replace fine craftsmanship, but they can certainly increase sales. With a little imaginative thinking on your part, you can probably come up with a good gimmick that will boost your sales, so don't be afraid to experiment with this idea, as well as the other suggestions in this chapter.

Develop Creativity and Design Ability

Your craftsmanship may be superior, but if your designs are poor (or worse, copied from other craftsmen) you may experience difficulty in selling, particularly to established shops and stores. Sophisticated buyers can spot copied designs and kit products a mile away. If you are serious about selling, don't waste your time copying the designs of others. Create your own and be done with it.

What? You say you're just not that creative? Nonsense. You may not be an artist, true, but there is a streak of creativity and artistry in each of us. In fact, creativity may well be merely the discovery of something that's been there all along. Perhaps you ought to think more like Oscar Wilde, who once said, "An artist is not a special sort of man, every man is a special sort of artist."

You *can* learn to apply your natural creativity to your crafts or needlework, and here are a few tips to get you started. The first thing you must do to sharpen your sense of creativity and design is develop a "seeing eye." In other words, don't just *look* at something, really try to *see* it. I'm sure that in the past you've looked at clouds and seen something in their formations, such as an animal or a tree, but have you ever really seen the intricate patterns in a seashell, the veins in a leaf, or the interesting design on your window as the setting sun casts a shadow of bare branches?

Designs are everywhere for the taking. You need only train your eyes to see them. Why, one

Designs are everywhere for the taking, like this owl who suddenly swirled into view as the electric beaters came out of a batch of cookie dough.

36

"Snow Lady" design, captured by the author one morning during breakfast. She was hiding in the guise of a clump of snow on a nearby tree, patiently waiting to be found by someone with a "seeing eye".

day last winter, I looked out the window and saw, sticking to a tree, a clump of snow that looked exactly like the face of a pompous old woman. She had a double chin, a pointed nose, and a mop of hair so amusing I had to sketch her quick before she melted. (My husband thought I was a bit daft, of course, since he couldn't see a thing.) Another day, while baking cookies, I noticed the design my electric beaters left in the dough and saw not cookies but a "kookie" owl perched on a branch, surrounded by swirling leaves. The cookie baking had to wait until I captured this bird on paper for a future piece of needlework. The interesting thing about these designs is that I couldn't have created them without the help of an outside "spark" of nature. I'm just not an artist, you see.

Try capturing a few designs of your own some day. It's not as difficult as you might believe. All of us drew things as children, and although your drawing may still be child-like, it is nonetheless a talent you can use, and, like everything else, it will improve with practice.

You won't see anything unless you really look, and ideas won't come to you unless you work to get them, so it may be necessary for you to study some design books to get started on the road to creativity. One of the best design books available to you is *How To Create Your Own Designs*, by Dona Z. Meilach and Jay and Bill Hinz, published by Doubleday. This excellent book will help you extract what you see around you and teach you how to put your ideas on paper, as well as apply them to your crafts and needlework.

Another book you might like is *Approaching Design Through Nature — The Quiet Joy*, by Grace O. Martin, recently published by The Viking Press. Here, the author shares her observations of nature and offers practical exercises to help the reader interpret nature in techniques such as simple weaving, stitchery, applique, and using thread, fabric, and yarn in imaginative ways. Both books should be available through your library, bookstore, or mail-order craft book sellers.

If you need inspiration for designs other than what you see around you in nature, you will be delighted to learn that there are literally thousands of copyright-free designs available to you today, and you don't have to visit a museum to find them, either. I'm talking about the amazing world of the *Dover Pictorial Archives*, a wonderful series of high-quality paperbacks, each of which contains hundreds of designs you can use in any manner or place you wish, without further payment, permission, or acknowledgement. All of you out there who claim you can't draw a straight line will really appreciate these books, and you will soon discover that you *can* add your own ideas to a design or pattern created by someone else. Remember that every artist through the ages has studied the work of others for inspiration and ideas, often lifting or adapting the best ideas of someone else for his own use. You can too.

There is an increasing interest these days in ethnic designs, and the Pictorial Archive books offer a real treasure of usable patterns, ideas, and authentic motifs from many cultures, such as the American Indian, Japanese, Chinese, African, Mexican, Russian and East European, North African, Egyptian, and so on. There are also books on American folk art, flora and fauna, geometric design and ornament, and Art Deco.

Here's how to use design books like this in an imaginative way. Study their overall content, then select several motifs or ideas you like. Next, consider how you might mix, match, or blend one or more in an unusual arrangement or design, and don't hesitate to change anything you like in the process. Before long you will find that you have created a design of your own. It's important to remember that the designs suggested for one medium are often perfectly suited to others; thus one craftsman's "original macrame hanging" may actually have been inspired by an ancient Egyptian weaving or ceramic pot, and a colorful quilt pattern may have been "lifted" from an unusual stained glass window somewhere in Europe. Many is the time I've looked through a book labeled "For Needleworkers" and seen remarkable designs that could just as easily be used by rugmakers, handweavers, mosaic craftsmen, and decorative painters, to name just a few. In turn, designs on ancient ceramic pots, Indian baskets,

37

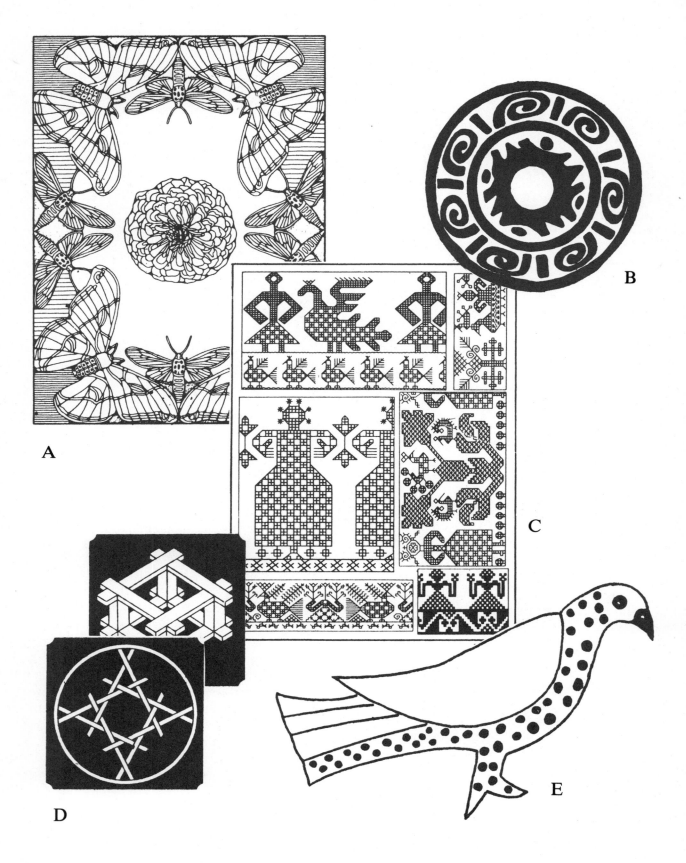

A

B

C

D

E

38

and African masks (all neatly captured for you in the Pictorial Archive books) lend themselves beautifully to needlework and a variety of crafts such as jewelry, papier mache, woodcarving, weaving, macrame, beadcraft, etc.

To become more creative you must first open your mind to the possibilities, and the best way to do this is *to open a few books*. For more informa-tion about the Dover design books, see the resource chapter, and in the meantime, give some thought to this idea, suggested by an unknown poet: "The universe is full of magical things patiently waiting for our wits to grow sharper."

NOTE: For more information about what makes a design "original," refer to "Getting Designs and Ideas Published," in Chapter 9.

Illustration opposite page.
Examples of copyright-free art from the Dover Pictorial Archives.
They are taken from the following:
(A) Art Nouveau Floral Ornament In Color
(B) Designs from Pre-Columbian Mexico
(C) Russian Peasant Design Motifs for Needleworkers & Craftsmen
(D) Japanese Design Motifs
(E) Early American Design Motifs

40

5

Putting Your Home To Work For You

Perhaps you'd like to have a shop of your own but just can't afford the large investment required to open a retail establishment. In that case, you might give some thought to starting a shop in your own home. Many people have done this successfuly on a temporary or permanent basis, beginning with a very small outlay of cash. Later I will discuss the legal aspects of having a shop in your home, but for now, read the following success stories to discover some good ideas that may work for you.

Before starting any kind of home shop or business, you ought to give some honest thought to this question, posed by Ginnie Wise of Tiffin, Ohio: "If big money profits do not materialize, will there be other satisfactions that will make it worth the time and effort?"

Home Gift Shops

Ginnie is a busy farm homemaker who has had a gift shop in her home for several years. Called Wises-on-High-Banks, it is filled with nature crafts made by Ginnie and her husband Ernie, a plumber by trade. The Wises' 240-acre farm is their "raw materials factory" since it contains 65 acres of river bottom that floods yearly, yielding many pieces of driftwood each spring. This driftwood and other woods, weathered by the elements and gathered from the ravines and hillsides, are combined with dried mosses, wayside

grasses, pods, and rocks to make a variety of natural gift items for their shop.

Although the shop is located "off the beaten track," it still attracts its share of customers. The rustic beauty of the surrounding countryside often

41

lures shoppers to its door, and of course the Wises advertise regularly and have a good brochure. In addition to exhibiting and selling at fairs and shows, the Wises invite various clubs to hold their meetings in their home, and afterwards Ginnie gives a little talk about the farm and shows some of her craft work. Then she invites the group to browse in the shop before they leave.

Do the Wises consider their home business a success? "Yes," says Ginnie, "but our success has not necessarily been in terms of making money. It is more in terms of *saving* money, in that when we go to arts and crafts shows, this is our vacation, so we have a paid vacation with possibly some profit in it too. We save money by having an avocation that more than pays for itself; it saves in that it probably substitutes for an active club and social life, and since craft work can be good therapy, I suppose one could say that it possibly saves on medical bills as well. More important, however, is the return I've had in terms of newfound self-worth, along with the ego-stroking that most of us need from time to time. The enjoyable friendships and acquaintances we have made through our craft is another good return on our investment. And, of course, ranking right up at the top would be the added sense of togetherness and closeness that my husband and I have realized as we have worked and traveled with our craft."

Dreams can, and do, become a reality for those who are not afraid to try. The Wises know that, and so does Miriam Fankhauser, another homemaker who always wanted a shop of her own. In fact, she had its name (and her first daughter's name) picked out long before she was married. Her mother's love of dolls started it all.

"I think I never quite outgrew dolls," says Miriam. "At any rate, I started making them in

42

1972, and when I began to shop for my baby girl, I realized I could design and make dolls that were more durable and beautiful than any I could buy.''

One thing led to another, and in 1974 Miriam opened her ''House of Pearl'' shop in the basement of her new home in Green Springs, Ohio. ''I had a corner of collectible fashion cloth dolls, three styles of doll heads, a few toys, and several other items,'' she recalls. ''In 2½ years, the shop has grown from a 10 x 12 foot area to a 10 x 40 foot showroom, with muslin and felt dolls, pin cushion dolls, a larger selection of children's toys, and a variety of doll furniture, including swings, highchairs, rocking and swinging cradles, canopy beds, and toy boxes.'' Miriam has a craftsman who does all the woodcutting, but she does all the sewing herself. She is confident her shop and business will continue to grow, but adds, realistically, ''While my success is not yet guaranteed, I now have no doubt I am going to do exactly what I have set out to accomplish.''

Miriam taught school for 7½ years, but, having resolved not to teach while her children were growing, she became a ''complete homemaker'' after her first daughter was born. Still, she is a woman with an alert mind that must be constantly challenged, and this, plus her interest in dolls and designing (she is also a certified interior decorator), just naturally led her to start her own business. Miriam's positive attitude reflects the feelings of many talented and ambitious homemakers today who have recognized that they *do* have certain creative abilities, and *do* have what it takes to meet a new challenge head-on. Philosophizing, Miriam sums it up like this: ''There are many things I am still trying to resolve, but I know this: When we venture into something new, we must not become discouraged, we must love what we are doing, and we must want what we are doing badly enough to keep trying until we realize our goals.'' With enthusiasm she adds, ''God bless every homemaker who dares to venture from her four walls, her TV serials, and her boredom to a world of unlimited horizons.''

One of the most interesting and amazing success stories I uncovered in my research for this book was that of Carol Ann Bernier, whose biographical sketch appears in the 10th edition of *Who's Who of American Women*. This is no small honor, indeed, since individuals gain a listing in this prestigious publication only because their career achievements or responsible position has made them the subject of considerable reference interest. Who is Carol Bernier, and what has she done? More important, *how* did she do it?

Married to Emery Bernier, a noted stained glass artist-craftsman, Carol is the mother of three children. The Bernier family lives in a wonderfully big house in Wentworth, New Hampshire, that serves as both home and shop. Called The Bernier Studio, it boasts 10 rooms, of which five are devoted to the works of more than 150 artists and craftsmen. There is also a book store, an antique shop, a gourmet room, and a women's clothing boutique.

Carol is currently managing The Bernier Studio and often travels the country in search of unique handcrafts and gifts. She also lectures on the art and technique of stained glass windows, as well as on crafts and craftspeople in America. A series of articles she wrote was published in *Profitable Crafts Merchandising,* and in 1972 she wrote a book entitled *Stained Glass.* She is a member of several business organizations and the president of one, as well as treasurer of the Wentworth Women's Club and president of her high school alumnae association. On top of all this, Carol somehow manages to remain a contented, well-organized homemaker whose house is as neat and uncluttered as her shops. ''The one rule we have in our house,'' she says, ''is NO CLUTTER. No one can leave anything lying around, whether it's school books, toys, or clothes. This is an indispensable rule for the working mother. It lifts your spirit. Without clutter, a house always seems to look clean, even when you know that up on that third shelf you could probably write your name in the dust.''

It seemed a bit improbable to me that a high school graduate who began her business career as a bank teller and secretary could have accomplished so much, so quickly, in a field so unrelated to what she had been trained to do. ''How were you able to do it?" I asked, and in a fascinating nine-page letter I wish I could quote in full, she told me. Perhaps Carol's story will help you realize your own potential for success.

It all started with her husband, Emery. Employed for 13 years as a stained glass artist for a Boston firm, he had often talked about starting his own business, but just didn't want to make that break from a steady income to "maybe's," as Carol called it. Once, while browsing in a small gift shop, the Berniers saw some cheap Mexican stained glass window mobiles, and Carol decided then and there that if those things would sell, Emery's superb work should sell easily. But he wasn't convinced.

"I decided I had to step in," Carol recalls. "I took a few days off work and experimented myself. I'm no artist, but I drew a star, a tulip, a candle, and a small heart, then proceeded to put into practice all I had watched Emery do during the three years we'd been married. I cut the glass,

44

(crudely) got lead around it, soldered, and there they were. Oh well. But they were as good as the Mexican stuff. Nothing compared to what Emery would have produced, but I had hounded him enough. He had to be convinced they would sell, and if he wouldn't do it, I would."

With shaky knees and shallow breath, Carol entered her first gift shop trying to look very businesslike. She didn't even know about markups, but when she walked out of that shop she had an order, and that was the start of The Bernier Studio. Emery then had the push he needed and together they started to build their business, with Emery producing, and Carol out looking for buyers. Eventually, Carol talked Emery into leaving his steady job and working on his own.

After a couple of good years, and the birth of one child, Carol started thinking of her own shop. "Why not?" she thought. "Other shops sell our stained glass; let's sell our own." They attempted a shop in their home, but felt the "vibration of the town selectmen," so they decided to move. It was then that they found their current house in Wentworth which, coincidentally, had been used as an antique shop by the former owner. "Antiques?" thought Carol, her curiosity aroused once again. "What a wonderful thing to sell!"

Although she knew nothing about antiques, except for the few auctions and flea markets she had attended, her business sense told her that the woman who had lived there before surely had some steady customers who would be coming back for antiques, so she'd better have some for sale. With her usual determination, she proceeded to learn the antiques business and soon became a self-taught expert. (She stayed away from expensive items, starting with bowl and pitcher sets, cups, china, and small woodenware.) "It was fun, interesting, and challenging," Carol told me, "and, actually, I did very well."

Another two years passed successfully for the Berniers, and soon Carol, ever the adventurer, felt an urge to expand a bit. "Why not handcrafted gifts?" she mused, thinking they would fit in well with their handcrafted glass. Off she went in search of craftspeople. Then she heard about gift shows. "Maybe there might be something there," she told herself, and sure enough, she discovered several gift lines that worked well with the crafted items. She even found some new craftsmen being represented at these shows. Eventually, the lines grew and Emery had to stop creating stained glass from time to time to take up hammer and nails and open another section of the house and barn.

Three years ago, Carol decided to try selling women's apparel. As usual, she started very small, offering a total of 40 dresses in assorted sizes, plus a few blouses and skirts. To her amazement they sold rapidly. Once again, Carol considered the possibilities. "Why not?" she thought. "Let's really get into it. Expand. Transform another section into an adaptable room and stock it with women's apparel."

Naturally, Carol has done well in this area, like all the others, because she is sensible and has a good head for business. But she admits that buying clothing is quite different from buying gifts and crafts. "There's a lot to learn," she says, with a warning to all aspiring businesspeople that boils down to this: ASK QUESTIONS. "Never hesitate about asking questions," she advises, "and then listen — really concentrate on what is being said. And see, don't just look. Absorb as much as you can. It's amazing, the wealth of knowledge that can be gained by just noticing things and people. Always be alert to all that is around you."

Like all people in business, the Berniers have had a few failures along the way. But, as Carol says, "In the long run everything we did or attempted to do has been an education. We feel we are better prepared for what the future may bring because of all the things we have gotten involved in to date."

I asked if they had any advice to pass along to those starting new businesses, and got these do's and don't's from them: Make the most of your time, be organized and keep your studio or workshop clean and orderly, keep good records, don't overextend yourself financially, don't borrow money thinking you'll sell or do very well, and don't talk yourself into a project by looking at only the good, and overlooking the bad.

One of the things I found interesting about Carol's success story was the fact that her primary goal in the beginning was not to become a success herself, but to help her husband achieve recognition. As she told me, "Very few people have Emery's talent and qualifications. I knew what he could do. I was and am very proud of him and his skill, and I wanted people to know about my special husband. He just wouldn't blow his own horn, so someone had to do it for him. Who was better qualified than I, his wife?"

As a final postscript to this story, I want to tell you how this energetic gal copes with life and "gets it all together." As determined and self-confident as she is, even Carol has her "downs." But she knows how to get over them, and other women might do well to follow her lead when they find themselves ready to throw in the towel.

"If I really hit a stumbling block," says Carol, "a good outburst of emotions — alone — really helps. That includes having a good cry. It might seem foolish, but expressing how disappointed I am in the outcome of a situation by getting angry with myself and crying, has always worked very well for me. I tell myself, Carol, you are failing. Go ahead and cry and be angry with yourself. Get it out of your system, then get up and fight back. There must be something you overlooked, so find it."

Right on, Carol!

Holiday Boutiques

If the idea of a permanent shop in your home is not desirable, or even possible, perhaps the idea of a temporary shop, such as a holiday boutique, would appeal to you. Here are several examples of boutiques and craft sales that different women have operated in their homes with considerable success.

One-day Christmas boutiques seem to be quite common all over the country. In checking with a group in the Chicagoland area that has had an annual Christmas boutique for several years, I learned how they operate. The spokesman for the group said that she is one of six women who plan and organize the sale, which until recently has been held in a different woman's house each year. She said they simply divide the various jobs to be done and share in any expense involved. For example,

45

Planning to turn your living room into a holiday boutique for a day or more? If so, this illustration will provide some ideas on how a variety of crafts might be arranged around your regular furniture. If an Easter boutique is preferred, the Christmas tree could be replaced with a gold-painted tree branch hung with Easter Eggs.

one will handle the bookkeeping, another the distribution of flyers in the neighborhood, a third will mail announcements to their mailing list, and so on.

That mailing list, by the way, is the group's most valuable possession, and the real key to their continued success. In the beginning they asked all visitors to sign a guest book with their names and addresses, but later found this wasn't necessary since most buyers paid by check and they could just as easily take the addresses from the checks before they were deposited. A file card is made for each buyer, and each year's purchases are noted. (Since many of the buyers on the group's choice mailing list make annual purchases in amounts as high as $80, these names are like pure gold to the craftswomen involved.)

Total sales have increased steadily through the years, reaching more than $4000 in 1976, a sizable increase over the year before. Part of this was due to the fact that several newcomers were invited to participate, and, as a result, the group decided to hold its show in a local church this year, rather than in one of the women's homes. (After so many years of having home shows, the women who started this have literally "had it" and will probably go the church route from now on.) Although they may let new artisans exhibit in the future on a one-time basis, they are naturally reluctant to bring any new women into their "working nucleus," for various reasons. Rather than ask anyone else to share the responsibility and expense of the show with them, they will simply be charging a small exhibitor's fee in the future.

In considering your home as a possible "one-day shop," do consider how this activity may disrupt normal family living, and think about such things as traffic patterns, both in the house and on the street. There's also the matter of the legality of it all, which seems to fall into a mysterious "grey area." Since people everywhere are doing this sort of thing, the question of whether it's legal or not doesn't seem to matter to most. It seems to depend on the kind of neighborhood you live in, the type of neighbors you have, and how strictly local laws are enforced. My advice would be to check into the matter carefully before you make definite plans to hold such a sale in your home.

If you decide to have a home boutique, it would certainly be wise to give consideration to your neighbors, not only extending them a special invitation to attend your gala event, but also telling them there will be a lot of cars parked on the street that day.

Turning your house, or that of a friend, into a one-day Christmas shop should prove not only profitable but pleasurable. Most women would have fun arranging and displaying beautiful gifts and decorative accessories in a home boutique, and the addition of little extras such as cinnamon-orange tea brewing in the kitchen will make the day even more enjoyable for you and all who come to buy.

If you can't arrange a group sale, don't be afraid to try this idea by yourself, especially if you have a good supply of merchandise to sell. Your one-day sale could even be held in the evening, and

need be nothing more elaborate than setting up a special room as your display area and inviting a few friends over for coffee and Christmas craft shopping. I started selling in just this way, inviting about a dozen friends over one evening early in December. To my surprise, I sold almost $100 worth of crafts, and that gave me all the encouragement I needed to walk into a local shop soon afterward and show the owner what I had to sell.

Carol Reeves of Riverside, California, a fine macrame artist and teacher, is very experienced when it comes to holding home boutiques, having had 15 of them by the end of 1975. (She discontinued them in 1976 because they had become too routine. But her regular customers missed her shows so much that she finally decided to have another boutique in mid-1977, as this book was being written.)

In the past, Carol's boutiques have been similar in nature to the one already discussed, except for the fact that Carol managed them by herself and generally had two-day sales twice a year. Her shows were presented in May, just before Mother's Day, and in November, in time for the Christmas season. Occasionally, she also had a Summer Boutique, or a "Mini-Boutique," just before Christmas. Usually, they were held on a Friday and Saturday afternoon from noon to 4 p.m. "It was fun," says Carol. "We served refreshments, and the boutiques always had the air of a party."

Carol always invited several other craftsmen to participate with her, selecting those whose products complemented her macrame work. "Craftsmen brought their work to my house on Thursday and I arranged it throughout my living room and dining room, and on the patio in warm weather," she said. "All items were marked by the craftsmen with the retail price. For my effort, I kept 20 percent of the price of items sold." Part of that amount helped defray the expense of invitations, postage, and refreshments. The remainder was Carol's profit. Naturally, she advertised her shows locally and sent out invitations to prospective buyers. Her mailing list numbers more than 400 names, but she estimates that only a quarter of those invited each year actually came.

47

Ruby Tobey has an interesting variation on the theme of home boutiques. Once a year, usually in the third week of November, she has a week-long open house in her basement, but unlike Carol, she sells only her own work. She can do this because she produces a variety of items, including a unique line of china painting, an annual calendar with poetry she writes herself, and note papers printed with her drawings. Like the other women I've discussed, Ruby also has a good mailing list of interested buyers, and she advertises in the local papers. (Of the 500 names on Ruby's mailing list, she estimates that about a quarter will actually attend, which coincides with what Carol Reeves said. This, then, would seem to be a good figure to remember when estimating the number of buyers you might expect, should you decide to have a craft boutique in your home.)

What are the advantages of an open-house boutique? Ruby said her sales are always good, but more important, the boutique gives her a chance to get to know people better — people she might not meet otherwise. She enjoys having the undivided attention of her customers, too. "This is the one time all year that the audience is all mine — not shared with others as it is at a craft show." And, with a chuckle, Ruby adds: "Probably the best thing about my open house is that we get the basement cleaned really well once a year."

Bonny Cook Lowry and her mother, Bessie Cook, are certainly "pros" when it comes to running a Christmas shop in their home, because they did this every year for 10 years in their Bainbridge Island home in Washington. Called "The Country Craftsmen," the shop was discontinued with sadness when Bonny and her mother moved to Long Beach, Washington, where they now have a year-round shop by the same name. (Bonnie, who recently became Mrs. William Lowry, is the enterprising fur weaver you met in the preceding chapter.)

"We made and gathered for our show all year long," says Bonny, "and we also displayed the works of many other craftsmen." Unlike Ruby's open house, however, their shop was open for two months, and occupied half the house. Their clever use of folding screens, plus collapsible shelves and tables, made it possible for them to make interesting and unusual displays, and their shop was a welcome event to the local residents each year.

Teaching in Your Home

Any artist or craftsman with a flair for teaching, and an extra room, basement, or garage,

If zoning laws permit the hanging of a sign in a window of your home, you might wish to design one that emphasizes your particular skills or the products you wish to sell. This macrame teaching sign suggests one way this can be done.

48

could easily turn that space into an income-producing area by starting an arts and crafts class or workshop. I'll be talking more about teaching in general in another chapter, but for now, I want to tell you about Carol Reeves' approach to teaching in her home.

In addition to having boutiques and running a macrame supply mail-order business, Carol has been teaching for five years. She told me how she got started. "Most of my teaching has been at home around the kitchen table, and these classes have been fun for everyone. Initially, I advertised in the local papers, but most people have found me by word of mouth." Carol sets aside one night a week for her classes, and occasionally her studio becomes a "field trip" for other macrame classes in the community. Instructors from the junior college, the school district adult education program, and the city parks and recreation department bring their students to see her work, buy the macrame supplies she sells, and perhaps learn a new knot or two.

"I like to teach people individually," Carol explained, "assisting them at their level of expertise with the project of their choice. Whenever I have more than six or eight students, I have someone help me teach. There is a fee per class and students may purchase materials from me or bring their own." The casual atmosphere of Carol's classes makes it easy to make new friendships, and some of her students return every year for a few more classes.

Carol sells craft supplies to her students, as well as by mail order. The advantages of doing this are obvious. By acting as a "dealer" (buying craft supplies for resale) Carol gains in two ways: (1) she is able to buy her own materials in greater quantity and at lower prices than she would normally have to pay; and (2) she can realize an excellent profit (approximately 40 percent) on all the supplies she sells. (As was previously discussed, in order to buy at wholesale prices, you need a business name, a resale tax number, and a professional image. But, even without these things, as a teacher you may find that many suppliers will offer you a special studio discount of 10 percent or more.)

Obviously, not everyone is qualified to be a teacher, and even those who are may have no desire to teach. But it cannot be denied that teaching is an excellent way for a talented and creative woman to earn extra money in the comfort of her own home. In addition, teaching often serves as a springboard to other interesting sideline activities, such as lecturing or demonstrating one's art or craft — topics I will soon be discussing in greater detail.

The Party Plan

Have you ever attended a Tupperware Party? If so, you already know what the "party plan" is all about. Although this is reportedly a popular method for selling handcrafted items, I had a difficult time tracking down someone who was experienced in this type of craft marketing. Fortunately, I discovered Joan McGovern, who lives in Mantua, New Jersey. She was kind enough to explain in detail exactly how she operates her party plan business, which she calls "The Final Touch."

"Basically, I take my samples and catalog into people's homes, present them, and take orders," says Joan, who had this idea a long time before actually starting anything. "My husband talked me out of it at first, but I kept turning it over in my mind, becoming more and more fascinated by the idea. I finally decided I had nothing to lose, except time, so I tried it."

Joan has been involved in crafts for as long as she can remember, but only in the past few years has she started to market anything. After selling for a while, she decided that selling her own crafts was just not interesting enough. "I wanted to get more involved in the craft world," says Joan, "and market other crafts besides my own." Financially, a shop was out of the question, but Joan reasoned that if clothing, jewelry, and kitchen items could be sold through the party plan, why not crafts?

After months of searching for just the right crafts to sell, Joan asked various craftspeople to send a sample of each item they wanted her to market for them, plus a color photograph and all pertinent information as to sizes, colors, etc. (She found everyone willing to do this, by the way, although some did not have photographs to send,

50

Women who enjoy meeting new people and talking about handcrafts would find party-plan selling an enjoyable way to earn money.

and she had to take a few pictures herself.) With the color photos, she made up a "catalog," which she knew would be necessary since everything couldn't be carried with her when she went into homes.

At this point she had everything she needed to start selling — except a place to go. (Exposure was, and still is, a problem for Joan who says, "Who has ever heard of The Final Touch?") Of course, Joan started where all beginning sellers seem to start — with friends. Eventually she arranged a number of bookings and also found a demonstrator who began to give parties for her. Together, the two women worked outward from their combined circle of friends, and Joan's business began to grow.

In presenting her parties, Joan follows the basic concept of the party-plan type of selling in that she first finds a hostess who will volunteer the use of her home and provide both guests and refreshments. Then Joan, as the demonstrator, presents her line of crafts and gives her demonstration — usually a talk about the people who make the crafts, or any interesting techniques that may be involved. Afterwards, the guests are invited to examine the merchandise on display and place orders for what they want. (NOTE: Guests do not pay at this time, but rather when the merchandise is delivered.)

Joan explains that there may be variations between the sample and the item people will receive, pointing out that no two handmade items will ever be exactly the same. And, she tells them that it may take four to six weeks to receive orders, since craftspeople will be making each individual item to order. Joan's hostess receives a small gift (usually something Joan has made herself) plus a 10 percent credit on sales (which is payable in gift merchandise, not cash). Joan also gives additional credit to the hostess if future bookings are realized as a direct result of the demonstration in her home.

The continued success of this type of selling depends, of course, on being able to continually find new hostesses, who will bring in new guests to buy the merchandise. Even more important to Joan, who wants to expand beyond the state of New Jersey, is to find reliable and competent demonstrators from all areas of the country. "If someone has a real love of crafts, and wants to make a reasonable amount of money — 20 percent of party sales — while having a lot of fun, demonstrating my line of crafts could be a very attrctive business proposition," believes Joan, who emphasizes that the fun aspect is considerable. "My demonstrations are usually on a week night, so my husband stays home with the children. It gets me out of the house and I have a great time."

After each party, Joan sends the orders out and the craftspeople ship the items directly to her as soon as possible. When everything is received, she delivers the order to the hostess who, in turn, is responsible for getting the items to the individual buyers and collecting payment. When Joan receives full payment, she pays the craftspeople. She told me this has always gone smoothly for her. "One problem I foresaw, which never came to pass, was unreliability on the part of craftspeople to meet deadlines," says Joan, who works primarily with people she has never met personally. "But everyone has been more than cooperative, and all orders have been filled satisfactorily and on time. In fact, in most cases we exchange little personal notes as the orders go back and forth, and I find I am dealing with a wonderful group of people."

Now, if you like the concept of the party plan, you have two alternatives at this point. You could consider becoming a demonstator for Joan, or you could set up your own operation in your area. But remember that it takes work, not only to organize such a business, but also to find reliable craftspeople who will be able to fill the orders you take. How did Joan find her suppliers?

I was delighted to learn that she had begun her search with "Guide to the Craft World," a directory I had compiled in 1975 for the readers of *Artisan Crafts*. By reading the various descriptions of crafts offered by the craftsmen in the guide, and writing many letters explaining her plan, she was able to find several good crafts to add to her line. Next, she placed an ad in *Decorating & Craft Ideas* magazine and received an overwhelming response. This gave her additional items she could sell. Between periods of letter writing, Joan also

51

went to many craft fairs, and often found one or more new craftspeople at each show who were interested in working with her. At present, Joan handles the work of more than 50 craftspeople, but the number of different items in her line is considerably more, of course. She will always be searching for new crafts because she will always need new items to show established customers in the future.

I asked Joan how much money could be made with the party plan, and she said that the least she ever made was at her first party when only four people came. Her largest sale to date has been $235, but she has been in business only a year and naturally expects this figure to rise in the future. She said that at least ten people should attend a party to make it profitable.

Perhaps the best thing about starting your own party plan business is that it requires a very small outlay of cash at the beginning. Joan's only expenses were for photos, albums, ads in local papers, business cards, order blanks, and "lots and lots of stamps and stationery." And don't forget the fun aspect of this kind of business. As Joan says, "The parties are really a social evening out because I meet new people, talk about my favorite topics, have cake and coffee, and a good time in general."

Home shops, holiday boutiques, teaching workshops, and party-plan selling can all be fun and profitable, but maybe you'd rather keep your home life a bit more serene and do your selling elsewhere — perhaps at the fair? It has a special lure of its own, and it's certainly a great way to break into the crafts business with a minimum of splash. (Which means you can get your feet wet without committing the rest of yourself.)

Beginning sellers will find in the next chapter a vivid description of the many pleasures and possiblities of craft fair selling, and even seasoned show-goers will find some new ideas and professional tips that might increase their sales.

6

The Lure Of The Fair

I have a friend who has a successful husband and a profitable home business of her own, yet she works two days a week in a bookstore for the minimum hourly wage. For a long time I wondered why she did it since I knew she didn't need the money. When I asked her, she gave me a grin and this perfectly logical explanation: "Because I love books and people and all the nice things that can happen in a bookstore. Besides, I'm sick and tired of doing volunteer work, and this is my new lifeline with the outside world."

Many people sell at craft fairs (my friend included) for the same reason — because they love crafts and people and all the wonderful things that can happen at a fair, which is their lifeline with the craft world. A good fair, festival, or show (call it what you will) is a joy for one and all because it offers so many opportunities to see, to touch, to learn, and to be entertained. Those who participate in shows go not just to sell their wares, but also to meet other creative people, to exchange information and ideas, to observe new techniques, and perhaps just to have a pleasant vacation away from their studios and workshops. In particular they enjoy the special pleasure that comes from selling something they have made themselves, and then seeing that pleasure reflected on a buyer's face.

Pleasures aside, there are several real advantages to craft fair selling. To begin with, fairs are the most profitable way for the majority of craftspeople to market their work. When you sell at a fair, you are selling direct to the consumer, which means you are also eliminating the "middle man" — the shop owner who generally takes a 25 to 40 percent commission on consignment sales, the wholesale buyer who expects 50 percent off the retail price, or the sales representative who requires a 10 to 20 percent commission.

Fairs will also provide you with an excellent way to test prices, gain confidence in selling, and meet the kind of people who can help your business. In fact, the contacts made at a fair are often more valuable to craftspeople than sales themselves. For example, you might meet one or more shop owners who will want to carry your work, be given a commission to do some special job, catch the eye of a writer or photographer who will give you free publicity, or be invited to participate in other shows and events.

Another advantage is that many fairs and shows offer prize money or special awards that are important to a craftsman's ego or reputation.

Professional craftspeople and hobbyists alike share similar advantages in craft fair selling, but when they also share tables or booths in the same show, there's bound to be some incompatibility. Like oil and water, professional craftsmen and amateur craftspeople don't mix well. For this reason, more and more craft shows are being juried today. Juried means that certain standards have been established for each show, and hopeful exhibitors must meet those standards to be accepted into the show. As a seller, however, the most important thing is not just that your work be up to the standards required for a particular show, but that the show itself meets *your* requirements.

Entering shows on a hit-or-miss basis can be a total waste of time, financially speaking, so it's wise to enter juried shows whenever possible, or at least have a clear understanding of the type of work that will be exhibited in any show you plan to enter. Simply ask yourself, "Is my work in the same category?" Of course, the standards committee of a juried show may sometimes answer that question for you by refusing to accept your work for exhibit and sale, but in that event, it's decidedly to your advangage. What's the sense in exhibiting in a fair that won't show your products to best advantage, or attract the kind of buyers you seek?

No one seems to know just how many selling craftspeople there are in America today, or how many craft fairs are held annually, but experts claim there are more than 6000 fairs staged each year, and as many as 52 million Americans who consider themselves handcraftsmen. Although I can't verify these figures, I do know from traveling all over Europe that America is unique in all the world for both its abundance of fairs and its number of selling craftspeople. With so much competition and so many shows to choose from, how do you pick the few best suited to your needs, let alone find them?

Finding the Right Shows To Enter

Serious sellers, as well as those who sponsor craft fairs and shows, will be glad to learn that a new directory of show listings is available. Called *Craftworker's Market,* it is a Writer's Digest book which has been around for a while under the guise of *Artist's Market,* a book that previously contained show information for both artists and craftsmen. In the future, this directory will concentrate purely on art, while the new directory will zero in on craft-related media. Listings include detailed information such as entry fee and commissions (if any), average attendance, jury requirements, whether demonstrations are allowed, if chairs and tables are provided, whether awards are offered, how the show will be publicized, and so on. (NOTE: Listings in this annual directory are free, so if you want to publicize the show you sponsor or produce, write the editor for a listing form.)

The above directory is just one source of information on shows. There are also several regional publications carrying show listings, such as *The Crafts Fair Guide,* which provides a calendar of West Coast shows and also evaluates individual shows based on reports from exhibiting craftsmen. There is also *S.C.A.N.,* which lists mostly southeastern shows, and the *Regional Art Fair List,* which covers the Midwest. For broader coverage, there is the well-known quarterly, *National Calendar of Indoor/Outdoor Art Fairs,* which includes craft fairs as well. Check the resource chapter for other publications of interest, and don't forget to ask your friends about shows they have entered. It would also be a good idea to attend as many local fairs as possible, to size up their potential for you.

Care should always be taken in choosing which shows to enter, particularly flea markets and small shows. Such events, when not juried, can often demean the quality of a good craftsman's product. You should also be wary of shows that appear to use artists and craftsmen as a drawing card, but seem to be promoting other things, such as antiques shows, concerts, outdoor picnics, horse races, or carnival-type attractions. Look instead for shows that emphasize arts and crafts for sale, and try to get into shows where the number of craftsmen per craft will be limited. This will automatically cut your competition and entice buyers, who will have a wider variety of crafts from which to choose.

"It certainly is important that you select shows with care," says Audrey Punzel, a Wisconsin rosemaler, "or you may end up wasting your time." Audrey subscribed to two show-listing publications when she first began to sell at fairs, but even that didn't provide any guarantees.

55

Craft fairs are a joy for participant and visitor alike because they offer so many opportunities to see, to touch, to learn, and be entertained. Experts estimate there are more than 6,000 fairs and shows staged each year, but no one knows for sure just how many people regularly enter such events to sell their work. It has been estimated, however, that as many as 52 million Americans consider themselves handcraftsmen.

"Picking the right shows was mostly a matter of chance at first," she says, "but before long, other artists shared their opinions and soon there were no more 'lemons.' One thing we did learn was that the big celebration with the beer tent and carnival rides was not conducive to good sales."

Another artist puts it this way: "I started out going to all the art fairs I could, just to try them all. Now I have reached the point where I attend only four or five of the bigger ones, about two in the spring and two or three in the fall. It's not that I think I'm getting too good for all the small town shows I used to attend, but rather that I just can't afford to go to the ones that don't pay. Sometimes I could stay home and work all day and be further ahead than If I were sitting at a show and not selling."

Any widely publicized craft fair will attract an ineresting variety of exhibitors, including craft professionals who rely on such shows for their entire living, part-time craftspeople who have other jobs and count on craft fairs for extra income, and homemakers and hobbyists who are trying to break into the field or gain additional selling experience. The real beauty of a craft fair is that it is based on the principle of free enterprise, so the spirit of competition is keen. It's every man for himself, or woman, as the case may be. Even though you may feel like a complete amateur in a class all by yourself, if your work is good, you can easily compete with anyone else in the show — provided you go to that show prepared.

Many do not prepare for their first selling experience, as evidenced by a letter I received from a woman who said she was chairing a Chamber of Commerce spring festival of arts and crafts. "I sure could use your book right now," she wrote. "All these little ladies are pulling their patchwork pot covers, quilled flower pictures, and string art from boxes to enter in this festival. They have no idea about pricing, setting up a booth, or displaying. They are too bashful to submit articles and photographs for publicity. They don't even know to ask questions about sales tax, labeling of certain fibers, the ethics of copying the work of others, or using kits."

Obviously, there are many things beginning sellers should know before they enter their first show, and the rest of this chapter is devoted to a discussion of points that are applicable to both small and large fairs. If you aren't a beginning seller you have probably worked out most of your big problems by now, but there is always something new to be learned, so don't overlook the many professional tips and guidelines which follow.

56

What To Know Before You Go (Or, What To Ask Before You're Sorry)

Let's assume you want to enter a local, indoor, one-day show because it seems right for you and your products. In order to be prepared for all the possibilities, you should ask the following questions before you enter the show:

1. Do you think you will sell enough to cover your expenses and make a profit? If not, will the

experience and publicity you receive compensate for any financial loss?

Consider not only your time, but the entry fee or sales commission that may be taken at show's end, plus all expenses such as gas, food, and parking. Find out if there will be additional expenses for extra lights, security, insurance, etc. Remember Ruby Tobey, the Kansas artist? She says, "Many people say if you break even at one of the art fairs you can count it good because you are getting publicity and exposure for your work. I guess I would agree, but that would depend on the distance you have to travel and how much work it is for you to set up your display." She adds, "Anyone who attends many art fairs soon learns that he must have many small items he can sell fast to earn back the cost of the entry fee, gas, food, and, in my case, a baby sitter."

2. Are you planning to do the show alone, or will you have the help of a friend?

If you think you can do a show alone, think twice. It's possible, of course, but difficult. Have you figured out how you're going to get everything loaded into your car, van, etc., then get it unloaded at the show, and finally get everything home afterward? (Find out in advance what facilities for parking and unloading will be provided by the show chairman or promoter.) Think about who will help you "cover base" during the show while you take a break or have lunch. When the crowd gets heavy, you may need someone to help watch for shoplifters, keep children's hands off fragile merchandise, or package sold items. Remember that craft fair selling, normally tiring in itself, is all the more so because it involves the emotions of the seller, who has placed not only his products on display, but himself as well.

3. Will tables and chairs be furnished, or will you have to bring your own? If you have things that must be hung, will a wall unit be provided?

Perhaps you will have to construct special displays for yourself — an added expense, but well worth it if you plan to do several shows. Find out if you will have sufficient lighting for your exhibit, and electrical outlets if needed. (For more information on how to display your merchandise,

see "How To Plan a Good Display" later in this chapter.)

4. How many people are expected to attend the show, and will you have enough merchandise to last? How much is enough?

There are no easy answers here, because even professionals can miscalculate in this area. So much depends on variables such as the weather, the publicity given to a show, or the individual whims of buyers. When possible, talk to other craftspeople who have been in the show you plan to enter. If such guidelines are unavailable, simply take twice as much merchandise as you can reasonably expect to sell and hope for the best. Better too much than not enough.

Audrey Punzel, mentioned earlier, sells most of her rosemaling at craft fairs, and is usually joined by her husband, Ray, who makes much of the woodenware she paints. They carried a lot of work home with them after their first three-day local show, which brought them only $200 in sales. Now, however, they often gross $1000 per day in the larger shows and they confirm that selling experience is the best guide for determining merchandise requirements for any show. (That's another reason why you should always keep good records of what you sell and where.)

5. Do you have a variety of products priced in a broad range?

What you sell may depend entirely on the price range of your merchandise. The Punzels, for example, carry items from $1 to $70, with a few special things (such as trunks) priced as high as $300. "We also carry what I call 'loss leaders,' a popular item or two that are real bargains," Audrey adds, giving an incident that reflects the wisdom of this practice. "A customer timidly stopped one time at a distant show, browsed and finally bought a $3 napkin holder. A few hours later she came back with her husband and bought a $60 table. I feel she never would have stopped if I hadn't had that $3 napkin holder that appealed to her." Audrey's story was continued recently when she was at another show. The same woman stopped and introduced herself, saying she had $200 to spend this time. "In the end," says

| WOULD YOU GIFT WRAP IT PLEASE? | WHAT • $25? WHY I COULD MAKE THIS MYSELF! | COULD YOU MAKE IT IN PURPLE? | DO YOU HAVE A PRICE LIST OR BROCHURE? | I ONLY HAVE $3. DO YOU TAKE CHARGE CARDS? | THE SHOP IN TOWN HAS ONE JUST LIKE THIS ONLY CHEAPER. | I THINK IT'S GOING TO RAIN! |

Audrey, "her order came to more than $200, and it was all a chain reaction starting with a three-dollar item."

6. Are you going to sell at retail prices only? If so, what will you do if a wholesale buyer approaches you?

You are the only one who can determine whether it is possible, or desirable, to sell at wholesale prices or not, but whatever your decision, make it *before* you go to your first show, and set your retail prices accordingly.

If, like many craftspeople, you feel you simply cannot wholesale your work, perhaps the method used by the Punzels would work for you. Audrey explains: "I'm afraid if we priced our merchandise too high, we'd have to sit and wait for the occasional customer, and this would be discouraging. For this reason we do not wholesale. We have, instead, developed a policy of giving 10 percent for cash (or payment within ten days) for those who buy $50 or more for resale. and they are then free to put any price on the items warranted by their trade area. I know of one gift shop owner who pays $18 for a small clock of ours and sells it for $32.50. They pay $22.50 for a purse they retail at $35. Snce they are constantly re-ordering, I know they move. We are, however, careful not to supply more than one gift shop in an area so we do not cause any hard feelings over pricing."

SPECIAL NOTE: Ordinarily, shops need to mark up merchandise a full 100 percent to cover the many expenses involved in running their shop, but occasionally, as in the case of the Punzels, shop owners will realize that certain items are going to sell very quickly in their area at a higher price than the craftsman is asking. In order to carry these items (which will be an attractive addition to their stock) they are sometimes willing to take a smaller markup, and a lesser profit.

Unfortunately, some craftsmen react badly to a situation like this. Often, when a shop owner tells a craftsman he can sell his merchandise at a higher retail price, the craftsman gets greedy and raises his retail prices accordingly. But this can be a bad move, indeed, for now the craftsman finds he cannot sell his work at this higher price, and in addition, he has lost the shop as a customer! Don't let yourself become this money-hungry. Be content to receive the price you know will yield a satisfactory profit, and when you find a shop owner who can help you sell your work, understand that he, too, is entitled to make a profit from the sale of your merchandise. That's the American way.

Finally, let me tell you that nothing upsets a shop owner more than discovering that a craftsman is wholesaling an item to him at, say, $10, and selling it at a craft fair for the same price. If the shop sells it for $20, then the craftsman should also sell it for $20. *It is unprofessional to do otherwise.* I urge you always to maintain your retail prices because, like the shop owner, you also have selling expenses that must be offset, and the time spent at a show (away from your studio or workshop) should yield some profit for you. Craftsmen are self-defeating if they decide to become wholesalers and then go out to a fair and sell at less than retail prices. They are then underselling their dealers. Only by maintaining your retail prices at all times can you hope to realize the profit that is rightfully yours, and only by operating in a professional manner can you hope to maintain good business relations with your shop customers.

In addition, you should not discount your prices. Your work is worth as much at the end of a show as it was at the beginning, and if you don't sell it, simply take it to another show and try again.

7. What if a shopowner asks you to place your work on consignment, or a customer wants a custom-designed item?

Before deciding whether or not to place your work on consignment, you should carefully weigh the many advantages and disadvantages of this type of selling, which is discussed in detail in the next chapter.

If you decide to take a custom-design order, remember that some people will order something, then decide later on they don't want it — after you have spent several hours and perhaps many dollars in materials. That's why it's a good idea to do one of the following things when customer orders are concerned: Either ask for a down payment sufficient to cover your actual costs (to be kept if the customer cancels later on), or make sure your custom-designed item is such that it can easily be sold to someone else.

8. How are you going to keep track of your sales at the show? Do you have a sales slip book? A money box? Sacks and wrapping paper?

Keeping records of your sales is very important (both for tax reasons and for projecting future merchandise needs for other shows) and you can buy the necessary sales slip books at stationery stores. For each item sold, you should write a sales ticket for the customer, and make a carbon copy for your own records. Show the name of the item sold (or its code number, if you have assigned one to it and recorded this information elsewhere), then the price, how much tax is being charged, and finally, the total.

Here's a valuable tip from George and Nancy Wettlaufer's book, *The Craftsman's Survival Manual:* "A good policy at a craft show is to take an inventory at the beginning and at the end of the day, then check it against your list and your cash box. This type of cross-check is a good way to figure out if anything is missing, and it is a quick and simple way to determine how much you sold and which items have been selling best."*

As for a money box, that's easy to make. One idea is to use a cigar box and add cardboard dividers secured with tape to keep coins and currency separate. Even better, use a fishing tackle box, which you may already have on hand. Keep your money box closed unless you are making change, and always be careful to keep bills out of the box until the financial transaction is completed. (This will protect you in case a customer becomes confused about the size of the bill he gave you.) Be sure to take a sufficient amount of change with you because you probably won't be able to get it at the show. Decide in advance whether you will accept checks or not, and what identification you will ask to see.

59

---

*From *The Craftsman's Survival Manual,* by George and Nancy Wettlaufer. © 1974 by Prentice Hall, Inc., and used with permission.

Once your sale is made, you can wrap or bag it in a number of ways. You'll find some bag sources in the resource chapter, but if you need to begin less expensively, use lunch sacks or even plastic bags for small items, or wrap things in tissue and tie with colored yarn. Some craftspeople simply use newspaper tied with twine because they know craft fair buyers aren't that fussy about how something is wrapped. The important thing is whether they can get it home safely or not.

9. Will you demonstrate your craft at the show, or wear a costume?

Demonstration of one's craft is sometimes required, other times not permitted or even advisable. When allowed, and when you feel a demonstration will help your sales, by all means demonstrate! Generally speaking, the craftsman who does something in his booth will always outsell the one who merely sits on a chair in the corner, reading a book or showing no apparent interest in whether customers buy or not. Naturally, if you plan to demonstrate, you must also plan to have some sales help. You can't do both efficiently.

10. Do you have printed calling cards? A price list or brochure?

Any seller who doesn't have a calling card, or some kind of printed literature with his name and address on it, is telling the world he's unprofessional. Even if you have to hand print a few cards to get started, take something to your first show with your name and address on it, so you can hand it to interested people. This often leads to additional sales and unusual opportunities. As soon as you can afford it, have printed cards made. They need not be expensive to be effective. (Also see "Promotional Materials" in Chapter 12.)

60

If you are making several standard items for sale, you should also have a price list or printed handbill, particularly if you wish to sell your work by mail. These can be handed out to people who stop at your booth, and may generate orders for weeks thereafter. (Not everyone buys on impulse.)

11. Are you aware of the many laws and regulations that apply to selling artists and craftsmen?

Clearly, many sellers and show promoters operate in defiance of the law. Some are aware of the laws but choose to ignore them; others are simply ignorant of the law, forgetting that old saying, "Ignorance is no excuse." Do you realize you may need a retail license or permit to sell in a show? If your state has a sales tax, you are supposed to collect (and report to the state) sales tax on all your sales. There are regulations that affect the raw materials you can use in your work, the labeling of your products, and consumer safety. Are you familiar with them? Have you registered your name with the county clerk? If you choose to ignore the laws applicable to sellers, then you must also be prepared to pay the penalty, which could be something as simple as having your booth closed down at a show, as bad as a stiff fine, or worse. (For more information on this topic, see Chapter 14.)

All of the foregoing questions are as applicable to local, indoor, one-day events as they are to shows of longer duration that are either outdoors or out of town. However, there are a few additional things to consider, namely:

12. If your display is to be left overnight for any reason — either indoors or outside — have you considered the possibility of theft or damage?

One couple I know who entered a large shopping mall show lost everything when the mall caught fire one evening. They never thought it would happen to them, so they had no insurance for such a thing. Do you? Also, are you aware that you could be held liable for any damage, injury, or sickness caused by one of your products? Discuss this matter with your insurance agent, and also refer to Chapter 15.

13. If exhibiting outdoors with no protection from the elements, will you be prepared for wind or rain?

Any outdoor show is a calculated risk, and many people have had their entire stock ruined in an unexpected rain or wind storm. It won't happen to you, however, if you take steps to prevent it.

14. If exhibiting outdoors in a tent, have you considered that it might leak?

Never leave your work unprotected at night. Even new tents have been known to leak, and water can also seep in under the tent flap, ruining anything on the ground. It would be wise to take duckboards with you, as well as large, waterproof coverings.

15. What major expenses will be incurred by an out-of-town trip?

Sometimes it is more profitable to exhibit in small local fairs than to travel out of town to the big shows and incur the accompanying food, gas, and lodging expenses. When traveling in a van or trailer to save on expenses, remember that you will still need a place to camp, and reservations should be made in advance. Don't forget to allow for changes in weather and take appropriate clothing so you won't have to buy something you don't really need. Some people also carry portable fans or heaters with them in case of extreme weather conditions. At any rate, make sure you take sufficient funds with you — or have access to additional cash — should you incur unexpected car trouble, illness, or serious injury.

And there you have the most important things to think about before you enter a craft show. As a seller, you may never make a shot heard 'round the world, but if you want to make a good bang, you'll need the ammunition for it.

Setting Up a Display

How you display your crafts at a fair is up to you. You can either do it like an amateur, and realize sales accordingly, or try to emulate the professionals and perhaps reap large profits, even in a small, local show.

Like commercial gift items, crafts and needlework need to be beautifully displayed in order to attract the attention of buyers, and you can get some good ideas for your table or booth simply by browsing in a nice gift shop. Note the interesting shelf arrangements, display cases, and background walls. They will probably give you several ideas for displays you can easily make, using inexpensive materials.

What constitutes a good display? Michael Scott, editor of *The Crafts Report* says, "A good display will show enough to demonstrate the range of work available and allow the customer to browse, but not so much that the customer gets confused and can focus on nothing." He adds, "It is *not* necessary to put everything you brought to a craft fair out on the table at one time."

There are several things to take into consideration when planning a display. Let's begin with the size of your selling area. The average display area at fairs is about ten feet square, and depending on what you are selling, you may or may not want your customers walking within this area. Therefore, you should design your booth to keep customers exactly where you want them — whether it's in front of you, down the center of your booth, or all around you. Do remember that not everyone in a crowd will be honest, and a poorly designed booth will be a real temptation to any thief, to say nothing of mischievous children. Since small, expensive pieces (such as jewelry) are the things most likely to be taken, they should always be kept in a suitable display case, or at least on a table near you where they cannot be reached without your knowledge.

A good display must be strong and sturdy in order to stand up against the press of the crowd, the whoosh of the wind, and the weight of your merchandise. At the same time, it should be lightweight, or at least portable enough to be easily carted to and from fairs. Ideally, your entire booth should be designed so it can be set up or broken down and packed by one person, since you may not always have someone around to help you.

If you plan to exhibit at outdoor shows, you might consider using cinder blocks as the basis for shelves to hold pottery or glassware. Although they are heavy to lug around, they can make a sturdy and attractive display. Be sure your display unit doesn't end up top-heavy. You wouldn't want it to fall over after it's loaded with your crafts, ruining them and possibly the booth of another craftsman as well. And here's another tip: When doing outdoor shows you might want to take an umbrella to protect you from the sun, and always take a waterproof covering that can be thrown over your goods in case of a sudden shower.

A common type of display unit, equally as good indoors or out, is the A-frame structure, which resembles a tall saw-horse. Such units are

61

This display unit, shown as it might look in the early stages of being set up, was designed by Audrey and Ray Punzel of Wisconsin. Ladders were stained and ornamented with rosemaling similar to the painted designs on their products, and pegboard was cut to fit the ends of the ladders. The combination of shelving placed on the steps of each ladder, with framed pegboard walls behind and a covered table in front, gives plenty of space to display a variety of differently shaped items. This type of display also allows for gradual enlargement as one's business grows.

especially suitable for things that must be hung, and it's always easy to add shelves when needed. Collapsible metal bookshelves might also work for you, and I'm sure you have seen shelves made by placing boards on the steps of two step ladders. In fact, Audrey and Ray Punzel built their entire display unit around this idea. I asked them how they did it, and what suggestions they had to offer to other craftspeople.

"Be original and practical," Audrey told me, "and be sure your display fits the type of merchandise you're selling. Our ladders and planks would hardly be suitable for fine jewelry!"

The Punzels began building their display by staining two ladders and two planks. Then they framed two pieces of peg board, mounting them (with carriage bolts and wing nuts) to the top plank between the ladders. A brace and bracket centered in the back holds them up and together. Audrey rosemaled the ladders and the planks, and they themselves are a conversation piece. This, plus a card table and chairs, was their original display.

"Then," says Audrey, "we added more items because we needed more space." First they framed two more pieces of pegboard and added "wings" at each end, mounted with pin butt hinges. The wasted space between the legs of the ladders was put to use by framing two more triangle-shaped pieces of pegboard. These held movable shelves, and could also be utilized for hanging things if the shelf items moved faster than the hanging items.

The Punzels' next display project was a combination cart and table, designed by Audrey. "My husband has always called me the Head of Design," she says, "and he's the Head of Manufacturing. According to him, if I designed a dinghy, we'd end up with the Queen Mary." Audrey explains how her "Queen Mary Cart and Table" was built: "Ray had steel plates welded to the frame of one-inch conduit. Two fixed and two swivel casters were mounted on the plates, and a plywood bottom was attached. Angle iron was welded across the top of each end to hold the table top." (This board is loose, and when used as a cart, it is just dropped to the bottom. The Punzels load it with their boxes of merchandise and wheel it into their van on two wooden rails they made to

hook over the back bumper.) "When we unload," says Audrey, "we roll it out to our site, unload the boxes, raise the board to table top height, and put our fitted cloth over the top. The table is also used for display and we have hidden storage space underneath."

If you don't have a van or station wagon, getting your display and merchandise to a show may present a problem, but you can work it out. An automobile can hold an amazing amount of goods when properly packed, and your goal is simply to design a display that will collapse and fit into the space you have available. When packing space is a problem, you might think about using small barrels or boxes that will hold your merchandise en route to a show, then double as display props in the booth itself. Boards placed on two boxes or barrels make very good shelves to hold merchandise.

By the way, did you note Audrey's mention of a fitted cloth used over her table-cart? Although this isn't necessary, it would certainly add a tailored look to any display table. A table covering should at least come all the way to the floor or ground. Not only does this look better, but also it enables you to use the area under the table for storage. Be sure to select a material that complements your crafts or needlework, remembering that the background should never overshadow the work itself. Suitable fabrics for table coverings might be felt, burlap, velveteen, or simply a colored sheet or bedspread. Or perhaps a large straw mat on the top of your table is just the thing that's needed to give your crafts the proper background. Experiment to achieve the best results.

Always think "contrast" when planning a display. Consider placing smooth surfaces against rough ones, and vice versa. Vividly colored items will look best on subdued or natural backgrounds, while items with little color will be more noticeable when placed against a brightly colored or rough-textured background. (Weathered wood, burlap covered walls, and painted pegboard seem to be favorite backgrounds for many craftspeople these days, but perhaps you can come up with something even better.) Glass looks terrific on bricks, and silver jewelry always looks most impressive when displayed on black velvet or plexiglas, which also

63

*A few display ideas that could be used at a crafts fair. (A) If you don't have
a shady spot at an outdoor crafts fair, an umbrella over your table will
provide welcome relief from the hot sun. (B) Don't forget that it could rain.
Take a large plastic cover to throw over your display. (C) An old barrel could
serve as a container when carrying crafts to the fair, then do double duty as a
display unit once you're set up. (D) An antique coat rack might add atmosphere
to a crafts display, as would an old trunk (E) that could be filled with
things like pillows, quilts, dolls, or toys. (F) An interesting piece of driftwood,
a couple of bricks, and a sheet of plexiglas make an eye-catching display
for a variety of crafts, as does an arrangement of boxes or cubes (G).*

complements many other crafts. A sheet of plexiglas, when placed on blocks of wood or bricks, can make a stunning display prop, and if you can also figure out how to include battery-operated lights in special displays such as this, it would add considerably to the overall effect of your booth— particularly when you end up in a dreary tent some day.

If you don't want to build your own props, visit flea markets and used furniture shops for things that will serve your needs. All it takes is a bit of time and imagination. You could probably do wonders with an old hat rack, trunk, or antique shelf unit. Also keep your eyes open for interesting nature items, such as small logs, driftwood, or gnarled branches. All would add flavor to many craft and needlework displays.

As you can see, ingenuity is the key to good display planning, along with originality and practicality. Your work may actually be judged by the overall quality of your display, so make it as clever and eye-catching as you can.

Your Personal and Professional Image

Good displays are vital to success in selling, but it takes more than that to be a successful seller. Also needed are craftsmanship, showmanship, and salesmanship, to say nothing of a neat appearance.

One's appearance is certainly important to one's professional image, and when exhibiting your work, it is wise to dress in a manner appropriate to your craft. For example, if you do contemporary work, regular clothing would be fine. If rustic or country crafts are your specialty, however, jeans and a plaid shirt or other homespun costume would probably look better. If you happen to do a traditional folk art, a colorful native costume would attract extra attention. When there are two or more people in a booth, something as simple as matching aprons, shirts, or hats can be a real eye-stopper. If needlework, quilting, or macrame happens to be your specialty, you might do some fancy stitching on your blouse, make a patchwork skirt or jacket, or macrame a fancy vest for yourself. Above all, be neat and clean. As Audrey Punzel says, ''Your 'bag' may be

jeans and a disheveled appearance, but most customers are neat, and they will appreciate neatness in you.''

Also consider that more and more people do not smoke these days, and the person who insists on smoking in his booth should figure on losing some sales from nonsmokers, many of whom simply won't go near anyone who is apt to blow smoke in their direction.

Next to neatness, friendliness may be most important. Artists who sit in their booth with arms crossed, staring at the crowd with a bored expression (or worse, reading a book) are *not* radiating interest and friendliness. As one buyer commented, ''These actions almost dare the customer to stop, and he usually doesn't. It takes action to get attention. Paint, whittle, tie knots, move about—but do something—and smile.''

Carol Bernier, the shop owner and crafts buyer you met in Chapter 5, told me that too few craftspeople greet her as she approaches their booth. ''It is amazing what a smile and a cheery hello can do,'' she said. ''For one thing, it stops me for a moment. If I seem slightly interested, why doesn't the person then say something like, 'Do you like the color?' or 'That's one of my new designs,' or anything to make me feel at ease and encourage me to pause and look his wares over a bit more.'' Craftspeople usually just sit and stay sitting, according to Carol, who goes to a lot of shows to buy merchandise for her shops.

''If they are talking with another craftsperson,'' she points out, ''they often continue talking as though I were not even there. Sometimes they sit on the floor or ground and I have to literally walk over them in order to see what's for sale. Maybe these people forget why they are there. They decided to show at this fair to sell their crafts, and here I am, a buyer. Grab me, sell to me. Don't ignore me!'' Carol says she cannot overemphasize the importance of a businesslike image, and she advises sellers to make the most of their time at a show and do what they originally set out to do: SELL. ''You can talk to friends and read books after the show,'' she concludes, ''when you are counting up all the sales you've made.''

Yes, I know it's hard to sell, especially when

you are emotionally involved with your products, as all artists and craftsmen are. But you must develop a different attitude at a fair and remember that, at a show, you are a salesman first, and an artist or craftsman second.

Some people avoid contact with the public simply because they are shy or lack confidence in their work; others just don't want to hear the usual discouraging remarks such as "Oh, I can do that myself," or any of a hundred other remarks made by thoughtless people. Negative feedback is one of the few disadvantages of direct selling that you will have to learn to accept. Although it hurts to hear it, it can sometimes be helpful when it reminds you that there is still room for improvement in some areas.

Carol Bernier has an interesting viewpoint on this topic that might help you cope with negative feedback. "Just because someone makes an unflattering comment about your work, it isn't the end of the world," she emphasizes. "A person may make a comment, but he is still a potential buyer. If not at this show, perhaps later, when his tastes may change, or your work has improved (if it truly is shoddy). Or maybe the next time you will have colors and styles to his liking. But if you reciprocate with a nasty remark to this potential buyer, he won't forget it. Just pass it off as his opinion, whether good or bad. You can't please everyone all of the time."

Even Zeuxis realized this way back in 400 B.C. Once, when he was criticized for something he had done, he said (smugly, I'm sure), "Criticism comes easier than craftsmanship." Remember that the next time you overhear a discouraging word and smile to yourself. For all you know, your most appreciative buyer could be right on your critic's heels.

Besides looking good and acting friendly in spite of what people may say, what else can you do to create a better image of yourself? In addition to demonstrating your craft, or at least looking busy in your booth, you should have printed sales literature or calling cards to give to interested people. And, individual tags on your work that tell buyers who you are and what makes your product special can add considerably to your professional image. You can design these yourself and have them printed quite inexpensively.

It is also important to stay with the times; you will have to study the new trends in crafts, gifts, toys, decorative accessories, clothing, etc., in order to keep up with your competition. If you are like most craftspeople, you will tend to return to the same fairs year after year, particularly if they prove financially successful for you. In that case, some of the people visiting these shows may be customers who bought from you in previous years. If you want them to have something to come back for each year, you will have to add new items to your line from time to time, or at the very least, change your colors, patterns, or designs so your work will look different to those who know you.

REMEMBER: If a field is to yield a good crop every year, it must be cultivated with care. And when you have learned how to cultivate repeat customers at a fair, you will have learned an important secret in making more money from your crafts.

Special Exhibitions And Prize Money Opportunities

There are some people who will never produce enough work to sell at a craft fair, but who would nonetheless enjoy having it seen and appreciated by others. For such people, exhibitions may be particularly appealing. And, when the possibility of cash awards exists, the temptation to exhibit one's work may be even greater.

Hobbyists and professionals alike enter exhibitions for similar reasons: to gain prestige or recognition in their field, and to compete for money awards. I know little about this from experience, however, so I asked Bucky King, a nationally known textile craftsman, for more information. Bucky, who thinks of herself as a "threadbender," teacher, designer, producing craftsman, and lover of fibers, has had her work exhibited throughout the United States and the United Kingdom. I asked her to explain the types of exhibitions craftspeople and needleworkers might enter.

"Basically, there are two distinct kinds of exhibitions," Bucky wrote. "There are the juried show and the nonjuried show. The juried exhibition may be open nationally, regionally, or locally. (This is always stated in the prospectus, as are all the rules for submission.) The best of these always offer good money prizes and are worth the trouble to seek. Selections are made by qualified jurors. The juried show for the professional craftsman offers recognition, not just in prizes awarded, but in the prestige of being accepted and the good publicity this brings. It also furthers sales, because of the publicity. The craft collectors in this country frequent these shows and are influenced by the work presented. Galleries go to these shows looking for future work for their shops, and magazines such as *Craft Horizons* review them, thus providing more free publicity and recognition for the craftsman.

"Amateurs usually have their work juried out of such shows," notes Bucky, "partly because the competition from professionals is keen, and partly because they submit unprofessional slides. In fact, about 80 percent of the national and regional open juried shows are by slide submission simply because it is easier to mail back the many rejects in the form of slides than it is to mail back the actual work itself."

There is always an entry fee for exhibitions, which you do not get back if your work is rejected, thus entering exhibitions can be expensive, particularly when a professional photographer must be hired to take slides. And without good slides, one has little chance of getting into a good show. In addition to professional slides, what else do jurors look for? Competence, for one, says Bucky. A command of your materials and the use of proper techniques. Innovative designing. "Work that

67

looks like things already on the market won't measure up here," she warns.

The other type of show is the nonjuried show, where everything submitted is hung or displayed, and might win a prize if it is offered. "About 70 per cent of all the needlework shows in the United States are nonjuried," says Bucky. "Awards, even money prizes, are offered, and everything submitted is shown. The jurors simply select the best pieces and award the ribbons or prizes accordingly. Naturally, since these shows lure many hobbyists, the quality of design is sometimes quite poor, although techniques may be excellent."

Juried exhibitions, then, are best for the more professional craftsperson or needleworker, while the hobby-craftsman or less experienced needleworker should try a nonjuried show for her first fling. Adds Bucky, "This is a good way to start, particularly if recognition is all the person cares about, and for many this is all that is important—to see their pieces hanging or displayed somewhere."

National and regional exhibitions and competitions are generally listed along with regular craft fairs in the various publications and show calendars mentioned earlier. You will also find an excellent list of regular, annual exhibitions in *Craftworker's Market*, an annual directory issued by Writer's Digest. Study the listings to find shows of interest, then write for additional information (a prospectus) before deciding whether you want to take this particular step on your ladder of success.

A word of warning, however. When it is necessary to submit the actual work itself (instead of slides) think twice before you mail your most prized creation to an exhibition, since the possibility always exists that you will not get it back in the same condition as you sent it. Perhaps the exhibition committee will not handle it as carefully as it should be. Or, if the exhibit isn't insured and your work is damaged or stolen, guess who loses?

Granted, this sort of thing is certainly the exception, rather than the rule, but it is a possibility that should be considered, and it would be remiss of me not to mention it. In the end, it all comes down to how much you desire recognition and the possibility of cash awards for your work. Many people enter exhibitions on a regular basis, often to excellent advantage, with no problems whatsoever. If you are primarily interested in selling one-of-a-kind pieces, or doing commission work (versus selling in a variety of shops), regular exhibition of your work could greatly enhance your image and increase your sales.

Exhibitions aside for the moment, there is another way to win recognition and prize money, with no entry fees or risk involved. You might enter some of the contests advertised in women's magazines such as *Woman's Day, Family Circle, Good Housekeeping*, etc. Here, men and women alike can vie for cash awards and the chance of having their work featured in an upcoming issue of the magazine, which is great for both the pocketbook and the ego. Occasionally such contests are given publicity in craft or needlework journals, but generally one learns of them simply by being a regular magazine reader.

NOTE: Magazine readers are obviously interested in such contests. A recent *Good Housekeeping* quilt contest attracted almost 10,000 entries. A 1976 *Woman's Day* crochet and knit design contest received more than 25,000 entries, and 51 winners were declared. First prize was $1000. Back in 1972, after a *Family Circle* needlework contest drew over 60,000 original designs with its offer of $10,000 in prizes, 200 semifinalists were asked to send their actual creations, and many winners were then selected and featured in the magazine.

Wholesale Fairs and Gift Shows

This section is for those readers who have considerable product to sell at wholesale prices, and who may be dreaming about, or actually gravitating toward, bigger and better shows. Tremendous sales possibilities await the craftsman who can meet the challenge of the big handcrafts fair, and to give you an idea of just how big this business has become in recent years, let me mention two of the largest retail/wholesale craft shows now being held annually.

The major marketplace for contemporary crafts in the United States — the Northeast Craft

Fair in Rhinebeck, New York, sponsored by the American Crafts Council — reported sales of $2 million in 1977, with public attendance of 44,000 and 2000 registered wholesale buyers. More than 2000 craftspeople applied for the 500 available booths in this show, which is open only to members of the American Crafts Council. The third Annual Frederick Craft Fair in Maryland, a show open to craftspeople all over the country, had sales of $1,250,000; 30,000 people came to buy from 500 craftsmen.

The above figures were taken from an article in the September 1977 issue of *The Crafts Report* (a newsmonthly for crafts professionals), which also gave sales figures for several other important shows. The article indicated that both sales and attendance are on the rise at quality craft fairs all over the country, *due in large part to craftsmen's increased awareness of the importance of professionally designed displays.*

Of course, one should not even consider entering a big show unless he is an experienced seller and fully prepared for all possibilities. In order to produce crafts in quantity, one has to have a certain psychological makeup. It can get to be very much like factory work after all, and few genuinely creative people can be production craftsmen for long. Those who can, however, may often sell as much as half (or more) of their annual production at one trade fair. They will work for months beforehand to build inventory, then go to the show and completely sell out their stock, returning with enough new wholesale orders to keep them busy for weeks thereafter. Then the cycle begins anew.

Many craftspeople have gone into trade shows not really expecting to sell much, only to be bombarded with orders and placed in a panic situation when they suddenly realize they have taken more orders than they can possibly fill. On the other hand, a craftsman might not receive many orders at all. Either way, doing a trade show can be something of a shock, as indicated by the letter I received from Mark Davis, a Wisconsin craftsman whose line of wooden toys is superior in quality and design. After exhibiting in a commercial gift show, Mark wrote: "I tried my first trade show in Kansas City, and it will be the last, as I lost my shirt on the deal. I can't compete with plastic imports." Later on, Mark tried one of the larger craft trade fairs and reported: "I didn't do real well, but I've received several orders since, and the experience really opened my eyes. I'll have to clean up my act and improve the overall image of the whole thing. For this to work, I must have a totally professional image and look as if I know what I'm doing — printed brochures, invoices, letterheads, leaflets, etc."

As you can see, even a professional craftsman can find a trade show intimidating, and entry into such a show is for the few, not the many. However, if you would like to learn more about trade shows, simply read the appropriate trade magazines. For instance, craft shows are discussed in the various periodicals serving this field, gift shows are listed in gift industry magazines such as *Gifts and Decorative Accessories,* and information about craft supply trade shows will be found in publications such as *Profitable Crafts Merchandising.* Also read "Exhibiting at the HIA Show" in Chapter 10, since it contains the trade secrets of a couple of homemakers who took their kits to the big trade fair and gave their businesses a tremendous boost as a result. The women agree it wasn't an easy job, but they are living proof that the average homemaker is often equal to such a challenge.

70

Whether situated in a rural or urban area, the typical crafts shop in America is likely
to be owned by people with a special interest in handcrafts and the American craftsman.
Often the owners of such shops are professional craftsmen themselves.

7

Selling Through Retail Outlets

Craft fair selling isn't the answer for everyone and, for some homemakers, it may even be impossible because of family obligations that require their constant presence at home. Marketing through retail outlets is always a possibility, however, and particularly desirable for those who wish to spend most of their time designing or producing instead of selling. An extra advantage of shop selling is that it can be done entirely by mail — a real plus for those who live in rural areas.

But inexperienced sellers often have a poor understanding of how shops operate, and thus, a poor understanding of how to deal with them. In fact, many craftspeople think shop owners are taking advantage of them when they take a 100 percent markup on their work. Let me set you straight on that right now. Financially speaking, most craft shop owners are in the same boat as craftsmen. Their profit margins are slim, their hours long, their problems many and complex.

In my experience as a crafts magazine editor, I have often had the opportunity to study both sides of this picture and have come to understand the problems faced by craftsmen and shop owners alike. Therefore, I chose to present in this chapter a picture few sellers have seen before: the craftsperson as he appears to the craft shop owner. Later on you will read what some shop owners have to say about dealing with craftspeople, what they expect of them, and what frustrates them most. Then you will learn what you should expect of them, and what precautions you should take when entering into any new shop relationship.

Shops and Galleries: How They Differ

Perhaps a general discussion of the difference between shops and galleries will help sharpen your focus at this point. Galleries aside for the moment, there are two basic kinds of shops with which you will probably be dealing: *craft* shops and *gift* shops. While both may carry handcrafts and imports, gift shops are generally associated with the commercial gift industry, craft shops with the handcrafts industry. What this means is that the owners walk different paths, read different publications, go to different shows, etc.

Gift shops and boutiques can be started by anyone with sufficient capital to buy inventory, and, generally, such people have little knowledge of crafts. It's true that more and more gift shops are now carrying a line of handcrafts, but often this merchandise is purchased from professional craftsmen who exhibit at craft trade fairs (such as Rhinebeck) or have sales representation at leading gift shows. This is not to say that the average craftsperson cannot sell to a commercial gift shop, only that his merchandise is going to have stiff competition, and he'd better know how to deal with the shop in a businesslike way.

Craft shops are usually started by people with a special interest in handcrafts and the American craftsman, and, often, the owners of such shops are craftspeople themselves. Of course, some are simply business-minded men or women who are dedicated to the idea of helping craftspeople market their work.

As for galleries, there are two kinds. One kind offers only fine art and the other sells art plus crafts or sculpture, weaving, needlework, etc. Craft galleries operate on a consignment basis similar to regular craft shops, with their primary difference being the way merchandise is displayed. Also, special exhibitions and sales are held from time to time to promote the work of one or more artisans or craftsmen represented in the gallery. Art galleries prefer to work only with full-time professionals, but craft galleries are ususaly interested in contact from any fine artisan or craftsperson.

Craft shops may operate on an outright-purchase basis, consignment arrangement, or a combination of both, but commercial gift shops and other retail outlets usually buy outright. If a craft shop takes work on consignment, a commission of between 25 and 40 percent of the retail price will be kept by the shop. Galleries may take an even larger commission.

Some craft shops work on a different basis, called "guaranteed sales," whereby the shop owner buys the craftwork outright with the understanding that the craftsman will exchange any pieces that have not sold after a certain length of time. In some ways this is similar to consignment, except it's better because you get your money before the work is actually sold. But if it doesn't sell, and the shop has kept it in good condition, you will be expected to replace it with other work of the same quality and price. Or, if you guarantee sales on wholesale orders, it would mean that if your work does not sell after a specified length of time, at a specified price, it can be returned to you (in good condition) and you will allow credit for it on the shop's next order.

The Consignment Controversy

Many professionals will advise you against consignment selling, arguing that shop owners who won't (or can't afford to) buy your merchandise outright will not work very hard to sell it, and will often ruin it in the process. Yet, for the beginner, consignment selling may be the best (or only) way to get started.

Since I have had both good and bad experiences with consignment, I am not going to advise you one way or the other. But I am going to present a picture of this type of selling from the viewpoint of both craftsman and shop owner, and show you the advantages and disadvantages to both. Then you can decide for yourself if consignment is the route you want to go.

First you should understand the basic difference between selling your work outright and consigning it. When you sell outright, you relinquish all control over your merchandise. Once you have been paid for it, the shop owns it and can sell it for any price it wishes. When you consign merchandise, however, you are merely transferring it to another who will act as your sales representative. Thus, you remain the owner of all consigned goods and will not receive payment for them until sometime after they have been sold. This can often take months, which is why some craftspeople prefer to wholesale their work. Even though their profits may be smaller, they at least get their money in hand as soon as possible.

What are the main disadvantages of consignment selling? We might begin with the increased bookkeeping and paperwork involved. For the craftsman, it's more than would be required for wholesaling, and for the shop, it's enough to give a trained accountant a headache. Considering that most shop owners aren't accountants, one can imagine their problems in keeping everything straight, particularly when they are just beginning in business. A new consignment shop may begin with as few as twenty-five consignors, but, as business grows, this number may increase to as many as five hundred people — all of whom are bringing in dozens of items that must be specially coded, inventoried, priced, and displayed. Ledger sheets must be accurately maintained for each consignor in order to make monthly reports and payments, checks must be written, envelopes addressed, etc. Meanwhile, the shop may be plagued with telephone calls and letters from craftspeople who want to know if this or that item has been sold and how soon they will get their money. Since the consignor remains the legal owner of the merchandise until it is sold, he is naturally the one most concerned about it.

And well he should be, for when many items are placed on consignment in several shops, it can mean that a great deal of capital is tied up in inventory. If the craftsman happens to be dealing with an undercapitalized shop, it is quite possible that he will not be paid promptly for work already sold (or worse, not paid at all).

Judy Bridge of Sarasota, Florida, is an example of what can sometimes happen in consignment selling. In a letter, Judy told me how she got started selling, and what problems she encountered: "My little sock babies have really done well for me," she wrote. "It all began when I prayed and asked the Lord to help me sell my things. Next day in the mail came my copy of *Decorating and Craft Ideas* magazine with the section on "Where To Sell Your Crafts." Now is that an answer to prayer? Wow! So I wrote to 18 shops, and got 17 answers in return. Everyone wanted my dolls. I was so excited! The following month I did the same, and before I knew it, I had to hire someone to help me keep up with all the orders."

Judy sold some of her dolls outright, and consigned many others. Unfortunately, her experience with some of the consignment shops listed hasn't been good. Eager to get started in selling, Judy was not too selective. She wrote to all shops listed, and practically all indicated an interest in her work, so she followed through and sent merchandise accordingly. Now she writes: "I'm getting to the point where I don't want consignment any more unless the shop sells well. Right now, I'm stuck for quite a bit. My dolls are inexpensive, but they add up. I have some shops who took half a dozen, and I've never heard from them since. A bunch of these shops can hurt, so I'm weeding out and putting them aside. I've written two or three times; I

73

can do no more. That's where the losses come in, and that is definitely a problem when you consign by mail. You don't know where the shop is or the people who run it. I've had shops that have had four owners in less than a year.''

I've heard Judy's story dozens of times from other craftspeople, so I know this sort of thing happens with regularity. Yet, there are many good consignment shops out there somewhere, if one can only find them. Later in this chapter you will learn how to do this.

Always a problem is the shop that fails, and there was a time not so long ago when more shops seemed to be failing than succeeding. To read now a crafts directory that was published only a few years ago is to hear the death knell of hundreds of shops that tried but failed to make a go of the retail crafts business. Perhaps too many were like the person who once wrote to *Artisan Crafts* saying: "I am just starting an arts and crafts store on a consignment basis, only handmade articles. I have very limited funds. I really don't know what I am doing. I have always sewn and done a lot of crafts. We do not have a shop of this kind here. I really believe it will work.''

I hope it did, but I strongly suspect that it didn't. When you encounter this kind of new shop, be especially cautious in dealing with it. Good and honest intentions do not make a craft shop successful. If you happen to be dealing with a shop when it goes out of business, you should realize that, as the legal owner of consigned merchandise, you have the right to take possession of your own work. (Here's one example of where accurate records on your part could make a big difference.) If the shop you are dealing with is miles from your home or out of state, however, it can be very difficult to get your work out of the shop. And if you eventually get it back, and it is damaged, what can you really do about it, except weep? Getting your money for items already sold can be next to impossible once a shop goes bankrupt and, regrettably, many people have been losers here. To lessen your chances of this happening to you, remember this important rule for consignment selling: Never consign more than a few items to a new or unknown shop until you have developed

some kind of satisfactory relationship with it, based on prompt payment after your first shipment of merchandise has been sold. This is usually a good indication of whether you're dealing with a responsible shop or not.

Now that I've talked about the bad side of consignment, let me show you its good side. There are advantages to both craftsman and shop owner, of course. From the shop's standpoint, the acquisition of merchandise on consignment means that less capital is needed to get started, and the shop does not have to worry about risk of loss if the goods do not sell. The craftsman benefits because he can (1) consign merchandise of his choice without the pressure of meeting a deadline date, (2) control the retail selling price of his work, and (3) use consignment to test the marketability of new or untried items. In fact, consignment selling is often the best or only way to market work of limited production, or expensive, one-of-a-kind crafts and needlework.

Many craftsmen have one or more consignment shops that sell their work regularly, and they usually enjoy a very satisfactory relationship with them. Ruby Tobey is one of those people. "I like working on consignment,'' she says. "It just happens to fit my way of life. I need the money for supplies, but I do not have to have a regular dependable income. I like to try new things and I feel that a shop is more willing to take new things and try them if it does not have to pay for them first. I do not like to be obligated by orders for so many dozen of any item. To me, it is much easier to do the work as I like, send it out to my shops, and around the first of the month, several checks come in.''

Ruby has found through experience that the shops that do best at selling her things are small craft shops usually owned by two or three women who are eager to make a go of their business. "Such women soon become firm friends,'' she says. "They keep in touch, send out checks regularly, let me know what is selling, pass on orders and suggestions, etc.'' Ruby does advise, however, to be cautious about starting with a new shop unless you know the owner.

74

Some craftsmen believe it unwise to consign work to any shop that isn't at least two years old. (Since the mortality rate in the craft shop business is high, anyone who can survive for at least two years is a pretty safe bet.) But, as you probably realize, many shops could not open at all if not for craftspeople willing to consign to them. Since many new consignment shop owners work especially hard to make their business a success, you should not automatically refuse to consign in a shop just because it's new, but you should check it out carefully and test it with a small consignment of merchandise to begin with. Given time, it could turn out to be an excellent outlet for you.

Tricia McManus is the owner of a new gallery/shop featuring crafts, graphics, painting, and sculpture. She told me she could not have opened if not for consignments, and her words echo those of many new shop owners I have corresponded with in the past: "We intend to try just as hard as all the others, and depend on getting trust from craftspeople. With this, our very good location, and a lot of hard work, we believe we will succeed. I love what I'm doing and I love most of the people who are taking a chance with me by consigning these first years while we find our market and get the experience we need to make the right buying decisions."

You will notice that Tricia said "most of the people", not *all* of them. She and scores of other craft shop owners do not love consignors who make promises and don't come through; those who send shoddy merchandise after promising good things; or those who take their work from a shop only two or three days after consigning it. "People like this are breaking their contract with me," says Tricia, "but I let them do it because I know they'll be nothing but future trouble for me. I hate the sight of my 'blackball file' (as I call it) that holds the names of people who do marvelous work, but who can't be trusted so much as a quarter of an inch."

Although as a seller you may feel that shop owners are the ones not to be trusted, I hope you are at least beginning to realize that consignment selling is a two-way street, and a cooperative form of marketing that will not succeed unless both parties work together. Here are some additional tips that might make consignment work better for you:

1. Don't consign your work to a shop that normally buys most of its products at wholesale from other craftsmen, or one that seems primarily interested in selling supplies, imports, or commercial gift lines.

2. Your products will sell better in any shop when many pieces are displayed. If the choice is between several shops who only want a few pieces, or one or two who will take a good supply, pick the latter, and offer a wide price range in the articles you consign. Obviously, the less expensive pieces will sell first, but your higher priced pieces will encourage the sale of the lower priced items. (Of course, I am assuming you will have investigated the shop thoroughly before consigning any substantial amount of merchandise to it.)

3. Promote the shop or gallery that is handling your work. If you exhibit at a craft fair, print flyers saying your work can also be found at certain shops and, by all means, make sure your retail prices are the same as those of your shops.

4. Finally, keep careful records and get everything in writing. Read all consignment agreements before signing them. If the shop does not offer a regular consignment form, you can prepare one of your own, or use a printed form such as the one available from The Unicorn. (Fifty forms may be ordered for $3. See resource chapter.)

Basically, a consignment agreement should cover the following points:

INSURANCE: as the owner of consignment merchandise, you must be concerned with risk of loss. Your work could be damaged or completely ruined, stolen, or destroyed by a fire or flood. A shop's insurance may not cover consignment merchandise, and if you do not want to run the risk of loss, you may have to take out an insurance policy

CONSIGNMENT AGREEMENT AND REPORTING FORM

I.   **NAME OF SHOP**_____

    ADDRESS_____

    CITY_____

    STATE_____ **ZIP**_____

    NAME OF CRAFTSMAN_____

    ADDRESS_____

    CITY_____

    STATE_____ **ZIP**_____

AGREEMENT NO. _____

AGREEMENT DATE _____

REPORTING DATES	AMOUNT PAID CRAFTSMAN
_____	_____
_____	_____
_____	_____
_____	_____
_____	_____

This consignment agreement is between the shop and the craftsman shown above. The shop agrees to display the consignment items properly and to maintain them in good, saleable condition for a period of _____ weeks, or until _____ (date). The shop will receive _____ % of the retail selling price of any item it sells.

II. ITEMS PLACED ON CONSIGNMENT	RETAIL PRICE	DATE SOLD	AMOUNT DUE CRAFTSMAN	DATE PAID
1.				
2.				
3.				
4.				
5.				
6.				
7.				
8.				

III. **TERMS**

    a. The items listed may not be sold for less than the retail price indicated. If any are sold for more, the craftsman is to receive his share of the higher selling price.

    b. If shipping is involved in getting the consigned material to and/or from the shop, the shop and the craftsman will share the cost of shipping equally.

    c. Unless this agreement is renewed, the craftsman agrees to pick up any unsold items, or have them shipped to him by the shop, within 15 days after the termination of this agreement.

    d. Any item which cannot be returned to the craftsman in perfect condition at the termination of this agreement will be considered sold and the craftsman will receive his share of the purchase price for it.

    e. Beginning 30 days after this agreement, and monthly thereafter during the term of this agreement, the shop will report which items, if any, were sold, and will attach a check to the craftsman in payment of his share of the items sold since the last report.

Signed: _____ Date _____   _____ Date _____
    FOR THE SHOP: NAME AND TITLE   CRAFTSMAN

© 1973 by the Guild of American Craftsmen

This consignment agreement form (copyright 1973 by the Guild of American Craftsmen) might be used as the basis for creating a form suited to your own individual needs; or you may order copies of this form for your own use. (See **The Unicorn** *in the resource chapter.)*

of your own. (See Chapter 15.) If you are sending your work to the shop by mail, who will pay for the postage and insurance? (Both ways. See "Return of Unsold Merchandise," below.)

PRICING AND SALES COMMISSION: Consignors are usually expected to set the retail price on their merchandise, but sometimes a shop will ask consignors simply to tell them how much they want for an item and they will set the retail price accordingly. This arrangement, or the exact percentage the shop will retain as its sales commission, should be clearly stated in your agreement.

PAYMENT DATES: How and when will you be paid? Monthly payments to craftspeople are customary for many shops, but there are many ways to keep consignment sale records, and the method of payment should therefore be spelled out in your agreement. In addition to a check each month, you should receive a report of the specific items sold so you can adjust your inventory records accordingly.

DISPLAY OF YOUR MERCHANDISE: Will your crafts be properly displayed and not left in the storeroom after you bring them in for consignment, or carelessly placed in a display window for weeks at a time, to be faded by the sun? Discuss the general matter of display in advance, noting in your agreement any special requirements you may have.

RETURN OF UNSOLD MERCHANDISE: How long will your work be on display, and how will unsold work eventually be returned to you? Will it be mailed back at your expense? If it's a local shop and you can pick it up in person, must you claim it by a certain date or forfeit ownership entirely? (Some shops have a clause that says that if unsold merchandise is not claimed within 30 to 60 days after the craftsman received notice to remove it, the shop can assume ownership of it and dispose of it any way it wishes.)

And there you have the case for and against consignment selling, one of the most controversial issues in the craft world tody. Gallery owner Tricia McManus still asks, "What's so awful about consignment selling?" and underscores the importance of a consignment agreement with these remarks: "A craftsperson won't get fleeced if he or she reads the contracts presented for signature and understands what is being signed. Properly and legally handled, consignment can bring more money and more orders to the working crafts professional than guaranteed sales or wholesale selling. Sixty-six and two-thirds percent is still better than 50 percent."

Wholesaling

Consignment selling has its problems, but so does selling outright, or wholesaling. To succeed in wholesaling, a craftsperson must be able to produce in quantity, which is why this kind of selling is out of the question for so many people. Pricing problems eliminate many others. Are your prices high enough that you can take a 50 percent discount and still make money? If so, and you can produce in quantity, maybe wholesaling is right for you. If and when you decide to try it, you'll need some guidelines. It takes courage to walk into that first big shop or store, see the buyer, and give your sales pitch, so let's get into the nitty-gritty of what you should know before you venture into this realm.

While craft shop owners are generally warm and friendly and eager to see the work of any new craftsperson, gift shop and department store buyers will need to be *sold* on what you have to offer. They prefer to see sellers by appointment, often on certain days of the week only. Good timing is always important, so don't walk into a store at its busiest time of day and expect the buyer to give you his full attention. Don't expect a store to give you a big Christmas order in November, either. Seasonal items will be of interest to buyers months in advance of the season itself.

While some buyers are still thinking in terms of ordering a dozen gross of one item, others now more enlightened about handcrafts and craftsmen are realizing that only so much can be produced. Recently a new trend has begun to emerge in department stores, some of which are beginning to feature demonstrating craftspeople in their stores as a promotion to attract new customers. The department store buyer who is looking for new products, concepts, and finishes may be very interested in talking to any craftsperson who can deliver them, even in quantities of one-of-a-kind or limited editions.

Ordinarily, however, it would be wise to think in terms of a buyer ordering at least two dozen of any item you offer, perhaps more. If a store should surprise you by offering to buy much more than you had expected to sell, and you are doubtful about when you can deliver the order, be honest with them and explain that you need to recalculate the time required to fill the order. Then go home, figure it out, and come back later to write up the actual order that will specify a shipping date you feel confident can be met.

When wholesaling your crafts, it is especially important to display them attractively for the buyer's consideration. You might make a special display case for this purpose, or at least carry an appropriate backdrop with you to make sure your products stand out from the clutter on a buyer's desk. Naturally, your samples should be the best you can produce. Never show work that requires an apology. Telling a buyer that what you will deliver to him will be better than what he sees before him is *not* what he wants to hear.

Each sample should bear a label or tag indicating its wholesale price, whether it comes in different colors or sizes, and what your minimum or maximum order quantity is for that item. If your work is too large or too heavy to carry around with you, you may have to prepare a special photographic presentation of your work (use only the best pictures you have). Or, take slides and a viewer with you. In fact, this might be helpful even when you have samples to show. Also include any press clippings or publicity your work has received, since this may give the buyer an indication of the interest your work will arouse in his shop or store.

You should have a printed price list, of course, with the retail prices on one sheet and the wholesale prices on another. (Shops report that their customers occasionally like to look at a craftsman's price list, but they can't show it if the retail and wholesale prices appear on the same sheet.) If you can include some simple line drawings to illustrate the items on your price list, so much the better. A brief description of each item should be given, including size and color.

Your price list should also state your conditions for new customers, such as "Check with first order," or "Three credit references must be provided." (The craftsperson who asks for references, *checks them,* and perhaps requires prepayment of the first order should have little trouble with non-payment of bills.) Also state your guarantee, if one is offered. Example: "Work that is unsuitable for any reason will be taken back," "Items shipped are guaranteed to be of same quality as samples," etc. Your policy regarding shipping charges should be included as well. Instead of charging the actual postage or shipping costs incurred, you may prefer instead to work on a percentage basis, such as 5 percent of the total order, and make that a standard shipping charge for all orders. This amount will probably give you more than the actual cost involved, and help reimburse you for the time you spend in packing. Few shops or stores would question this amount, especially when you ship via United Parcel Service (UPS), which is prompt and dependable.

Business Terms and Definitions

In order to converse intelligently with a buyer, you will need to understand certain business terms and be familiar with standard business forms. Here is an explanation of the ones you will most likely encounter:

MARKUP: This is the percentage or amount a retail outlet adds to the price it pays for any item. For example, if you wholesale an item for $5, the store will probably mark it up 100 percent to arrive at a retail price of $10. (Although, as you have already noted elsewhere, some stores may mark up items 150 percent or more, depending on what they think their customers will pay.)

DISCOUNT: You will be mainly concerned with two kinds of discounts. First, there is the cash discount, which is the percentage or amount subtracted from a retail price to get the price a store will pay for merchandise — the wholesale price. If you give a 50 percent discount off your retail price, it simply means that your wholesale price is half that amount. A $10 item would wholesale for $5. Thus you can see that a 50 percent discount relates to a 100 percent markup, and it all means the same to you in terms of actual dollars received.

Then there is the quantity discount, or the percentage that applies to the price if a purchase exceeds a certain amount. When you buy raw materials, you may get a discount by ordering more than a specified amount, and when you sell your crafts, you may wish to give your buyers a special discount for ordering your work in substantial quantity.

PRO FORMA: If you're dealing with a shop you feel might have financial problems, or one that has no credit credentials to offer you, it may be wise to ask for your money in advance, before you ship or deliver the work they have ordered. This is known as selling on a pro forma basis.

2/10/30 or 2% 10 DAYS, NET 30: You must decide whether you want cash with order, full payment within 30 days from date of invoice ("net 30 days"), or if you will give a 2 percent discount when payment is made within 10 days ("2/10/30" or "2% 10 days, net 30"). Craftspeople generally request full payment within 30 days, but some do offer the 2 percent discount in order to get their money in hand as soon as possible. Unfortunately, some buyers pay the invoice a month later and still take the discount, in which case the store should be invoiced for the difference. After 10 days, the full amount is due.

F.O.B.: This means "Freight, or free, on board." These initials, and the name of a place immediately after them, indicate the point to which the seller will pay the freight. If the buyer is to pay all shipping charges, you would indicate on your invoice, F.O.B. followed by the name of your town or city. If you have to pay the freight, however, this notation would read F.O.B. and the name of your customer's town or city. (NOTE: This F.O.B. notation could be very important in the event goods are damaged in transit because, legally, title

of the goods changes hands at the F.O.B. point. So, when you ship F.O.B. from your town or city and the UPS driver, mailman, truck driver, etc. takes the box or carton, the buyer is then responsible for the merchandise from that point on — even if he never receives the goods.)

ORDER FORM: As a buyer is telling you what he wants, you will be preparing an order form. An all-purpose sales form can be obtained from a business supplies store, or you can simply write the order on a piece of your stationery, making a carbon copy. A smaller shop may sign the original copy in your presence, to make it official, while a larger shop may ask you to send a typed version of the order after you get home. Others will use your order form to prepare their own purchase order, a copy of which you will receiver later. Your order form should specify the date on which you have agreed to ship, and it is important to meet this date. Future orders could depend upon it. If you do not plan to deliver your order in person, your order form should specify the method of shipping — parcel post, UPS, truck, etc.

PACKING LIST: Once you have prepared your order and are ready to deliver or ship it to your customer, you will need to prepare a packing list. Make two copies of it, one for you, one for your customer. It should agree in description and number with the information shown on your invoice, and be a complete record of what you have packed in each box or carton being shipped. Describe all items, grouping them under headings such as: "Contents of Box No. 1" (then list all items in that box); "Contents of Box No. 2" (list the items); etc. You need not show prices on your packing list. Include a copy of the completed packing list in one of the boxes or cartons being shipped, placing it on top where it can easily be found. When shipping more than one box or carton, be sure to mark the cartons themselves by writing on them, "Box No. 1 of 4 boxes shipped;" "Box No. 2 of 4 boxes shipped," etc., so your customer will know when all have been received.

THE INVOICE: You can buy simple three-part invoices from a business supplies store, or order

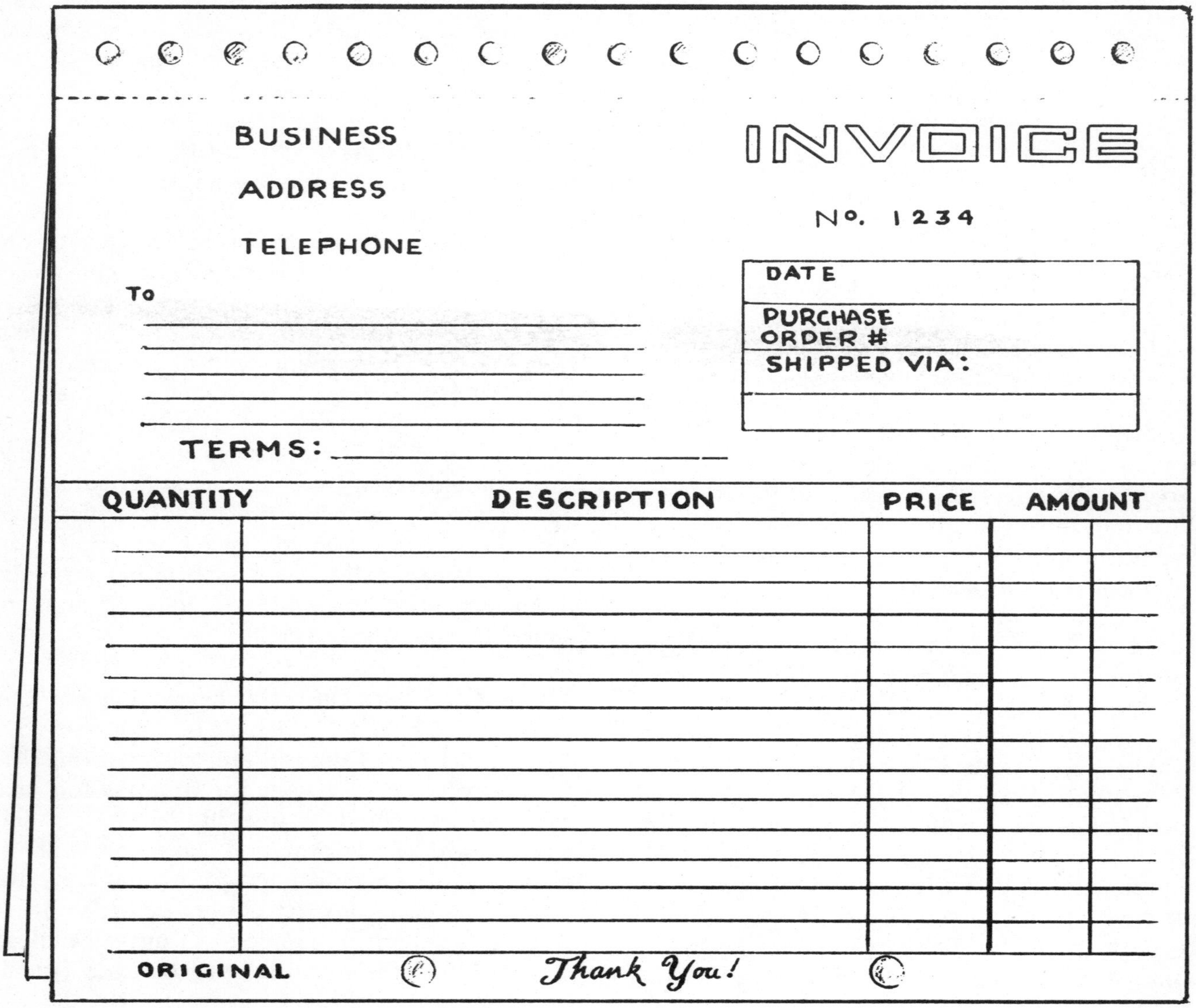

INVOICE

BUSINESS

ADDRESS

TELEPHONE

No. 1234

To

_____
_____
_____
_____

DATE	
PURCHASE ORDER #	
SHIPPED VIA:	

TERMS: _____

QUANTITY	DESCRIPTION	PRICE	AMOUNT

ORIGINAL   Thank You!

80

Simple three-part invoices like this can be purchased in stationery stores or ordered by mail from office supply companies. Imprinting can be ordered if desired.

them from one of the sources in the resource chapter. The last copy of the invoice is for your files, the first two are for your customer, who should return one of them to you along with his check. Mail the invoice by first class mail, separately from the shipment, and send it the same day you ship the order so it will arrive before the order and alert your customer to its arrival. Here's what your invoice should contain in the way of information:

1. Your name and address, your customer's name and address, and the ship-to address (if it is different from the sold-to-address).
2. The date of the invoice, and the date merchandise is being shipped.
3. Method of shipment (parcel post, UPS, truck or busline, etc.)
4. Invoice number. Use any four-digit number (1001 is a good place to start) and thereafter number all your invoices accordingly.
5. Customer's purchase order number. Smaller shops and stores may not require a P.O. number, but larger stores will need it for identification purposes.
6. Terms of payment. (Net 30 days, or 2% 10 days, net 30, as you prefer.)
7. Quantity and description of items, their unit price, and total amount. Refer to your packing list in preparing your invoice, to make sure the information on both forms is in agreement. List the wholesale price of each item in the "price" column, then calculate the figure for the "amount" column by multiplying the number of items shipped by the wholesale price. Then total the amount column.
8. Shipping costs. Generally, the buyer is expected to pay shipping costs, but this should be confirmed at the time you take the order. If the buyer is paying it, simply add the actual amount of postage to the total of the amount column, or charge your usual percentage for shipping costs. Then indicate the proper F.O.B. notation somewhere on your invoice.

A STATEMENT: Contrary to popular belief, a statement is not a request for payment, like an invoice, but merely a summary of a financial account showing the balance due. Unless you are making several shipments to a major account each month, a monthly statement should not be necessary. If a customer doesn't pay your invoice when it's due, simply send a duplicate invoice, only this time, write the words "second notice" at the top. Usually this will be enough to get action. (There are standard invoice forms available that have extra carbons with gentle reminders like this already printed on them.)

If you run into the situation where an account does not pay you, even after a polite "second notice," send another notice and start charging interest. They are using your money and should be paying for the privilege. If this doesn't work, telephone them, and continue to call regularly until they pay. Let them know you mean business (but no threats, as this is illegal). When all else fails, consider the use of a collection agency, which is less expensive than suing the debtor on your own behalf.

Once you have established a few wholesale accounts, it will be necessary to follow up on them later on since they probably won't call you when they run out of your stock. If your shops are local, call on them regularly, taking any new products you may have developed since your last visit. Leave your price list and brochure with them if they do not wish to re-order, since this may prompt an order later on.

If you have several wholesale accounts you have dealt with by mail in the past, or a number of outlets you are still trying to sell, take the initiative and send them copies of your new price list, brochure, or catalog. For a minimum cost in postage and printing, you may gain some repeat orders from old customers or bring in two or three new accounts. At least it's worth a try.

When you do receive an order, immediately send back a copy on your stationery, indicating when you will ship, and any problems in filling the order stock shortages, etc.). The craftsperson who deals with his retail outlets in a business-like manner will probably continue to receive orders from them in the future.

Sales Representatives — Working With Them or Becoming One Yourself

Producing craftsmen often discover that only about one-third of their time is actually being spent in production. The other two-thirds may be tied up in less satisfying jobs such as selling, advertising, doing paperwork, making deliveries, etc. Although most craftsmen would automatically assume that a sales representative is out of the question for them, a careful evaluation of the situation might prove otherwise. If an additional one-third, or more, of their time could suddenly be freed for additional production, perhaps it would more than compensate for the commission a sales representative would charge.

Generally, a sales representative will take about 10 percent of the wholesale price as his commission, although some take as much as 30 percent. As the link between manufacturer and retailer, it is the sales representative's job to get the order for the manufacturer, who must then ship and bill the customer. The sales representative receives his commission only after the manufacturer has been paid.

There are several ways to find representatives, beginning with trade magazines such as *Gifts & Decorative Accessories* or *Gift & Tableware Reporter,* which carry notices placed by sales representatives looking for new gift or handcraft lines. The telephone books of many major cities have a category, "Expositions, Trade Shows, and Fairs," which will guide you to some appropriate wholesale centers. Call them and explain that you are a manufacturer looking for a representative. You might also ask a few shop owners in your area for the name of a good representative they may be dealing with.

In selecting a sales representative, it is important to find one that is interested in you and your work. Otherwise he won't be able to sell it well. Naturally, he will only be interested in new products that are compatible with his existing line and accounts. In order to sell your line, a sales representative must have complete information about you and your work, including background information about yourself and the processes involved in the making of your products. He will also need price lists, order forms, and samples of the items to be sold. You should have a written agreement with him that defines his sales territory and commission, as well as your terms of sale, credit policy, delivery dates, discounts, and shipping and packaging policies. There should also be a clause that stipulates how either party can break the relationship should it prove unsatisfactory for any reason. (Example: You may not be able to make as much as he can sell, or he may not be able to sell as much as you make. Either way, the arrangement would be mutually unprofitable.)

Depending on his territory, a sales representative may be able to introduce your product line in areas you cannot easily reach — either a particular city or state, or a particular type of retail market. Sales representatives often take their line to trade shows that cater exclusively to wholesale buyers in many different fields. Some have their own showrooms and others simply stay on the road most of the time, visiting countless department stores, gift shops, mail-order houses, and other retail outlets. The small manufacturer who needs new accounts but can't afford his own sales staff (or just doesn't want one) will therefore find the sales representative a valuable addition to his business. Although few individuals can produce in a quantity sufficient to interest the average sales representative, there are exceptions, of course, and you may be one of them. If not now, then perhaps later.

Maybe you are not a producing craftsman at all, but merely one who is interested in selling the work of others. When a craft shop is desired but there is simply no capital with which to launch such a venture, you might consider becoming a sales representative. Craft know-how and selling expertise could be put to work for you on a schedule of your own making, in a sales territory as limited or extensive as you care to make it. It is the concept here that is important. There will always be craftspeople who love to produce, but hate to sell. You might represent several craftsmen who live in isolated, rural areas and need additional retail outlets, or you might start a party-plan marketing operation such as Joan McGovern did, or take the work of several producing craftsmen to a big gift show. Corporate executives are often looking for unusual Christmas gifts, shops might be delighted to stock the line of handcrafts you represent, and your own ingenuity will no doubt turn up other buying markets.

There seems to be a growing need today for qualified craft sales representatives, but a very tight lid on the pot that holds all the how-to's on being one. I wrote to three craft representatives who had received mentions in trade papers, asking them for comments and information about their experience in this field. None replied. Then I discovered Gail Steinberg of Jasmine and Bread Inc., in Yellow Springs, Ohio.

Gail, the sole owner, buyer, and trouble-shooter for a corporation that now employs 15 women, was both interested and willing to help. At one time she was a sales representative for craftsmen, but now her business has grown to the point at which this activity has had to be curtailed. These days she thinks of herself as a "brainstormer, chief saleswoman, strategist, and developer of new markets." She writes: "We now manufacture and import goods, all handcrafts, in 11 different product categories, and have our collective arms full, selling just our own lines. In fact, we could use more marketing services ourselves, and are very interested in representatives who deal in handcrafted items."

Gail passed my request for additional information on to Rosanne Hauser, the woman in her organization who is in charge of all sales, representatives, and promotions. She was kind enough to offer the excellent suggestions below. Rosanne says they are all basic, but easy to forget. Interestingly, her advice is as appropriate for the craftsman doing his own wholesaling as it is for the budding sales representative:

1. Handcrafts are unique and special, and so are the buyers of these crafts. Make them feel that way. Give them individual stories or selling points or histories on each item that catches their eye. The added extras make each item a treasure, and something that the buyer, in turn, can pass on to his customers. (This, of course, implies knowing your product inside out — processes in-

volved in its making, histories of the people who make it, personal anecdotes, etc.)

2. Use all available resources for leads — trade journals, yellow pages, magazines — and know your competition. Most wholesale shows mail exhibitors lists of those buyers who attended. If you're not exhibiting at these shows, at least go to see what is around and get hold of the buyers' lists and use them as leads.

3. Any help you can give the buyer about how to display products will make sales easier. Buyers are always concerned with their space limitations and display problems. Be able to give them suggestions about these areas.

4. Organize your time. Keep accurate records of all leads and follow-ups. Call and follow up on clients on a regular basis. Leave literature even at places that don't place an order. Who knows when they might change their minds?

5. Be thoroughly prepared and competent before walking in to see a client. That way you can concentrate on the buyer's moods and attention spans, speeding up when you're losing him, slowing down when he displays interest. If you have to spend most of your energy looking at your own samples or familiarizing yourself with your products while with a client, you miss out on the subtle ways of judging and getting to know your buyer.

Finally, says Rosanne, don't let buyers tell you when they're through buying. "If you still have more to show or sell, let them know that. Often it's easy to change their minds with 'just one more thing'."

How To Find Good Craft Shop Outlets

If you exhibit at craft fairs, you will surely learn about good shops and galleries from other craftsmen or be contacted by interested buyers themselves. If you don't sell at shows, perhaps you know a few shops nearby that might be interested

SOME RETAIL OUTLETS TO EXPLORE

CRAFT SHOPS & GALLERIES
in your area or
listed in directories

GIFT SHOPS
in hospitals & nursing homes
boutiques • bridal shops
card & stationery stores

DEPARTMENT STORES
bridal or baby departments
decorative accessories
needlework departments
housewares • giftwares • "notions"

84

OTHER RETAIL STORES
hardware stores • restaurants
shoe shops • office supply stores
clothing shops • specialty shops
sports stores • florists

in your work. If so, visit them in person and take samples of your best work with you to show the owner or manager. If there are no shops near you, however, you will have to establish your retail outlets by mail, and many craftspeople do this by simply sending a letter to a shop and enclosing a few slides or photographs of their work. Once you have a list of craft shops and some knowledge about what they might want in the way of merchandise, you can begin to find new outlets too.

As with craft fairs, there are special publications that list shops and galleries interested in buying crafts outright or handling them on consignment. Two directories that contain such information are the *Contemporary Crafts Marketplace,* compiled biennially by the American Crafts Council (ACC), and *Craftworker's Market,* issued annually by Writer's Digest. The ACC directory lists approximately 1000 shops and galleries that offer American contemporary crafts to the public. Although this directory does not indicate what each outlet wishes to buy or receive on consignment, it does specify the type of crafts carried, and also includes the year in which the business was established.

Craftworker's Market, compiled especially for sellers of art/craft merchandise, is recommended to all who seek a direct avenue to craft retailers. Its listings are choice and very detailed, and number approximately the same as the ACC directory. A typical shop listing will explain the kind of crafts desired by the owner and often includes the price range preferred. It tells how to query the shop owner and indicates such information as who pays shipping costs for exhibited work, what kind of customers frequent the shop, and which months are heaviest buying times. Indeed, this is a fine guide for serious sellers.

Although it may seem pointless to say it, it is a waste of time to try to sell your work to a shop unless you know it is carrying merchandise similar in nature to yours. Some shops will have no interest in your work, not because it isn't good, but simply because it isn't compatible with the rest of their stock. While cornhusk dolls might be extremely good sellers in dozens of shops around the country, they would not be of interest to the shop that sells only contemporary crafts. That's why you should study shop listings carefully before contacting any shop by mail, and look at the merchandise in local shops before going in to make your presentation. All shops are different, each with a personality of its own. What one shop can sell, another cannot. Your goal as a supplier is to give the right product to the right shop.

It will be easier to do this if you understand what shops mean when they ask for specific kinds of craft merchandise. For example, "contemporary crafts" means work that is new, modern, and innovative in design or technique, while "traditional crafts" refers to objects made in proved patterns and forms from older design concepts. "Ethnic or folk crafts" are those that are characteristic of a people or region. Everyone has seen examples of folk or traditional crafts such as apple dolls, quilts, mountain woodcarvings, and tole painting, but many people have had little exposure to fine contemporary crafts, and a better understanding of them could be gained by reading a few issues of magazines such as *Craft Horizons* or *Canada Crafts.* Other magazines such as *Fiberarts, Glass,* and *Fine Woodworking* also feature photographs of outstanding contemporary work.

Shops often indicate an interest in work that is "utilitarian" or "decorative," categories that are self-explanatory and applicable to all kinds of merchandise. You will also note that there is a continuing demand in good craft shops for work that is "unique" and "one-of-a-kind," and I only wish that someone would come up with a couple of new adjectives that aren't as overworked as these.

Naturally, anyone who sells crafts should subscribe to several craft periodicals, not only to stay abreast of the latest marketing information, but to find new outlets and other important leads. Shop openings (and closings) always receive attention in the various craft publications, and each one carries news and information that could be vital to your success. One monthly, in particular, is worthy of note here since it focuses entirely on marketing. *Quality Crafts Market* (formerly called *Craft Market News)* provides its subscribers with a continuing source of leads for new markets, retail

85

and wholesale alike. It watches trends in crafts and reports on what is selling around the country. It lists newly opened shops and galleries, gives profiles of buyers, and explains their specific needs. One section reports on craft classifications (such as wood crafts, miniatures, handcrafted kitchenware, etc.) and markets that are gaining new importance. Another section is devoted to a discussion of the "Mastercraft Market" — shops and galleries carrying crafts retailing for $1000 and up.

Other Retail Outlets To Explore

In addition to craft shops, there are many other places to consider when seeking reliable retail outlets, and some of them may be right under your nose. Craft shops are an obvious possibility, but you might tend to overlook the kind of shops found in hospitals and nursing homes, or the bridal, baby, or gift shops of department stores.

Incidentally, according to articles in various publications, crafts seem to be selling well in large department stores such as Lord and Taylor, Saks Fifth Avenue, Marshall Field and Company, etc. But getting your work into prestigious stores such as these is not easy, and even when you succeed, you may encounter problems you never even thought about. In one article I read, a woman reported an unusual experience she had had with a big department store. They liked her work but didn't want to buy it. Instead, they wanted it on consignment, which is quite unusual. (Obviously, they weren't sure her work would sell.) Eager to have her work in this store, the woman gave them more than $500 worth of merchandise that she had priced for retail. They said they would take 50 percent of that amount (not 40 percent as is the custom elsewhere for consigned mechandise). She agreed to this. When she returned a month later with a second delivery she found, to her surprise, that the store had marked up her prices on some items as much as 150 percent, making them, in her opinion, too high to sell. But there was nothing she could do about it because she did not have a formal consignment agreement with the store.

As you can see, the above arrangement was quite advantageous for the store, which was obviously experimenting to see if crafts would sell, and completely disadvantageous for the craftswoman, who had a major portion of her crafts inventory tied up in a store that had priced most items too high to sell.

Perhaps other retail outlets would be better for you, such as garden or floral shops, which might be interested in any art or craft relating to flowers. Hardware stores might add handcrafted kitchenware and unusual gifts to their giftwares section. Home furnishing stores might be interested in wall hangings or decorative accessories, and restaurants might desire special floral arrangements, centerpieces, macrame planters,

stained glass lamps, or sculpture. Shoe stores might appreciate a line of originally designed handbags, and clothing stores might be interested in carrying special items you have knitted, crocheted, sewed, or macramed. Or perhaps you could offer to do decorative stitching or embroidery on their line of sweaters, or provide other custom design services their customers would appreciate.

An article in a recent issue of *Quality Crafts Market* pointed out the accelerating demand for handcrafted gifts for men and gave several suggestions worth exploring. For example, men's clothing and specialty shops might be interested in craft wearables and accessories; office suppliers might like to see handcrafted desk accessories, lamps, wall hangings, or sculpture; game and leisure shops can always use handcrafted chessboards, backgammon, and other adult games or toys; sport shops need quality items for participants and spectators alike. And don't overlook boating and yachting shops, because nothing is ever too expensive for a man's boat.

"Consumer interest in crafts is booming," says Flissy Benjamin in a recent issue of *Gift & Tableware Reporter*. She also notes that two out of five Americans are now involved in some type of craft as a leisure activity. This accounts for the fact that there is now a greater appreciation for quality handcrafts on the part of consumers, she said, and a growing awareness among retailers of the market potential for contemporary crafts.

Any store that concentrates on a concept of selling, rather than quantity of merchandise, is a possible market for craftspeople these days, and selling them on your products may require nothing more than just letting them know you are there, ready to supply them with quality merchandise.

Being a Good Supplier

Without dependable suppliers, it is difficult to stock any kind of shop, so if you want to rate high with your retail outlets, simply become a supplier they can count on. Once you have made a sale to a retailer, call back in a month or so and try to get a re-order. When a merchant realizes that you are going to be available to provide goods and service on a regular basis, he will begin to develop confidence in you and be more interested in working with you. Retailers are simply not interested in dealing with craftspeople on a one-shot basis.

Most craftspeople are unreliable suppliers. If you don't believe me, ask any craft shop owner. A letter from the owners of Crafts Incredible in Prairie Village, Kansas, explained the kinds of things that can affect the shop-supplier relationship: "Working with individuals is both trying and enjoyable," says Donna Adam, speaking for her partners, husband Claude and friend Irene Marsh. "We find a source we think is great, and the next thing you know, the craftsman is doing something else and we are left to find a replacement.

"Even though we certainly have no objection to children," Donna continues, "we find that when one of our sources had a child, her production of crafts is cut severely or completely — often for as long as three years. Also, as craftspeople grow in their craft their product changes, sometimes for the good of both parties, sometimes not. Again we must search for a replacement. Sometimes the product must increase in price and we feel it becomes too high for good turnover, and we are out searching again. I am sure this will be the case in the coming months, with fuel costs rising and causing price increases in shipping and raw materials."

Most craftspeople do not realize how hard shop owners work to find them. In fact, many spend a great deal of time and money trying to find good suppliers, and some become quite frustrated in the process, as evidenced by one letter I received from the owner of a consignment shop.

"Why should shop owners travel all over the place looking for good people to deal with?" she wrote. "And why are we treated as some passive animal sitting in a lair waiting to be found by some enterprising innocent looking to be fleeced? I'd love to contact good craftspeople directly by phone or mail, and would, if I could find them."

After about a year and a half in business, the owner of a crafts gallery in New York City gave me an interesting picture of three kinds of craftsmen who were represented in his store at that time.

87

His comments below, reprinted from an article in *Artisian Crafts* magazine, are as timely now as they were in 1973, and should help you understand how shop owners everywhere view their craft suppliers:

> Over the past year I find that I am dealing with three categories of craftsmen — the *hobby craftsman,* the *artist-craftsman,* and the *professional craftsman.*
>
> The hobby craftsman is the person who makes something at his leisure, maybe has fantasies of leaving everything and just 'doing his thing,' but in reality has many other priorities before producing his craft. These people are nice to have in the store, but they're not a reliable source of income.
>
> The artist-craftsman produces beautiful one-of-a-kind work, and his pieces add a lot of quality and uniqueness to my store, but do not turn over much because of the price.
>
> Finally, there is the professional craftsman. He is into a product line. The professional craftsman has developed a group of items that seem to have a consistent appeal to the public after being marketed through a retail outlet. The professional craftsman has come to terms with the reality value of his product, independent of his labors. It is this craftsman that supports our store and contributes to making it a viable operation.*

It is unfortunate that so few craftspeople can separate the art from the marketability of the objects they create. As this gallery owner explains in his article, "The hobby craftsman is more interested in selling the object than the monetary return he receives. The artist-craftsman wants to be paid for both his concept and his time (research and development), and he would rather not sell his work at all if he is not to be adequately rewarded for it. The professional craftsman usually creates a product for a specific market, or finds a market for a specific product." *

To increase your sales, try creating a coordinated line of products. Just one or two of something in a shop does not offer much of a selection, so shop owners will be especially interested in the seller who offers them at least four to six items in a line.

To create a line, think in terms of what will go together. For example, if you are selling hand-painted cutting boards, you might include in your line several other useful and decorative kitchen items such as a set of canisters, salt and pepper shakers, recipe box, napkin holder, etc. In creating a line you must also think in terms of what will sell. As a consumer, you know what you would like to buy, and this is certainly one indication of what others will want to buy as well.

Although most craftspeople seem to prefer making one-of-a-kind pieces, these are not the items that turn over easily in the average retail store. One-of-a-kind pieces may provide the cream for your table, but if you need bread and butter, do what the professionals do: Develop a line of crafts that is moderately priced to sell quickly.

* From "The Reality of a Crafts Store," by Bob Fireman. © 1973 *Artisan Crafts.*

8

Selling by Mail

Mail order. The great American dream.

All kinds of people are fascinated by mail order because it is a business that can be started with a small investment and operated on a part-time basis out of one's home. But few people who get involved in it have the necessary requirements for success. What does it take to succeed, and do you have it?

The most important qualities for success in mail order are: organizational abilities, an enjoyment of detail, and a willingness to work hard. The ability to do many different jobs, from writing advertisements to packing products for shipment, is also very important. Having the right product is the most important thing of all.

The first part of this chapter is devoted to general information about the mail-order business, followed by a discussion of the three types of mail order: (1) selling through magazine or newspaper advertisements; (2) direct mail; and (3) selling through a catalog. As the chapter unfolds, you will meet some interesting men and women who have developed successful mail-order businesses, and much will be learned from a study of their techniques.

The Best Mail-Order Products

What type of craft item sells best by mail? Kits, patterns, designs, supplies, instructions, books, and services are easier sold through the mail than finished handcrafts, whose sale so often depends on eye appeal and buyer impulse. But handcrafts will sell when they meet certain requirements, and the following guidelines will help you determine if you have a good mail-order item or not.

First it must be unusual and not readily available elsewhere. It must also be familiar to people, so they will not hesitate to buy it sight unseen. A good rule to remember is that you should offer the same type of product that others are selling, since a really new and innovative item probably will not sell well. (People won't buy something if they don't understand what it is, or why they should have it.)

A product offered by mail must be one that can be easily described and illustrated in an ad. Study the mail-order sections of various magazines to find out how others do this. At the same time you will discover certain categories of merchandise that are obviously good mail-order sellers, such as unique seasonal items, kitchenware, unusual gifts, needlework kits, and various other objects designed to fill specific needs.

Mail-order items must be attractively priced, and by that I mean they must give the impression of being a good buy. Mail-order specialists advise that items priced under $10 usually sell best, but a beginner in mail order would be wise to select something that can be sold for even less. Since people are often reluctant to buy anything from an unknown company, the lower the price of your first mail-order item, the better.

Incidentally, the price of a mail order item should be at least five times what it cost in materials and labor to produce, according to Michael Scott, author of *The Crafts Business Encyclopedia* (Harcourt Brace Jovanovich). In his book, he points out that this high markup is necessary in order to compensate for increased overhead costs. In addition to advertising and regular postage and shipping costs, you must also consider the cost of packaging supplies and the time spent in packing, shipping, and corresponding with customers about lost shipments, damaged goods, or complaints. And don't forget that your first big ad just might pull in more orders than you anticipate. You might have to hire

90

someone to help you fill them, and if your price isn't high enough to begin with, you could lose all your profit as a result.

You realize, I hope, that a mail-order item has to be produced in quantity. If you can't do this, or don't want to do it, then you should forget about selling by mail.

Finally, the best items to sell by mail are those that are nonfragile and easy and inexpensive to pack and ship. The more fragile the item, the higher your shipping costs will be since you will need special packing materials for it. Keep in mind that anything that can be easily damaged in shipment will probably result in your having to replace merchandise from time to time.

Good Advice for Beginners

The following words of advice are from Marian Mumby of Costa Mesa, California, a woman who is experienced in mail order. Her entire family is currently involved in The Mumby Bead Company, a manufacturer of ceramic beads and accessories.

Marian stresses the importance of getting reliable advice when starting any new business venture: "People who start a business are apt to take the advice of friends, fellow craftsmen, or anyone who happens to sound as if they know what they are talking about. But are these people really qualified? Are they, or have they been, successful in a similar situation or business? Do they know enough about your actual situation or problem?"

Marian also warns about carrying too large an inventory. In the beginning, she said, they offered many more beads than they do now. In order to be able to ship immediately upon receipt of an order, it was necessary to keep a tremendous inventory on hand. "This is a drain financially as your money is tied up too long in an inventory that may or may not move," Marian told me. "We had too many different kinds of beads for the size of our business, so we streamlined the number of kinds of beads, and things are running more smoothly now."

Beginners in mail order would be wise to heed this advice. If you are selling handcrafts or kits,

begin with a small line of perhaps half a dozen items. Then you won't have to invest too much in inventory right at the beginning. Run a few test ads to gauge order response; then build your inventory accordingly and prepare for more and bigger ads in the future.

Packaging and Shipping Tips

The packaging of a craft or needlework product is important. If you need a special presentation case or package to house your product — such as a piece of jewelry, needlework kit, set of printed patterns, etc. — you might consider the vinyl zipper bag. 20th Century Plastics, Inc., in Los Angeles offers this item in several sizes, from 3 x 4 in. to 12 x 15 in., and they can also imprint the bag with your business logo or content instructions. Although you must order in minimum quantities of 1000 of any size, prices are still reasonable. This company is listed in the resource chapter along with others who can supply bags and boxes suitable for packaging all kinds of items. Similar companies can be found in the yellow pages of any large city, under headings such as "boxes," "plastics," or "cellophane."

Shipping cartons will probably be a problem because, as you will learn when you approach a box manufacturing company, minimum orders are usually too high for the small businessperson to meet. At the very least, you will have to think in terms of 500 or 1000 of any size box or carton when ordering from a company such as United States Box Corporation in Newark, New Jersey. (They also have a $100 minimum order.) If you can't afford to buy boxes directly from such a manufacturer, you will have to use your ingenuity to find some local sources. Perhaps a store or company in your area that ships merchandise would agree to sell you some of its boxes, just to get you started.

Once you have decided how you are going to package your mail-order product, you should make a test package, wrapping it exactly as you plan to do when shipping it to your customer. Be sure to calculate the cost of all wrapping supplies, and try to determine an accurate wrapping cost per package. Then you should weigh the package and

You Can Bank On A Package When It's Wrapped Like This!

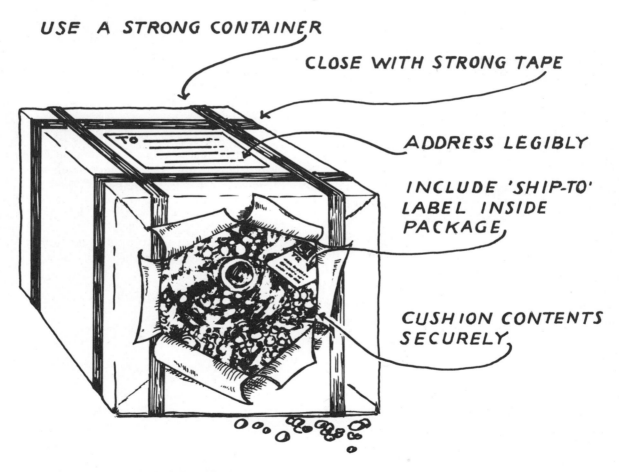

USE A STRONG CONTAINER

CLOSE WITH STRONG TAPE

ADDRESS LEGIBLY

INCLUDE 'SHIP-TO' LABEL INSIDE PACKAGE.

CUSHION CONTENTS SECURELY

TO

Illustration idea courtesy of U.S. Postal Service.

There are many different kinds of packaging materials that can be used to ship crafts by mail. Ideally, a shipping container will be both strudy and light in weight.

decide how you are going to ship it. Will you use the mail or United Parcel Service? Will you insure your package or run the risk of its being lost or damaged en route? How much will this cost?

Here's an important tip to remember: Do not tie your shipping carton or package with string. Instead, use fiber or paper tape with a 60-pound test weight. A package tied with string can easily get caught in the sorting machines being used by the Postal Service. And, once this happens, a package's contents may be seriously damaged or totally destroyed.

Frankly, I do not recommend using parcel post unless absolutely necessary, since UPS is so reliable and so readily available to everyone. When I telephoned them recently they advised that they will pick up packages at any home (even in isolated rural areas) for just $2 a week, and will come as many times during the week as necessary. It is not necessary to pay for this service on a 52-week basis, either; simply call UPS when you need them. They will deliver anywhere, even to a post office box number or rural route. With a box number address, or someone they cannot locate in the country, they will send the recipient a notice through

the mail requesting additional delivery instructions.

You can send any package or carton so long as it does not exceed 108 in. in length and girth combined, or does not weigh more than 50 pounds. No more than 100 pounds may be shipped to one destination in a day, but you could conceivably ship as much as 100 pounds a day for five days in a row for the same $2 charge mentioned above. You must, however, weigh each package before shipping and call UPS to find out how much it will cost to send, giving payment to driver at time of pickup. For additional information, call your nearest United Parcel Service office.

If you do decide to ship via parcel post, I urge you to insure everything you mail, and test your mailing package very thoroughly. Try throwing it out the upstairs window a few times, or kick it downstairs with gusto and see how it holds up. This in no way duplicates the type of handling usually given to fourth-class packages as they are dumped from trucks to conveyor belts and tossed from one bin to another, but it will give you an idea of whether your product is going to reach your customer intact and undamaged. If you need

93

more padding for the inside of your shipping carton, consider the use of air cushion bags or foam padding, which is available in rolls. Crumpled newspaper may also do the trick, and it's a lot cheaper.

NOTE: If saving money on shipping costs is of primary importance to you, you should be aware that it is less expensive to ship small parcels (up to 50 pounds) by parcel post than it is to use UPS, particularly for shipments in the local zone, and for heavier parcels in zones three through eight.

Mail-Order Rules and Regulations

The law is especially important in mail order.

Above all, you must be concerned with truth in advertising. You cannot in any way misrepresent your product or your business, use deceptive prices, or imitate the trademarks or trade names of others. Every word and picture in your advertisements must be true. Mail-order expert Julian L. Simon explains this clearly in his book when he says that an advertisement must not fool even gullible or ordinarily trusting people. "If you fool any substantial portion of your public," he warns, "you are in the wrong. And what counts is not your actual words, but what people believe after they have read your ad."* Mr. Simon emphasizes that a customer must get from the seller exactly what he expects to receive, and must not feel he has been gypped. (Note, however, that a customer can feel dissatisfied without feeling gypped. Being unhappy isn't the same as feeling cheated.)

In addition to truth in advertising, you must also be aware of Federal Trade Commission (FTC) laws that pertain to consumer safety and the labeling of certain products, most notably textile wearing apparel, wool products, and items with concealed fillings. The FTC offers several free booklets that explain trade practice rules for various industries, and you should order those that pertain to you. (Also see Chapter 15.)

Another FTC ruling states that all orders must be shipped within 30 days of receipt, or the customer is entitled to a refund. If for some reason an order cannot be shipped within this period, the seller must advise the customer accordingly and give him the opportunity to cancel the order or indicate a date beyond which he will not wait for shipment.

Finally, you will have to register the name of your business with the county clerk if you are using any name but your own. This simple matter is discussed further in the legal chapter.

Selling Through Advertisements

If you were to go to the library and check out a good book on the mail-order business, you would probably discover that the average person needs $2500 or more to start even the smallest mail-order business. And with this amount he would still be dangerously undercapitalized.

But the craftsman who is currently selling with success at fairs or through shops could hardly be called "average" in this instance. Actually, a producing craftsman has an important edge on mail order due to the fact that he manufactures the very product he sells and is thus in complete control of his source of supply (unlike the average mail-order seller). A craftsman can easily control the growth of his business and the number of orders to be filled simply by placing more, or fewer, ads.

Many people who begin selling at craft fairs gradually expand to selling by mail, and in a case like this it will not require $2500 to get started. In fact, it is quite possible to launch a small mail-order business with a couple of classified ads and a good illustrated price list. Although it is a lot easier to start a business if you have a thousand dollars or more to invest, there is no rule that says you must begin with a $600 display ad in a prestigious publication.

Mail-order items can be advertised in newspapers or magazines, but experts advise that daily newspapers are not a very successful mail-order medium. Certain magazines are not likely to be profitable media either, which is why it is important to study the mail-order sections of many magazines in order to find the ones right for your

94

* From *How To Start and Operate a Mail Order Business* by Julian L. Simon. © 1964 by McGraw-Hill, Inc. Used with permission of McGraw-Hill Book Company.

products and pocketbook. Most classified ads are quite inexpensive, but the cost of a small display ad can run anywhere from $100 to $600 and more in magazines such as *House Beautiful,* whose "Window Shopping" pages have carried more mail-order advertising than any other magazine in the world. TIP: Regardless of where you advertise, be prepared to advertise continuously once you start, since repetition of your ad will build customer confidence.

Although you can start out in mail order with just one item, it is much wiser to have a line of several; otherwise you will not be able to benefit from repeat business. Following is the approach most often used by the successful mail-order seller: One item is selected from his line — usually his most unusual product, the best seller, or the one that is sure to grab a reader's attention. A photograph of this product is featured in a display ad, and often the ad copy will mention the availability of a catalog. (If people do not order from the ad itself, they may later order from the catalog they have requested.)

When an order is received for the advertised item, the seller will fill it promptly, being sure to include his advertising literature and/or catalog showing his complete line. The quality of the advertised product, and the manner in which the initial order is handled, will have a great deal to do with whether the customer will order from this company again. Once a seller has a mailing list of satisfied customers, he will probably use direct-mail techniques to obtain additional orders from them, sending new advertising literature or catalogs as they are issued. In mail order, repeat business is the name of the game.

Direct Mail

I do not recommend this type of mail-order selling to any but experienced sellers since it can be quite expensive and the results are often discouraging as well. For the benefit of those who would like more information, however, here's a brief explanation of it.

Direct mail is exactly what it sounds like: One approaches prospective customers directly, using a letter, brochure, or catalog. In mail-order jargon, this is known as "mailing cold" because the addressees have not requested information and may have no interest in it once they receive it. Whether such a mailing will yield orders depends on many things, such as the quality of the names being mailed to, the quality and content of one's mail piece, the uniqueness of one's product(s), the time of the year the mailing is being made, and other variables.

Large direct-mail advertisers send several thousand pieces of mail each year, and, upon buying a special postal permit and paying an annual fee, they are entitled to special bulk-mail rates. The small-business owner who is thinking in terms of sending out only 100 fliers once or twice a year will have to think in terms of mailing at first class or regular third class rates, since bulk mailings must be made in quantities of 200 pieces or more.

If you have developed a good mailing list of satisfied customers and other people who have expressed a serious interest in your work in the past, perhaps a small mailing would work well for you. But, before conducting even a small direct-mail campaign, be sure to calculate all your printing and postage costs, then weigh this total against the number of orders (and dollars) you could reasonably expect to receive. The answer will tell you if direct mail is something you should try.

What kind of response can you expect to receive? Let's suppose you have a new illustrated price list or catalog you'd like to get into the hands of about 100 people, as a follow-up to some ad you've placed recently. If all of them are satisfied customers of yours, you could realize an order response of perhaps 20 percent or more. Or, you might get only one or two orders. Or none. The only thing certain about direct-mail advertising is that one cannot be certain about the final outcome. It's a risky business, so don't try it unless you can easily afford to lose the cost of your printing and postage.

Two Mail-Order Success Stories

In order to uncover some techniques and ideas you can use in your own mail-order business, let's take a look at how a couple of craftspeople operate their businesses.

95

A study of the history of Love-Built Toys & Crafts of Tahoe City, California, illustrates how a business can be launched with just one product and a small classified ad. Starting with one set of wood toy plans in December 1972, Dale C. Prohaska, Jr., has since developed an impressive catalog of ideas and supplies for the wooden toy maker, including plans, wooden wheels, books, and toy-making supplies.

Love-Built Toys is a retail-wholesale business, doing 99.5 percent of its business by mail. New customers are obtained through magazine advertisements. When a customer orders through a magazine ad, he receives the company's catalog and may order from it also. The company's goal is to provide ideas and supplies to parents so they can make imaginative and safe toys for their children, but many customers have now begun to make toys to sell at craft fairs, and they are able to buy from the company at special bulk prices. A 15 percent discount is usually given to purchasers such as schools or Scout groups.

Dale's first ad, a $16 classified in *Workbench* magazine, read: "Ten Wooden Toy Plans, $1" That ad yielded 55 orders. The following year Dale put out a small four-page mimeographed catalog showing about 25 designs and again advertised in the classified section of *Workbench*. The next

year, a 12-page brochure was printed with photographs showing plans, wheels, and doll patterns. A problem developed at this point, however. Says Dale, "After advertising in nine magazines to send out a free catalog, we nearly went broke paying for the postage. Eventually we had to find a new printer for the catalogs."

Love-Built Toys took a giant step when it placed its first display ad in the August 1974 issue of *Workbench*. "It was only 1 in. high and 2½ in. wide," recalls Dale, "but it tripled our business. By February of 1975 we were experimenting with several other magazines and in August we began printing our catalog in newspaper format, which reduced the price of our catalog to about one-sixth of what it was before." At this point, Dale also changed the format of his woodworking plans to a large folded sheet. Since then, many new plans and supplies have been added to Love-Built's line, and business continues to grow.

(Pay special attention to Dale's remarks about the expense of mailing free catalogs, and note how a different format lowered his costs.)

Mail order is a great way to sell all kinds of patterns and designs, but few people realize the work that is involved in getting such products into a customer's hands. Colette Wolff, a successful designer-craftsman from New York, gave me a brief education on this process, and her frank comments paint a vivid picture of just what a person lets himself in for when he starts any kind of mail-order business.

Colette designs fabric toys for other people to make from patterns that she publishes and sells through the mail. Her company is called Platypus. Here's how she gets her product from the drawing board into the customer's hands.

"First of all," she explains, "I have to have an idea for a toy that can be interpreted in stuffed fabric. Then I have to design the toy — make the patterns and work out all the details of execution. Then I convert the process of making the toy into step-by-step instructions. I leave the sewing machine for the typewriter. Then I proceed to design and lay out — arranging those instructions into a certain size and number of pages. I illustrate

FUNNY PEOPLE
Pattern
Booklet
- $4.00 -

© by Colette Wolff

An illustration taken from Colette Wolff's catalog, which includes numerous toy and doll patterns to stitch and stuff. Among them is a pattern for a basic doll body that can be turned into the nine personable characters shown here — characters Colette calls her "Funny People." Good drawings like this would add considerable interest to any crafts catalog.

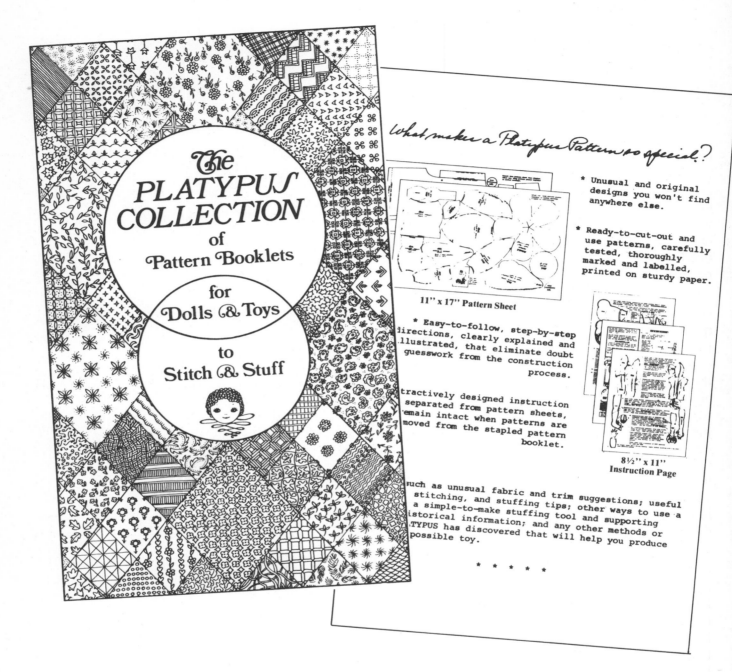

The PLATYPUS COLLECTION
of Pattern Booklets

for Dolls & Toys

to Stitch & Stuff

What makes a Platypus Pattern so special?

11" x 17" Pattern Sheet

* Unusual and original designs you won't find anywhere else.

* Ready-to-cut-out and use patterns, carefully tested, thoroughly marked and labelled, printed on sturdy paper.

* Easy-to-follow, step-by-step directions, clearly explained and illustrated, that eliminate doubt guesswork from the construction process.

ttractively designed instruction separated from pattern sheets, emain intact when patterns are moved from the stapled pattern booklet.

8½" x 11" Instruction Page

such as unusual fabric and trim suggestions; useful stitching, and stuffing tips; other ways to use a simple-to-make stuffing tool and supporting istorical information; and any other methods or TYPUS has discovered that will help you produce possible toy.

* * * * *

98

Note the front cover of Colette Wolff's well-designed mail order catalog, which creates a warm first impression, then "makes its pitch" on the inside front cover by answering the question, "What makes a Platypus Pattern so special?" Colette takes this opportunity to list the important selling points of her product, such as (1) unusual and original designs; (2) ready-to-cut-out-and-use patterns; (3) easy-to-follow, step-by-step directions; and so on.

On the inside back cover (not shown here) Colette explains how her pattern booklets may be ordered, and the outside back cover has her return address and her Platypus logo, plus space for the mailing address and a special bonus: instructions on how to make a quick-and-easy stocking doll, illustrated with drawings.

the steps in the instructions, working with a light box, Rapidographs, photographs, and other artists' materials, plus oceans of rubber cement. After the copy is prepared for the printer, I must find/choose a printer to do the actual printing.

"Then," Colette continues, "I sell the product, or pattern booklet as I call it. That involves becoming a copywriter; placing ads in magazines; and writing, designing, and illustrating a catalog and fliers. When orders come in I become an office worker and record them, stuff envelopes, type labels, and deal with the U.S. Post Office. It's a one-person operation at the beginning, and perhaps for a long time afterward."

Mail order is a business with a peculiar nature that Colette describes like this: "It runs you, I think, as much as you run it. If someone just wants to make toys to sell, that's an activity that can be controlled, more or less, by the toymaker; and if the toymaker gets sick, wants to go into another activity, take a vacation — whatever — the toymaker, after dealing with outstanding orders, just stops. Not so with a catalog mail-order business. It goes on every day the mail is delivered. Orders come in from catalogs that were mailed out years before. It requires constant attention. And if you get bored with it, or want to 'close up shop,' a mail-order business dies a very slow death, and can dribble on for years."

Colette began Platypus with a $7 ad and a borrowed mimeograph, much like Dale Prohaska of Love-Built Toys. Her business has stayed at the level generated by the kind of advertising she does. (She is still working only with classified advertising in small needlework and hobby publications because this is bringing her all the business she can handle by herself.) "In order to get to the next level," Colette says, "I will need a much higher advertising budget for display ads, more space to store all my pattern booklets, files, and materials, and machinery to help process the daily mail."

A note in Colette's advertising material offers a tip for mail-order sellers. She is not equipped to send out extensive mailings whenever her catalog expands, but she does maintain a file of large, stamped, self-addressed envelopes from customers who want to be informed about new publications as soon as they are in print. Perhaps this idea would work for you, too.

"One of the nice things about what I do," concludes Colette, "is that when I finally have a design in print, in booklet form, the returns on that title are endless until I decide to take it out of circulation or not to reprint it. My kind of approach to the craft business builds the longer you stay in it."

Creating Your Own Catalog

In Chapter 12, under the subhead "Promotional Materials," you will find information on how to create your own letterhead, calling cards, brochures, etc. A catalog can be created in much the same way, and it can be something as simple as one sheet of paper or as complex as the 42-page catalog offered by Alfred Atkins of Spencer, New York.

Al is a specialist in miniature wrought iron and unquestionably the most amazing craftsman/catalog designer I have ever encountered. I asked him to give me some sage advice that could be passed on to others who are interested in creating their own catalogs, and while he was at it, would he also tell me more about his mail-order business.

"Yeah," he replied. "It started like this. Caye MacLaren wrote an article about me in *Nutshell News* after I made some clumsy trinkets for her. Did I ever get mail? A rhetorical question, the answer to which is yes, I ever got mail. It wasn't that I was so great; there just was nobody into metal minis, so I was in the position of one who had invented booze or baseball. Soon I was writing the same kind of letter to many people explaining, 'Yes, I can make a spiral staircase for you. It will cost by the inch of vertical rise, and I do mean COST, etc.' Finally I realized I was writing letters all the time and getting no work done. Had to get out a catalog."

If you are writing letters all the time, explaining what you can and cannot make for your customers, perhaps you need a catalog, too. Whether it is one or two sheets of paper or a nice booklet, make sure it represents you and your work. If you have the money to spend on layout

99

and design, it will be well spent on the creation of a professional catalog, but if not, you can create your own. A typewriter helps, but it's not necessary. Many craftspeople create hand-written, hand-drawn catalogs and brochures that are real attention-getters. If you can do simple line drawings, or have a friend who will do them for you, that's fine. Photographs are better than drawings, but they do add to your printing costs.

The content of your catalog should be clear enough for anyone to understand, and items for sale should be accurately described. Do *not* show prices in the catalog itself, but print loose sheets (and order forms) that can be inserted. Then, when it becomes necessary to change a price (and it will) you can simply have the price sheet reprinted. New items can be added to your catalog by printing additional loose pages until such time as you can afford to reprint the entire catalog.

When describing your products, give color, size, texture, and materials used. If space allows, include additional information as well — perhaps something about the history of your craft, the origin of your materials, or anything that makes you or your products unusual and interesting. This kind of information will give your catalog a special personality all its own.

Perhaps that's why I like Alfred Atkins' catalog so much. Not because it has 42 pages, but because it has lots of personality. So much, in fact, that it is always getting free publicity. (Everyone who sees it wants to share it with others.) It is not just a catalog of "metal minis," but the personal statement of an artist who obviously has a zest for life and a love for people. (Even if he doesn't trust anyone over 6½ inches tall.) After a lifetime spent in occupations far removed from the world of miniatures, Al, at the age of 61, is now doing the kind of work he loves best and wants to do from here on in. His unique catalog reflects his humorous approach to life and the great pleasure he receives from his work. A study of it is something of an education in itself. How did he produce it, I wondered.

"I was a commercial artist," he explained, "so had no trouble on illustrations, layout, typography, and production know-how. Always wanted to write a book but never had any message or viewpoint on anything before, so I was all set for copy. For anyone without that precise background, however, I scarce know how to advise that person to go about making up a catalog. Pathetic ones are made by many who rush in where copy-writing artists shuffle in sideways. Yet, if you put the making of a catalog into the hands of a professional, you are into, like, MONEY. The work I put into my catalog (and it isn't all apparent) I wouldn't have done for $25,000 for anyone else. I designed and wrote it all with help from any artist whose work was no longer in copyright. I admired the Caswell-Massey compendium, the Dixie Gunworks Catalog, and Mark Twain (Sam Clemens), Kipling, Shakespeare, and Dr. David Emanuel Jack, and I decided my catalog would be a compendium of these and would stand or fall or crawl in that form because I had done my best and didn't know how to do any better."

And there you have the best advice anyone can give you. Do your best with what you've got to work with. You don't have to be an artist, illustrator, or layout technician to put out your own catalog, but you do have to have some common sense and good judgment. It will also help to study the techniques of preparing camera-ready copy (see Chapter 12) and you should also study the catalogs of other craftsmen for ideas. It's all right to emulate the style of catalogs that strike your fancy, but please don't copy another person's ideas or artwork. Finally, it is a good idea to get the response of a couple of objective friends once you have planned your catalog. As the person creating both the handcrafts and the catalog they're featured in, it will be very difficult for you to play the role of a would-be customer trying to order from that catalog. What you can understand, another may not. The criticism of an objective friend could be invaluable to you.

If, in the end, you think getting out your own catalog is just too much for you, drop me a line. After five years of putting out a quarterly magazine, I am something of an expert at preparing camera-ready copy for a printer, and I'd be happy to discuss the possibilities of creating a catalog for you at a price you can afford.

100

THE VILLAGE SMITHY

Miniature Catalogue

R.D. 5 ✳ Hemlock Trail
Carmel, New York ✳ 10512

$3⁰⁰

a paltry figure when you consider that this is positively the last catalogue by

A. Atkins
Blacksmith &
Designer

SPECIALIST IN
MINIATURE
WROUGHT IRON

101

...a surprise... to see all this mini stuff coming off my anvil.

a. Atkins

Cover of Al Atkins' unusual catalog, and a humorous self-portrait of the artist, originally drawn for Artisan Crafts magazine.

Although a good catalog can be expensive to produce and print, please note that it does not have to be given away. Few catalogs are offered free these days. If your catalog price seems a bit high to you, you should consider the practice followed by Al and many other craftsmen: Offer a refund of the catalog's price on a customer's first order (usually given in the form of a credit on the order). In advertisements, simply show your catalog's price with the word "refundable" after it.

If you decide to create your own catalog, remember that it will take you some time. Al had so much fun doing his first catalog that it took him a year to complete it. "Got behind in my work," he says. "Actually, the catalog was out of date by the time it was printed. So I announced my second one at $3 (tired of losing money on each catalog

| TO: | **P L A T Y P U S**
P. O. Box 396
Planetarium Station
New York, N. Y. 10024 | Date_____ |

Please send me the following PLATYPUS PATTERN BOOKLETS:

Title of Booklet	No. of Booklets	Cost

	TOTAL COST	

MAILING CHARGE

When the cost of the pattern booklets ordered totals ...
    ... less than $ 5.00 – add 40¢
between $5.00 and $10.00 – add 60¢
    more than $10.00 – postpaid

Sales Tax (N. Y. State residents only)	
MAILING CHARGE	

TOTAL AMOUNT ENCLOSED —

Mail immediately to:_____

Please print clearly!

Left.
Colette Wolff's order form occupies a whole page in her catalog, which is printed to size 5½ x 8½ in. The back of this page has been left blank. Although this form has been prepared in a style different from the one at right, it contains the same basic information. Together, these samples will provide clues on how to design an order form that will suit your own special needs.

Opposite page.
A sample order form from Al Atkins' catalog. Because it is printed to size 8½ x 11 in., two order forms can be placed on one page. (Note: The back of this page is a continuation of the two forms, for customers who wish to order more than eight items.)

THE VILLAGE SMITHY **ORDER FORM** DATE _____

204 Hulbert Hollow Road
Spencer, NY 14883   FROM: NAME _____

STREET _____

(607) 589-6166   CITY _____ STATE _____ ZIP _____

QUANTITY	CATALOGUE NO.	Description	Price Each	Total

MINIMUM ORDER $5.00
NOTES:

Add Shipping & Handling	1	50
N.Y.S. - add tax		
Total Enclosed with Order		

continue on other side

THE VILLAGE SMITHY **ORDER FORM** DATE _____

204 Hulbert Hollow Road
Spencer, NY 14883   FROM: NAME _____

STREET _____

(607) 589-6166   CITY _____ STATE _____ ZIP _____

QUANTITY	CATALOGUE NO.	Description	Price Each	Total

MINIMUM ORDER $5.00
NOTES:

Add Shipping & Handling	1	50
N.Y.S. - add tax		
Total Enclosed with Order		

continue on other side

mailed at $1). It took me about 2½ years to get this one out. It got so a day's mail would average three catalog requests and one refund demand. Trouble was, every time I read over a page for final approval I got an irresistible idea for a change or addition. Fun, but you never finish. Had to force myself to reform.''

Frankly, I don't think Al will ever reform, and I hope he never loses his sense of humor either. On the cover of his catalog it says: "$3 — a paltry figure when you consider that this is positively the last catalog by A. Atkins, Blacksmith & Designer.'' Recently Al told me that his next catalog will probably cost $5 and take at least 3 years to complete. Meanwhile, he continues to wrought his miniature iron wonders for customers who are willing to wait months for them to come off the anvil. Al always has more orders than he can fill and wonders if he ought to raise his prices. "I know I am not overcharging,'' he says with a wink, "because I remain poor.''

A woman once wrote Al saying she couldn't believe he made a living from miniatures. His reply? "It's a *miniature* living.''

Special Handcraft Catalogs For Craftspeople

Relatively new to the craft world are handcraft catalogs that feature the work of crafts professionals. Although inclusion in such catalogs can represent thousands of dollars of advertising for each exhibitor, there is often little or no charge involved. This type of marketing is the perfect answer for the craftsman who wants to sell by mail but doesn't want the bother and expense of putting out his own catalog. Inclusion in someone else's catalog means the craftsman only has to fill and ship orders as they are received.

Handcraft catalogs fall into two basic categories. The first kind is sold to consumers who order direct from the craftsman, whose address is listed in the catalog. The second kind is either sold or sent free to consumers, who order through the catalog. (The craftsman's address is not listed.) The catalog publisher may buy outright from the craftsman, retaining small inventories of each item

and re-ordering as the need arises; or, he may simply forward orders to craftsmen for fulfillment, taking a percentage of the retail price as his commission. In either case, the publisher takes care of all photography, printing, and mailing costs of the catalog, and also handles correspondence relating to orders.

Sounds good, doesn't it? Too good to be true, maybe? I had planned to give you two excellent examples of this type of catalog, but during the year it has taken me to research and write this book, the two new and promising mail-order crafts catalogs I was going to review here have discontinued publishing. They simply came and went, as is so often the case with new craft businesses of any kind. But there will be other catalogs in the future, I'm sure, because there is a definite need for them, and someday someone will recognize that need, and fill it. You will learn about such catalogs if you read publications that are edited for selling craftsmen.

But all is not lost. Fortunately, there are at least two mail-order catalogs for craftspeople at the present time, and both fall into the first category I mentioned. In corresponding with the two publishers, I learned more about their individual operations, and the following information has been taken from their letters in order to help you evaluate each catalog's worth to you, as a seller.

The Goodfellow Catalog of Wonderful Things: Christopher Weills, who compiled this catalog, is also publisher and editor of *The Goodfellow Review of Crafts,* a newspaper that has gained a devoted following since it began in 1973. The first edition of *The Goodfellow Catalog* (1974) received critical acclaim and fine reviews in such prestigious publications as the *New York Times* and the *Washington Post.* The second edition of the catalog was published in 1977 by Berkley Publishing Company, New York, and Chris told me that 15,000 copies were printed on the first run for distribution through book stores and by mail. The directory is now in its second printing.

"The work of some 600 people is included in this catalog,'' says Chris, "and all fields of handcrafts are represented.'' The book also includes a comprehensive resource section designed to aid and inform both the amateur and professional craftsperson, making it well worth its price of $7.95.

In answer to my question about the handling of orders, Chris told me they are sent directly to the individual craftsman whose address appears along with his product description and biography. "Craftspeople must assume all responsibility for orders," says Chris. *"The Goodfellow Catalog takes no commissions on sales."*

About 1500 craftspeople made application for *The Goodfellow Catalog* last year, and even more are expected for future editions. "We have a large file of inquiries about the third edition, and are now thinking that we'll do a catalog every two years," says Chris.

The editorial board of *The Goodfellow Review* serves as jury for all crafts to be considered for inclusion, and interested craftspeople must submit professional slides or photos of their work, along with complete descriptions of the products they wish to sell. Acceptance into the catalog is based on such things as excellence of craftsmanship, salability of items, and uniqueness of design. Of primary importance to the publisher is the professional attitude of the seller, who must show evidence of the fact that he is, indeed, a seller who approaches his business in a professional manner and one who will fill all orders received through the catalog.

Brochures and applications for the next edition of the catalog are available and interested readers can stay informed of the catalog's progress by reading *The Goodfellow Review*. "We're expecting to include color in the next catalog," adds Chris, "and we hope it will become an alternative Sears, Roebuck catalog."

The CraftsPeople Directory 1978 * : This is a new regional directory serving artisans in the three-state area of New York, New Jersey, and Connecticut. It is being advertised to the general public nationally in such publications as *McCall's* and *Better Homes and Gardens*. It is also available in several New York bookstores. The purpose of this directory, priced at $2.95, is to "allow the individual searching for a truly unique craft masterwork or a particularly expressive gift to find just the right craftsperson to fulfill his needs." In short, it's a consumer guide that enables buyers to deal directly with craftspeople. The publishers assume no responsibility, and no profit, for such dealings.

Carol Binen, Dianne Dolowich, and Lucretia Steele are the three women behind this directory. All three, mothers of young children, happen to be craft enthusiasts, as well as present or former teachers of English and language arts. In a letter I received from Dianne, she wrote: "I wholly support your concept of encouraging women to get out and do something about their ideas. From the conception of the idea to the stage we have now reached (promotion of the 1978 and planning the 1979) this endeavor has been a most thrilling experience."

The three women searched for craftspeople at various shows in the tri-state area and approached only the best ones found, inviting them to be included in their first directory. When I asked if participants were actually juried, Dianne said there was a natural process of elimination "because only the committed craftsperson would pay for advertising and be willing to undertake wholesale work, commissions, etc."

Each of the 100 craftspeople included in this directory designed his own entry and paid an advertising fee that covered the initial printing of the directory (2500 copies) and some of the publishers' overhead expenses. "We don't expect to make a profit this year," says Dianne, "since all revenue from the sale of the directory will be put back into advertising and promotion to build interest in future editions. The next edition will be published in August 1979, and we expect 400 to 500 participants. The book has gotten good press and participating craftspeople are reporting good response."

Dianne says they welcome contact from others in the tri-state area who would like to be included in future editions, adding, "We hope that soon we won't be limited to this geographical area,

105

---

* Shortly before going to press we learned that this directory will be called *The Artists and CraftsPeople Directory* in 1979.

however, as we have been contacted by some people who are interested in forming directories in other locations."

Other Catalog Markets

In addition to selling through special handcraft catalogs such as those just discussed, you might consider marketing through mail-order companies such as Miles Kimball Company in Oshkosh, Wisconsin. I wrote them and asked what a craftsperson had to do to sell through their catalog, and received an interesting response from George R. Hagene, vice president of merchandising.

"Because of the fact that most individuals are not able to produce handmade items in sufficient quantity," he wrote, "I hesitate to encourage you to mention us in your book since I feel that, in all probability, the individuals that your book will appeal to will not be in a position to supply the demand created by our catalog. It is extremely important that anybody who writes us concerning their idea or their product have facilities for producing the article in quantity. The latest Federal Trade Commission rulings make it necessary that merchandise be shipped promptly, and, therefore,

it is impossible to hold a customer's order for an extended period of time waiting for the production of the merchandise."

Mr. Hagene's remarks remind me of those made by one of the publishers who recently discontinued publication of this handcrafts catalog. "Although the catalog was well received," he wrote, "we had some difficulty obtaining the quantities of craft items as quickly as they were needed."

No catalog can be successful if there is difficulty with its suppliers, and, as a seller, you should not try to sell through any type of catalog unless you are prepared to handle all orders received. If you are the rare craftsperson who can produce in quantity, you may wish to contact a mail-order firm such as Miles Kimball Company, whose products include jewelry, kits, stuffed toys, and Christmas ornaments, among other things. When writing this or any other mail-order firm, be sure to submit a sample or a letter indicating what your product is, including full information as to weight, packing, terms, F.O.B. point, the cost on a jobbing basis, and the intended retail price. Also give sizes and colors when these are a consideration.

9

Needlework And Design Markets

According to *Ladies' Home Journal Needle & Craft* magazine, almost 40 per cent of the women in the United States do some sort of needlework—including needlepoint, embroidery, knitting, crocheting, and quilting. It's anybody's guess as to how many of these women are trying to sell the products of their nimble fingers.

In Erica Wilson's newspaper column, *Needleplay,* a reader once asked where she could sell her crewel work and needlepoint, to which Erica replied, "Have you ever thought about giving needlework lessons?" That says a lot about the market for finished needlework.

One woman wrote to me saying, "I have sold extremely few made-up embroideries. It's terribly difficult to price if you count your labor at any fair rate to yourself. Besides, most people prefer to do their own." This particular woman eventually solved her problem by creating a line of needlework kits that she wholesales to stitchery shops across the country.

Markets for Needleworkers

Selling kits and giving lessons are certainly two options open to needleworkers who want to make money, but they aren't the only ones to be explored. For example, if you can chart needlework patterns, this talent may be of special interest to shops. Perhaps a customer will bring in a design she wants translated to chart form, in

order that she might work it herself. Or, if you are a designer, a shop might buy the charted patterns you have published (printed) yourself. Hand-painted canvases are always in demand—the more original and unique, the better. Read needlework journals to stay abreast of new developments in this area.

In an earlier chapter, Connie Stano remarked that a woman can, indeed, make a career from needlework, but it takes great motivation, experience, and creative ability. She believes that a woman working by herself in her own community can be very busy today merely by running an ad in her local paper offering to finish kits, frame, or design custom pieces. I asked Connie to elaborate on this topic a bit.

"There really is a market for embroidering kits for money," she told me. "Not just for people who are too lazy or inept, but more often for people who are just too busy, or not interested in doing it themselves. There is no law saying these people cannot enjoy embroidery enough to want to buy it. It is a unique operation and word-of-mouth advertising works well on a local level. Some of your best customers will be women who started a kit and lost interest, or found they couldn't do it. Others will be people who bought a kit and then never had time to start it."

Why not take your lead from Connie Stano to sell some of your needlework? Place an ad in your local paper offering to do custom designed needlework, blocking, or framing, depending on where your talents and interests lie. Or, approach a needlework shop and find out if they can use your services as a custom designer. Not all shop owners have the time, talent, or inclination to do custom designing themselves, and they may be delighted to learn your services are available to them. I checked a new needlework shop in my area shortly after it opened and asked if there really was a demand for custom work, and they gave me an enthusiastic yes. In fact, the first week they were open, three women requested custom jobs. One asked to have an antique footstool refurbished with fresh needle-point, another wanted a humorous sign made for her kitchen, and a third needed a small clutch bag to complement a new evening gown.

Don't forget about small items, such as jewelry, Christmas ornaments, eyeglass cases, and trim items that might be added to dresses or suits. Collars, pockets, and belts might be of interest to a custom-made dress shop, to say nothing of special items such as evening jackets, vests, and handbags. Once you enter the fashion field, you can command prices more in line with the hours actually spent on a piece of needlework.

Finally, since needlework of any kind is so time consuming and so hard to market profitably, perhaps you ought to consider the ever-growing miniatures market and doll-house collectors who are willing to pay large sums for miniature master-pieces. The needlepoint picture or rug you cannot afford to sell as a full-size item might be very profitable indeed when done in miniature, to dollhouse scale. Read magazines such as *Nutshell News* in order to learn more about the miniatures market.

Embroiderers should explore the possibility of doing stitchery for specialty shops. Offer a line of designs from which customers can select a motif to be added to items purchased in the shop, such as sweaters. Depending on the quality of the shop and the price of its merchandise, you might receive a large sum of money for a small amount of hand-work.

Connie also emphasizes that professional blocking and framing of needlework—all kinds—can bring in money, too. This is a skill you can learn by studying needlework instruction books and from simple trial-and-error experience. (Practice on your own work first, of course.)

If there is an interior decorator in your area, find out if he or she is interested in a good source of supply for custom-made pillow covers to complement special room decors. Or maybe you have created some other item that makes a good decorator accent. Home decorating magazines will provide additional ideas that can be adapted for needlework items.

Special Tips for Quilters

Quilting falls into the same category as other forms of needlework in that one never receives in dollars and cents what is put out in time and talent. Yet women continue to make and sell quilts, not just for the money, but mostly because they love to make quilts. Since they can't keep all the quilts they make, they simply sell them for the best price they can get.

In an interview with Lassie Bradshaw of Georgia Mountain Arts Products, Inc., a cooperative, I learned something about the value of quilts. "Is there a good market for quilts?" I asked. "Yes," said Lassie, "there sure is. The week before we came up here we sold twelve in one day."

I met Lassie at a show in Cincinnati called Appalachiana Festival '77, a four-day show then in its seventh year. The cooperative was enjoying brisk sales during the show, especially of its quilts. The average price was around $100, depending on the size and pattern. Lassie explained that quilts in the co-op's shop were priced even lower than this. "Some quilts we can get cheaper," she said. "Like, a craftsman comes in and the quality's not really good, but it's good enough that you can sell it, so we price it at $50."

When I said that even at $100, the maker of a quilt was not being well paid, Lassie agreed, but made an important point, especially concerning quilters in the Appalachian region. "When our cooperative first started," Lassie said, "you could go out and buy a quilt for $7 or $10. After we started the co-op and realized there was a good market for the quilts, we raised the prices. These ladies are now getting a price that is double or triple what they used to get. They've learned the value of their work, which they didn't know before. They used to work for nothing, practically."

Even though they are still not receiving full value for the time spent in quilting, Lassie made me realize that it means so much more to them now because it's more than they had before.

Understandably, urban quilters and more sophisticated sellers can command higher prices for their work than women who live in rural or economically depressed parts of the country. Quilting enjoyed a countrywide revival in 1976 as young and old alike made Bicentennial quilts in uncounted thousands, and today it is not unusual to see fine quilts priced in the $500 to $1000 range.

In a conversation with Evelyn Mendes of The Patchwork Company in Wilmette, Illinois, I learned that she often pays as much as $175 to $300 for a hand-stitched quilt. (The lower amount is for patchwork or applique quilts; the higher figure for more difficult patterns such as Lone Star or Cathedral Window.) Says Evelyn, "We are paying our quilters much more now than ever before because we know we will lose them otherwise. We appreciate the fact that they are artists, and believe they should be paid for their artistry. Many of our quilters have great color sense, and this is especially important to buyers."

Does machine quilting reduce the value of a quilt in a buyer's eyes? "Most definitely," said Evelyn. "Quilting by hand really makes a quilt come alive. While machine-stitched quilts have a good market, especially for use in children's rooms and college dorms, there is a greater demand for quilts that have been entirely patched and quilted by hand."

109

The Patchwork Company, owned by Evelyn and her partner, Maryan Bogg, accepts some quilts on consignment and buys others outright, taking a 100 per cent markup. Some shops take as much as 300 per cent, however, so it might pay you to shop around when trying to establish a good outlet for your quilts.

I must inject something here. I know one quiltmaker who consigns her quilts to a local shop that retails them for about $300. She also takes similar quilts to craft fairs and sells them for about half that amount. I can see her point. She wants to sell her quilts and feels the $300 price the shop puts on them is too high. She may be right. But she is certainly wrong when she undercuts the shop's retail price. This is very unprofessional, and, if the shop finds out, they will probably refuse to accept additional quilts from her. Think how aggravated their customers would be if they paid $300 for a quilt, then went to a craft fair and saw the same quilt for half that amount.

If you find yourself in a similar position, I urge you to either raise your retail prices to match those of the shop you are dealing with, or don't sell at both fairs and shops. There are specialty quilt shops who are interested in developing relationships with quilters who can supply them with quality merchandise on a regular basis, and you should try to find them. "When we find good quiltmakers," says Evelyn, "we treat them as the valued suppliers they are, and pay them accordingly. We're interested in hearing from quilters from all over the country."

The demand for fine quilts currently exceeds the supply, so don't settle for less than what you know your work is worth. Study listings in directories such as *Craftworker's Market* and the *Contemporary Crafts Marketplace* to learn about other shops and galleries who want quilts, and read the *Quilter's Newsletter* to stay abreast of new developments in this field.

A Little-Known Market For Knitters/Crocheters

There is, unfortunately, little demand for knitted or crocheted garments. Too many women knit and crochet today to be interested in buying this kind of work. Yet I continue to see ads for crocheted and knitted items in the classified sections of various women's magazines, and have often wondered just how much of this work actually sells. I directed my wondering to Barbara Hall Pederson, editor of *Stitch 'n Sew,* asking if she had any indication of the amount of money women were making from the sale of such handmades.

"I have no actual figures on the profit made from selling handmades," she wrote. "From the letters I receive, I would conclude that while there is enough financial gain to make an ad worthwhile, nobody is going to get rich that way. Most of our ladies are either supplementing Social Security, or are mothers of small children using extra time for a bit of fun and profit."

My correspondence with another magazine editor led me to the discovery that there is at least one good market for needlework that is generally overlooked. Jane Luddecke, editor of *American Home Crafts* explains: "There is a great need for anyone who can write the how-to instructions for knitted and crocheted garments. The older women now doing this sort of thing are quickly diminishing, and younger ones are not taking their jobs. The pay is good for this type of work."

Sometimes a person will create an original knitted or crocheted piece "off the top of her head" and is unable to write the instructions, Jane told me. A magazine editor may buy a finished piece, but then she has to find someone who can duplicate it and write the instructions for use in the magazine. Jane emphasized that anyone who can look at a finished garment and figure out how it was made—and put those details down on paper—has got a great, salable service to offer all craft/needlework magazine editors.

"Further," says Jane, "once those instructions have been written, the magazine editor must have someone else double-check them, and the pay is also good for this—perhaps $45 to $50 for doing a sweater." One would simply have to make the sweater, exactly following the instructions given, indicating any corrections, errors, etc., as well as verifying the amount of yarn required. Someone always double-checks every pattern published in a magazine, and you might be that someone.

Here are three ways a design for a sweater might get into a magazine, and they will suggest how you can approach magazine editors and yarn companies:

1. A yarn company has come to the magazine editor with an original design it has purchased from a designer. The company would like publicity for its yarn and may give — or sell — this design to the magazine in return for the publicity it would receive by having its yarn mentioned in the instructions.

2. The magazine has purchased the design/pattern/instructions from someone, and it goes to the yarn company and asks if it has a designer who could make it up for the magazine.

3. A person goes directly to the magazine editor offering any or all of the above.

If any of the foregoing suggests an idea that will work for you, by all means follow up on it by contacting some editors and leading manufacturers of yarns and threads. In other words, don't hide your talents in your needlework basket; bring them out into the open and see what unravels. (NOTE: Any presentation concerning your talents should be backed up with good photographs of your work and information about your background and experience.)

Getting Designs and Ideas Published

Because there are so many needlework and craft magazines being published today, there is

111

naturally a good market for designs and ideas. Yours may be good, but are they truly *original*?

A design is not original if it is merely an adaptation of something you have seen at a craft fair, in a shop, in someone's home, etc. Making changes in color, size, or decoration does not constitute originality, either. To take someone else's idea or design and have it published as your own is to invite legal trouble for both you and the magazine. Many craftspeople are copyrighting their designs these days and fighting back in court when people "lift" them for commercial use.

"There are subtle distinctions between that which is original and that which is adapted from, inspired by, or just plain stolen from something else," says Barbara Hall Pedersen in an editorial in *Stitch 'n Sew* magazine. Barbara gave me permission to quote from her editorial to help my readers understand the problem so often encountered by craft editors everywhere.

"If we as a magazine were to deal exclusively with professionls," Barbara says, "we might have a reasonble assurance that the material offered us could be published without fear of violating someone's copyright or design patent.

"In a magazine like *Stitch 'n Sew* where reader participation is encouraged, we have an altogether different situation. Many of our contributors are not professionals; they are simply talented and experienced needlewomen who enjoy exercising their own creativity to turn out something unique. They will often start with a basic commercial pattern and modify it or improve it each time they make it up until they feel that the resulting product is truly their own creation.

"Sometimes it is hard to tell whether a design qualifies as an original. We suggest that if you have done any borrowing at all from another source, it would be best to mention it when submitting your idea, and let us decide."*

This is good advice, and I'm sure all craft and needlework magazine editors would appreciate the same consideration from their contributors.

Most editors have some kind of standard

112

* Editorial from *Stitch 'N Sew,* January-February 1977 issue. © 1977 Tower Press. Reprinted with permission.

release form they send to people whose ideas are of interest to them. The one used by *Decorating & Craft Ideas* magazine, for instance, asks the person signing the release to certify that the material submitted is of her "own design, not previously published nor utilizing any part of previously published material." Joyce Bennett, editor of *Crafts* magazine and former crafts director of *Decorating & Craft Ideas* says, "Too many people do not understand how magazines of this type operate. We are not out to rip anyone off or swipe a good idea, so we require a release. We are just as likely to get stuck in the middle because so many people add to or adjust things that often no one knows who is the originator of an item. I'm for everyone being protected."

There is not much formality on craft magazine staffs, and usually you will encounter friendly editors such as Jane Luddecke of *American Home Crafts,* who works with contributors on a simple correspondence basis. "We have a very limited free-lance budget for ideas," says Jane, "and no standard release form is sent because it would cost just as much for us to copy a person's design as it would to buy it. We really get some very good things from our readers, and we like people to send in their ideas from different parts of the country."

Most of the editors I corresponded with told me that the best way to make an initial presentation of an idea is to send a couple of photographs and a brief letter explaining it. This will give the editor the knowledge necessary to make a decision as to whether your idea is one the publication can use. If so, you will be contacted for further information. TIP: It would be wise to send a self-addressed stamped envelope with your initial inquiry if you want your photographs returned. And, if an editor requests samples of your work, Jane Luddecke says to be sure to finish things properly. In particular, needlework should be properly blocked. "A great design that isn't properly executed and finished will turn off any editor," she warns.

Assuming that one of your ideas is accepted by an editor, what then? And how much money can you expect to make? This varies with each magazine. For example, Kay Dougherty, editor of

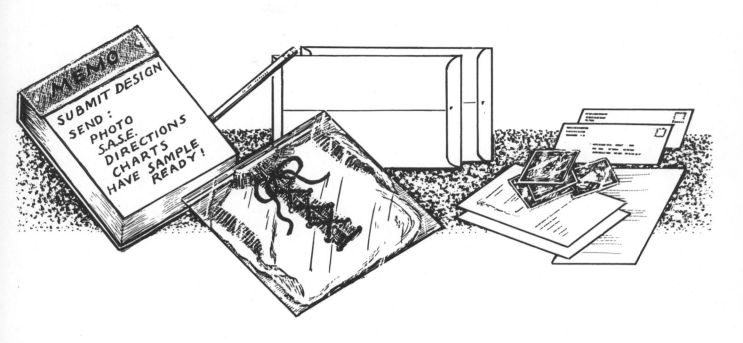

Good craft designers must be organized, as well as creative. A neat, professional presentation will improve the chance of a sale.

Crafts 'n Things says, "We will need either four-color transparencies or the actual item for photographing once we have accepted the article. We do reserve the right to edit instructions, and rate of payment depends upon the length and complexity of each given article." Kay welcomes unsolicited ideas and asks that craftspeople send detailed descriptions of their ideas, with photos if possible.

Margaret Gilman, managing editor at *McCall's Needlework & Crafts Publications* says they are interested in made-up original handcraft items in a variety of techniques — with the directions and diagrams or charts for making them. "We take all of our own photographs," she says, "and all of the material is copyrighted by us. Price offered for items will be in ratio to originality and quality." As with other magazines, *McCall's* asks that a snapshot (not sketch) be submitted before the complete made-up item is sent in. Unfortunately, many items submitted to *McCall's* cannot be used because the designs or quality of workmanship are not up to its standards, so before sending samples of your work, study the contents of

several issues to be certain your work is comparable in quality and design. (This applies not only to *McCall's,* but to all other magazines as well.)

Other tips from *McCall's*: Submissions of work must be accompanied by complete, clear, specific directions that are legibly written. Made-up items must be carefully constructed and spotlessly clean. When wrapping merchandise for shipment, make sure it is properly packed. (Many items have to be rejected simply because they are poorly packed and damaged in shipment.)

In addition to craft magazines, you might consider selling your ideas to consumer publications such as *Good Housekeeping* or *Better Homes and Gardens,* both of whom indicated they were interested in hearing from designers and qualified craftspeople. Understandably, it is more difficult to be published in magazines like these than in others whose entire content is devoted to crafts or needlework, as Cecelia K. Toth, director of needlework and sewing at *Good Housekeeping* explains. "Most of the designers whose work you see in our magazine are individuals well known in our field," she says. "We do, however, sometimes

113

find new and good designers by having individuals send photographs of their work. Frankly, 90 percent is awful, but the 10 percent that is beautiful makes it worthwhile. Initially, photographs are probably the best way of giving us an idea. Payment can be for photograph rights or for the purchase of the item. Rates differ and are individually negotiated."

Ciba Vaughan, crafts editor at *Better Homes and Gardens,* welcomes submissions of craft ideas from free-lance designers but prefers to see slides, Polaroid shots, or detailed sketches of items before finished projects can be commissioned. For small items, such as Christmas ornaments, finished samples are preferred, along with a brief typewritten description of the technique and materials involved in making the item. "The amount we pay for a given craft design depends entirely on the project and how we plan to use it in the magazine," says Ciba. "All purchased craft items become the property of the magazine."

If you plan to sell your craft ideas and designs to magazines, you will need good photographs of your work, and if you cannot take them yourself, you will have to find someone to do this for you. Stuart W. Goodwin of South Ryegate, Vermont, currently offers a photographic service to writers, craftsmen, and hobbyists that may be of interest to you. You can send him light mailables such as craftwork, crocheted items, sewing, dolls, afghans, etc., and he will photograph them in black and white and return them to you. (You pay postage, of course.) A free brochure is available upon request, and readers who use Stuart's service will receive a 15 percent discount on their first order if they mention this book in their correspondence. (See resource chapter, "Special Services.")

114

Can Craftspeople Sell To Manufacturers?

"I have completed a project using felt, beads, and sequins that can be made into a kit," one woman wrote. "I found the address of one company, which I wrote, but never received an answer. Could you tell me how to find the names and addresses of companies that would be interested in my project? I would like to sell my idea to them."

I'm sorry to say that the above idea is not marketable, at least not to a craft supply manufacturer. What the average craftsperson does not realize is that craft manufacturers have designers of their own, either full-time employees or freelancers who work on special assignment. Very few craftspeople have the required background and experience to design for the craft industry, and even those who do are not likely to get the time of day from manufacturers, who want not just ideas, but complete marketing programs.

While I was researching this topic, one authority in the craft industry told me that individuals who try to sell to manufacturers are more likely to have their designs and ideas pirated than purchased, and often, the larger the company, the greater the chance of this happening. A manufacturer may say "Yes, I'm interested" when a brief explanation of an idea is submitted, and "Sorry, not interested" once all details have been provided. A year later that same idea may be on the market, only the designer won't get anything for it. It will have been cleverly adapted or subtly changed or, in other words, stolen.

This is not to say that all manufacturers operate this way, nor that individuals cannot sell a good idea to a reputable company, but unknown designers have always had difficulty in cracking this market. The picture may be changing though, because recent articles in craft publications indicate that many companies are currently seeking new designs and ideas for their craft lines and inviting contact from creative craftspeople. As an experiment, I wrote to a few of these companies and confronted them with the rumor I'd heard: namely, that manufacturers often pirate designs and ideas from unsuspecting individuals who believe the whole world to be honest. I also asked them to tell me how a person could protect designs and ideas during the submission process. I received two very frank replies that I'm quoting to give you a new viewpoint on this matter and to help you in any negotiations you might have with craft manufacturers.

From Fredrick Allen Fortune, art director, Open Door Enterprises, Santa Clara, California (a craft kit manufacturer): "You may tell your readers that, though lengthy and somewhat unwieldly, some type of nondisclosure agreement is advantageous if they have what they feel is a good, marketable concept. Rarely have I received in the mail, unsolicited, a usable product for inclusion in any of our lines. Unfortunately, most designers have an inflated idea of their design's worth as a marketable item, and have little, if any, idea about the expense and effort in turning this concept into a profitable seller. A manufacturer incurs the major burden when undertaking research and development on a new product category; that is, cost-time components, merchandising strategy, packaging, advertising, ad infinitum. Your readers should be made aware of this especially since it is the main reason the ideas that the designer has such high hopes for may not be accepted by a manufacturer for promotion (in addition to the fact that few ideas are really new)."

From Al Silverman, needlepoint merchandise manager for Bucilla in Long Island City, New York: "We are constantly on the lookout for fresh, new ideas. For some years now, we have been able to work most successfully with a great many free-lance designers who are responsible for successful designs in our stitchery, needlepoint, and latchet rug lines. Practically all of the designers still work with us today and I would venture to say that they are all most satisfied with their arrangement with Bucilla.

"As I am sure you understand, an arrangement with a free-lance designer has to be one of mutual trust by both parties. Speaking for Bucilla, we have never, nor will we ever, 'pirate' a design from a free-lancer, and by the same token, if we include something from a free-lance designer in our line, we certainly would not expect her to sell a first cousin of that design to another company.

"I receive many inquiries from aspiring needlepoint designers from all over the country. From time to time we do find designs or ideas that can be utilized in our product line. However, these are few and far between since 99 percent of the material that is sent in to us is not what we consider marketable. Therefore, under the circumstances, we would not want you to direct all would-be designers to our attention."

If all this sounds discouraging, that's the point I'm trying to make. Very few readers of this book are apt to be qualified to design for manufacturers, but if you think you are the exception to the rule and really do have a great product or idea, here are some guidelines that may be of help when dealing with a manufacturer:

1. Do not send an unsolicited idea to any company, since this constitutes "public exposure" of the idea, according to both the Patent and Copyright Laws, and automatically gives a company the right to steal it from you.

2. Be certain the people you are offering your idea to are reputable and presently showing an interest in the type of product you offer. This will save a lot of time.

3. Your initial letter to a manufacturer should describe your idea in general terms only and should include some information about your background and experience. In this letter you should predetermine the company's interest in the possibility of looking at your idea and ask it to sign an agreement that says, in essence, that it will receive your idea in confidence, and will protect your rights to it.

4. If you approach a manufacturer and receive a special submission agreement or waiver to be signed, be sure to read it carefully. All rights should remain your property unless otherwise agreed upon by all parties concerned. Think twice if a company offers you a small flat fee and asks you to relinquish all rights because it is not always wise to trust a company about your design's originality and value.

5. Never send samples of anything until you have a satisfactory contract, and never send original copies of designs or informational materials since they might be lost in the mail.

6. Copyright all designs before submitting them to anyone. (See next section.) Safeguard other ideas by keeping records of how and when they were conceived. Include sketches, notes, and other things

115

which give a full understanding of the subject matter. Sign and date them. Show this material to a trusted witness and ask him to also sign and date the papers. This will prove the idea originated with you on a particular date. Some people put such information in a registered letter to themselves, then retain the unopened letter in a safe place until such time as it might be needed. (NOTE: The U.S. Patent Office offers a special service, "Idea Disclosure Document," where, for $10, it will officially date, number, stamp, and return one copy of any document you send in, keeping the other copy in its file for two years. For complete details about this program, write the Patent Office.)

Finally, heed these words of advice from a woman who designed and manufactured two craft kits: "The most logical thing to do when you have a good idea is to sit down and THINK. Don't believe everything anyone tells you. WHY are people telling you thus and so? Always look for their motivation, and use logic to reach a sound conclusion."

Design Copying and the New Copyright Law

As already stressed, people who sell their creations should use only original or copyright-free designs. To use a copyrighted design can mean legal trouble, yet craftspeople everywhere continue to reproduce for sale such well-known designs as the Walt Disney cartoon characters, Snoopy, Winnie the Pooh, Raggedy Ann and Andy, and others. All of these designs are copyrighted, and lawsuits have been brought against some craftspeople in the past for using them illegally, including homemakers who were only selling reproductions of them in church bazaars. You might make a copy of some design thinking no one will ever know about it, but don't be too sure. Anyone can inform on you, and might, so it's best not to take chances. Making minor changes in someone else's design doesn't protect you either. *In the eyes of the law you can be held liable for copying if your design so much as resembles a copyrighted design.*

If you must copy, be sure to use designs currently in public domain. Such designs are available to everyone for use without payment or permission. Copyright protection does not last forever, and once a work has fallen into public domain, copyright is lost permanently. According to the "General Guide" issued by the Copyright Office, a work falls into public domain when (1) the copyright owner has authorized publication of the work without the notice of copyright, and (2) when the first 28th year term of copyright expires without renewal. Fairy-tale characters and other designs found in old books are likely to be in public domain, and I have already discussed the thousands of copyright-free designs available to artists and craftsmen in the *Dover Pictorial Archives.*

Originally, copyright protection lasted 28 years and could be renewed for another term of 28 years if desired. The new copyright law that took effect January 1, 1978, has changed that, however, and now provides an extension of the second 28-year term to 47 years instead. Copyrights in their first term must be renewed in order to receive the full new maximum term of 75 years. For writers, the new law provides a term lasting for the author's life, plus an additional 50 years after the author's death. (Interestingly, Mark Twain asked Congress to do this 70 years ago. "I think that would satisfy any reasonable author because it would take care of his children," he said, adding that the grandchildren could take care of themselves.)

Speaking of authors, many people mistakenly believe that copyright protection extends only to printed works, but that is not true. The purpose of the copyright law is to protect *any creator* from anyone who would use his creative work for his own profit. Under the new copyright law, claims are now being registered in five different classes, including Nondramatic Literary Works, Works of the Performing Arts, Works of the Visual Arts, Sound Recordings, and Renewal Registration. Because the readers of this book will be primarily concerned with only two of the above five classes, my discussion will be limited to them: Nondramatic Literary Works and Works of the Visual Arts.

Nondramatic Literary Works (Class TX) applies to any work written in words, and specifically relates to Chapter 13 of this book. Works of the Visual Arts (Class VA) relates to several chapters in this book since it applies to pictorial, graphic, or sculptural works and covers a lot of ground. Quoting from a booklet issued by the Copyright Office, this category includes the following:

> ... two-dimensional and three-dimensional works of fine, graphic, and applied art, photographs, prints and art reproductions, maps, globes, charts, technical drawings, diagrams, and models. Such works shall include works of artistic craftsmanship insofar as their form but not their mechanical or utilitarian aspects are concerned; the design of a useful article, as defined in this section, shall be considered a pictorial, graphic, or sculptural work only if, and only to the extent that, such design incorporates pictorial, graphic, or sculptural features that can be identified separately from, and are capable of existing independently of, the utilitarian aspects of the article.

The language of the Copyright Office is not exactly easy to understand, but I interpret the above to mean that most original designs and art/craft objects can be copyrighted. (As you will note a little later on in this section, it is not necessary to send two actual copies of three-dimensional objects with a copyright claim — photographs or drawings are sufficient.)

Statutory Copyright can be obtained only by placing the copyright notice on your work and filing a claim with the Copyright Office. Regardless of whether you have written something, or created a "pictorial, graphic, or sculptural work," the copyright notice shall be composed of:

1. The word "copyright" or its symbol (a "c" with a circle around it)
2. The date of "publication" — the year in which work was first placed on sale, sold, or distributed for sale or exhibited in a public place
3. Your name — either your personal name or your business name

Example of a copyright notice:
Copyright © 1979 Mary Jones

The copyright notice must be readable and permanently affixed to the object, and this means it can be stamped, cast, engraved, painted, printed, etc., on the object's surface. In the case of fiber crafts where this is not possible, some kind of label must be added. In the words of the Copyright Office, the notice "shall be affixed to the copies in such manner and location as to give reasonable notice of the claim of copyright." In the near future, the Copyright Office expects to set forth in regulations a list of examples of specific methods of affixation and positions of the notice on various types of works that will satisfy this requirement. But even this list will not be considered exhaustive, and a notice placed or affixed in some other way might also comply with the law.

One thing about the new copyright law that has many people confused is the fact that one does not have to register a copyright claim and pay the $10 fee just because the copyright notice is placed on a piece of work, But, it *is* mandatory to deposit two copies of all "published" works for the collections of the Library of Congress within three months after publication. Failure to make the deposit may subject the copyright owner to fines and other monetary liabilities, but it does not affect copyright protection. No special form is required for this deposit.

Only the "best edition" of a published work is to be deposited with the Library of Congress, and the Copyright Office has a list of criteria that determine exactly what the "best edition" is in each case. For example, in printed matter, the best edition would be a hard-cover book instead of the paperback edition; for other graphic matter, the best edition would be that which is in color, rather than black and white; that which is larger, and so on. When in doubt as to what you should submit, ask the Copyright Registrar for additional information.

If you plan to register your copyright, the new law contains a special provision under which a single deposit can be made to satisfy both the deposit reqirements for the Library and the registration requirements. In order to have this dual effect, the copies must be accompanied by the prescribed application and fee. Any deposit received by the Copyright Office without said application and fee will automatically be sent on to the Library of Congress for its collections or other disposition. If you later decide to register a copyright claim, you would then have to send an additional two copies of the work with the application form and fee.

Ordinarily, two actual copies of all things bearing a copyright notice must be deposited with the Libary of Congress, but certain items are exempt from deposit requirements, including all three-dimensional sculptural works, and any works published only as reproduced in or on jewelry, dolls, toys, games, plaques, floor coverings, textile and other fabrics, packaging material, or any useful article. Also exempt are greeting cards, picture postcards, and stationery.

Although "publication" of an item with the required copyright notice is all that is required under the new law, one cannot sue for infringement of his rights *unless and until he has registered his copyright with the Copyright Office in Washington, D.C.* Therefore, it is suggested that you always file a copyright claim if your design is of real value to you and could easily be reproduced by others. While placement of the copyright notice on your work may discourage others from stealing it, there are no guarantees to this effect. If you really fear infringement and want to protect your rights to the design, file a copyright claim. Simply request the proper form, then complete it and return it to the Copyright Office with the $10 fee and two copies of the "best edition." (NOTE: In the case of three-dimensional works, photographs or accurate drawings will be accepted in lieu of actual copies.)

Here are some additional points concerning copyrights:

1. Names, titles, and short phrases or expressions are not copyrightable, but brand names, trade names, slogans, and phrases may be entitled to protection under the provisions of the Trademark Laws, discussed next.

2. Inventions are subject matter for patents, not copyrights.

3. No copyright protection is available for ideas or procedures for doing, making, or building things. Although ideas cannot be copyrighted, the expression of an idea, as fixed in a tangible medium, may be copyrightable, such as a book explaining a new system or technique.

4. The Copyright Office does not compare deposit copies to determine whether works submitted for registration are similar to any material already copyrighted. It is the sender's responsibility to determine the originality of what is being copyrighted.

Finally, let me add that the new copyright law is extremely complex and difficult to interpret. The information given here is meant to serve only as a general guide, since it would require a whole chapter just to touch on all the points applicable to artists, craftsmen, and writers. If you have additional questions, please write the Copyright Office for information.

(NOTE: The Copyright Office is primarily an office of public record, and regulations prohibit it from giving legal advice or opinions concerning the rights of persons in connection with cases of alleged copyright infringement, "or the sufficiency, extent, or scope of compliance with the copyright law." Several pamphlets are available, however, and noted in the resource chapter for your convenience.

Trademarks

A trademark "includes any word, name, symbol, or device, or any combination thereof adopted and used by a manufacturer or merchant to identify his goods and distinguish them from those manufactured or sold by others," according to the Trademark Act of 1946. The primary function of a trademark is to indicate origin, but in some cases it also serves as a guarantee of quality.

A trademark may be owned by any individual, firm, partnership, corporation, association, or other collective group, and one may apply for the registration of a trademark by making application to the Commissioner of Patents. (A brochure on trademarks is available from the Superintendent of Documents in Washington, D.C.)

10

Marketing Your Own Craft Or Needlework Kit

Kits continue to fill an important need as thousands of hobbyists look for new and interesting ways to spend their leisure hours, and smart craftspeople are beginning to capitalize on this fact. Even professional craftsmen who feel that kits are beneath their abilities (or dignity) agree they can often be good money-makers. If you have created an unusual craft or needlework kit, you do not need to rely on a big manufacturer to get it to market. In fact, you will probably be money ahead if you manufacture and market it yourself.

In designing a kit, there are certain things you should keep in mind. Commercial kit manufacturers figure that a kit should cost no more in materials than one-fifth of its retail price; that is, a $1 kit should have no more than 20 cents' worth of materials in it, a $5 kit no more than one dollar's worth, and so on. Most craft kits are designed to appeal to beginners and inexperienced handicrafters and they require a minimum amount of time and skill to complete. All necessary materials, instructions, or tools are included.

Needlework kits, as most women know, are a bit different and come in two basic types: quick, easy, and inexpensive, and time-consuming, difficult, and costly. The kind of craft or needlework kit you design is entirely up to you, of course, but you should remember that the higher priced and more sophisticated your kit, the smaller your market. Also, remember that it is easier to sell a line of several kits than it is to sell just one. Your "line" can be based on one idea, of course, but it should at least include variations on the theme.

Whether you are trying to reach an art needlework market or the 7-to-97 group of crafters, you are bound to encounter certain stumbling blocks in the beginning, as did the five women you are about to meet. After I've introduced them, I'll let each of them tell you about the packaging and marketing problems she encountered and eventually solved.

Five Kit Manufacturers

Margaret Thompson, Oak Ridge, Tennessee: Margaret has designed a variety of counted thread cross stitch sampler kits and graphs she calls "Maggie's Mini Mottos." Margaret discovered counted thread cross stitch at a gift show in Atlanta. She bought some sampler kits for the shop she and her husband owned at the time and, later, when she decided they weren't going to sell unless they were made up, worked them herself. "Then I was totally hooked," she wrote. "One thing led to another and I started tentatively designing a few on my own. With the encouragement of friends and family I had the graphs printed, designed a package, found sources for supplies, and I was on my way."

Connie A. Stano, Greenfield, Indiana: You met

119

Connie in a previous chapter. She and her sister, Mary Lou Nowak, are The Greenfield Needlewomen, and together they have designed and marketed several crewel embroidery kits. "I was doing commissioned designs for a long time," says Connie, "and eventually an idea began to grow. In October of 1975 I presented a small line of my own needlework kits to The Stitchery catalog in Boston, and three of the designs were accepted and included in their catalog. The Greenfield Needlewomen thus became a kit manufacturer. My sister and I do the designing and my husband, a lawyer, keeps the books and me out of all sorts of business trouble." For a while the kits were manufacturered in Connie's basement with the help of part-time employees, but recently the business was moved to a small factory, the made-over first floor of an old house.

© Tree Toys, Inc.

In quilling, thin strips of paper are wound and pressed into various shapes, then glued together to form interesting designs like these, from Tree Toys, Inc.

Betty Christy, Hinsdale, Illinois: Betty and her partner, Doris Tracy, own Tree Toys, Inc., a national manufacturing company that produces quilling supplies, kits, and instruction booklets. Betty, the mother of four grown children, has a background in crafts that goes back to 1946 when she started selling wooden Christmas ornaments called "Tree Toys." Later, she and another woman opened a retail handicrafts shop that eventually grew to include decoupage classes in the back room. "This was in the early days of the craft industry," says Betty, "when many of today's now-popular crafts were totally unknown to most people." When Betty sold out to her then-partner, she began to think about all those wooden items she had been decoupaging, wondering what other crafty uses they might have. When she discovered quilling and realized its tie-in with wood, she began to develop her ideas. Later, when a student in one of her classes asked her why she didn't put up her designs in kit form, the suggestion struck a responsive chord. "Doris joined me at this time," says Betty, "and together we launched our quilling kit business."

Carolyn Klein, Sarasota, Florida: Carolyn entered the kit field recently with a line of expensive needlepoint kits called Indian Images. When an interesting job in Italy fell through a couple of years ago, Carolyn decided it was time to start moving in a new direction. But what to do? At that time she was living in the Chicagoland area with her older brother who had a collection of American Indian ceremonial masks she admired very much. She couldn't afford to buy them herself, but she could needlepoint them, and did. After doing about three pieces, she looked at them and thought, "This is what I'm going to do — I'm going into business for myself and sell these things." Carolyn began with four pieces — got them framed and photographed and did all the backup work (stationery, brochures, etc. — her background in graphics helped here). Then she packed up her samples and kit packages and hit the road.

Lois L. Moyer, Des Plaines, Illinois: Remember Lois? You first met her in the pricing chapter when I was emphasizing the importance of including all costs in your pricing formula. Four years ago, Lois was an average homemaker who did all kinds of decorating, made presents for the family, and sewed all her children's clothes. Today she is a successful businesswoman whose company, Lo Lo Bags, has grown to such an extent that it can no longer be operated from her basement workshop and office. In fact, Lois rented a nearby building recently and turned it into a kit factory. Her clever line of Stitch 'N Sew Craft Kits includes pin-cushions, pillows, dolls, nursery items, shoe bags, and tennis accessory kits, with more new items coming. Her first big order got her into the mail-order section of a national magazine, and when it came out Lois was so excited she ran over to her mother-in-law's house whooping, "I've made it! I'm going to be busy for the rest of my life with this one mail-order house!" But, the volume wasn't as expected and it was at this point that Lois took a realistic look at her business and really got down to work.

Although the women you've just met have many things in common, you will note that each entered the kit field through a different door. There are no set rules here; anyone can become a kit manufacturer. But designing a kit is just the first step. Getting it packaged and sold is quite another.

Packaging Problems and Solutions

"Packaging is important," says Margaret. "My kits have on the 'cover' a picture of the sampler, the contents, size, materials used, and a warning: *'Caution—may be habit forming'.*" Margaret's cross stitch sampler kits are packaged in a zip-lock bag with a hole punched in the top so it can be hung up in shops. Her "header," which shows the contents of the kit, is printed on ivory paper in red and black, with a black and white picture of the finished sampler printed in the center. Her kit package is effective, proving that expensive color sheets are not always necessary to sell a needlework kit. The fact that the embroidery floss is visible from the back of the package helps, I'm sure. Needleworkers can look at the colors and get a good idea of how the finished kit will look.

Lois's original kit, a shoebag, was also packaged in a plastic bag with a cardboard header done by a local printer. The sewing instructions

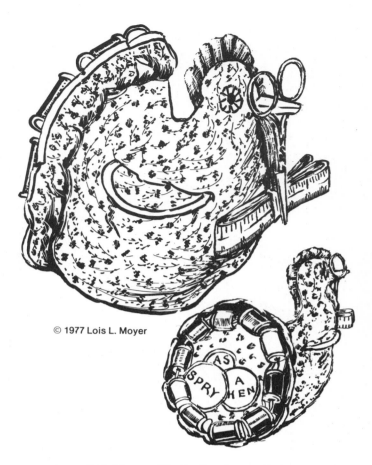

© 1977 Lois L. Moyer

Lois Moyer of Lo Lo Bags knows that the right combination of cleverness and practicality in a kit product will make a good money-maker. Shown here is her unusual sewing kit, currently one of her best sellers.

were simply typed and printed, and included a drawing Lois had done of her boy-and-girl kit designs. She sold her kit in this form until she made enough money to be able to afford the expensive and impressive color sheets she now uses.

"Printing costs are HIGH," Margaret notes. "I didn't feel at this time that I could go to color separations on the package, although I would very much like to. Printing and packaging are a large part of the cost of the kit."

Carolyn knows exactly what Margaret means. She really ran into packaging problems when she tried to get her art needlework kit on the market,

121

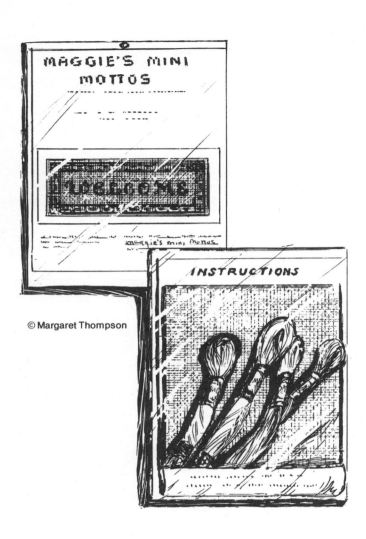

© Margaret Thompson

Margaret Thompson's needlework kits are simply but effectively packaged in clear plastic bags that can be hung up for display.

them either. The cost of full-color artwork was also staggering. Finally she realized her kit package, as originally envisioned, would take thousands of dollars to produce in quantity, and she just couldn't do it.

Her solution? She is no longer selling a kit as such. At least, her "kit" does not include yarn. Now she sells only the hand-painted canvases to shops (and to individuals by mail order) and each canvas comes complete with a small plastic bag of accessory items stapled to one corner, along with a card that gives the history of the piece. In another corner is stapled a color photograph showing how the finished piece will look. Carolyn has worked out the yarn requirements for each of her designs, computed for Paternayan yarn. This information is given to each shop owner who can then direct customers in the purchase of yarn, whether Paternayan or some other brand.

And now I want you to listen to the words of a woman who shall remain anonymous, a kit designer whose product never got on the market in spite of the fact that she tried to do everything in a professional manner. I'll call her Mrs. X.

"Beware of hiring a professional to do your package design," she warns. "I went to a marketing consultant who spent hours talking to me about my kit, at the rate of $50 an hour. He hired a box designer who took three months to produce a simple package I could have done myself. Then he suggested we call a manufacturer's agent into the picture. He wanted to handle my kit, but not in the package that had been designed. Then I signed a contract for a different designer to do the prototype and found that a revision in the original package would cost another fee."

At this point, Mrs. X had spent several months and over a thousand dollars with very little to show for her effort. In the end she decided to do her own manufacturing and created her own package, a plastic bag with a printed cardboard header folded over the top and stapled shut. I tried to reach Mrs. X by phone recently to see how her kit business was progressing and found her phone had been disconnected. I'm afraid things didn't work out well for her.

122

and eventually had to change all her plans. Her 12 needlepoint designs, each based on authentic American Indian artifacts, are dimensional and incorporate such accessory items as feathers, beads, shells, leather thongs, copper wire, etc. Because Carolyn originally hoped to sell these kits in great quantity, she explored silk screening and heat-transfer methods of getting her designs on canvas. But they proved impractical as well as extremely expensive. When she investigated the cost and minimum quantity requirements of plastic bags with firm handles, she found she couldn't afford

Point of story? Your own ideas and simple packaging methods may be just as good as those of a professional, and they are certainly going to be a lot less expensive.

Presenting and Promoting a Line

In a letter Connie Stano sent me, she said: "I presented a small line of my own needlework kits to The Stitchery catalog in Boston, and three of these designs were accepted for inclusion in their catalog." I wrote back asking if it was really as simple to sell a line as she made it sound.

"It is just that simple," she replied. "You can just present your line to a customer and wait for acceptance, or more often, rejection. It is also just that complex, as most good things look simple on the surface." Then Connie got to the heart of my question with these remarks: "Before the line can be presented, months of work on the products must be completed, preceded by almost a year of market research, letter writing, reading, and management decision-making, preceded by years of practice and experience in the field. It must be remembered that the product you submit is the product they expect to order. Availability of supplies, their cost, and a complete plan of the actual production are necessary before the line is submitted. You must be prepared for complete rejection all the way up to being killed by success. In other words, there are literally a million details and bits of knowledge beyond the craft itself that are needed to market a product nationally and professionally."

Connie concluded by saying that the best advice she could give to any craftsman who wishes to sell commercially is to "stop thinking of himself as a craftsman and start thinking of himself as a *businessman.*"

That remark reminds me of one made by Ray Martell, the jeweler craftsman you met earlier in the book: "An illusion that seems to die hard among craftsmen is that you can run a business without being in business. It's a lovely dream, but it's very hard to make enough money with one's eyes half closed. It's often difficult enough to make enough money with ideals stripped,

pragmatism wide open, and nothing between you and the goal post."

Back to Connie. Her mention of The Stitchery needlework catalog prompted me to drop them a line and inquire about their interest in needlework kits from individual designers. Susanne M. Knowles replied, saying they were always looking for suppliers of *good* needlework kits, and that they buy some designs outright and others on a royalty basis. (Interested suppliers can write Ms. Knowles sending information, prices, and sample kits. If accepted, a finished model would be required for photography.) Perhaps other needlework catalog companies work on a similar basis, and kit designers should contact several and see what happens.

Lois Moyer's marketing approach was quite different from Connie's. She didn't do a lot of market research or planning and never read any how-to books like this one. She just dived into the pool figuring she'd sink or swim. Sure, she made mistakes in the beginning, but she corrected them as time went on and learned from each experience. Her incredible success now, just four years after she began, attests to just how well and how quickly she learned.

Lois sold finished items in craft shops for awhile but eventually got tired of hearing people say they could "do it themselves." She decided to let them do just that, and worked up some kits. They sold, bringing in $30 to $40 a month for awhile, "which didn't excite me," Lois recalls. "I wanted to see bigger figures." She finally decided she was either going to do something big with her kits or forget them, and she entered the field with the attitude of "I'll never know unless I try."

She began her marketing campaign by contacting a couple of catalog houses. At this point she had a line of boy-and-girl shoebag kits to sell. She picked up the phone, asked to talk to a buyer, and came on strong: "This is Lois Moyer of Lo Lo Bags, and I have a line of shoebag kits I think you should see."

"Well," replied the interested buyer, "we're just closing a catalog. Why don't you send me some samples."

123

She sent them. The buyer called back shortly saying he was interested. "We're gonna run it," he told Lois. "What's your pricing?"

SILENCE. Then, "What do you mean, what's my pricing?" When the buyer heard that, he suddenly knew he was dealing not with a professional, but with "a little lady in her house," to use Lois's words. But the buyer was kind. He told Lois to think about it, sit down, and figure it out.

At that time Lois was still buying her fabric from the local store she had always dealt with, doing all the work in putting the kits together, and sewing all the necessary samples herself. Because she didn't know what her actual costs were, she could only guess at a suggested retail price. So she got on the phone and started calling suppliers saying she had a large order to fill. (Fortunately, she had filed for a resale tax number earlier, which entitled her to buy at wholesale prices.)

Lois recalls her feelings at the time. "All of a sudden I had to react quickly and come up with what I thought was a decent price, and what I thought I could make money on." She finally called the buyer, gave him her price, and got an order for 120 kits. "Wow!" she thought, and then, "How am I ever going to do it?"

The buyer featured Lois's kits in an ad in the *Ladies' Home Journal* craft catalog, and like so many other beginners in mail order, Lois figured she was going to get rich from this one ad. But the volume wasn't as great as expected. (She had forgotten to consider the percentage of people who respond to an ad.) Later, she realized she wasn't going to make it on one account and began to call other buyers. She also began to expand her line of kits at that time.

She found her first sales representative quite accidentally in a buyer's office. He saw her work and asked to carry it. At his suggestion, Lois got a price list printed and made up some samples for him to use. Soon the representative was presenting her line in several states. For the first year Lois worked with only one representative, and he offered a lot of guidance. He called on some New York magazines and got her items in *Good Housekeeping*. But that presented problems Lois hadn't counted on. *Good Housekeeping* looked at her "Ernie the Engineer" shoebag and decided they would have to have something suitable for either a boy or a girl; so Lois took the same fabric used in the engineer shoebag and created two new shoebags, "Freddie and Franny Farmer," with striped pants. But *Good Housekeeping* only had room for one kit, so Lois had to package a special kit to enable readers to make either one or the other — boy or girl — a lot of extra work to meet the magazine's particular requirments. Of course, the national exposure for her company justified all the time and effort it took. "It's part of being in business," says Lois.

After she exhibited in the Hobby Industry Association of America (HIA) trade show in Houston in 1977, Lois's business really picked up and she acquired many new customers and several new sales representatives as well. Currently she has 11 representative organizations promoting her growing kit line to retail stores, chain distributors, and catalog houses all over the country.

When Carolyn Klein was ready to sell her line of Indian Images needlepoint kits (before she switched over to selling just hand-painted canvases) she tried an idea I thought quite interesting. She entered a needlework exhibition in Des Moines, Iowa, that promised to attract some 8000 people. The idea was that her work (finished pieces of needlepoint) would be exhibited with a sign that said where, in that city, people could buy her work. She bundled up her best pieces, delivered them to the exhibition and asked where to find the best needlework shops in town. Then she visited them, told them about the exhibition, and sold several kits before driving back home to Evanston, Illinois.

Results? Interesting. Carolyn got no re-orders from any of the shops (but agrees she didn't prod them for re-orders, either). The exhibition committee wrapped up her work and sent it back air freight, collect, which not only cost $36 to claim but necessitated a trip to the airport to pick it up. This, added to the gas and other expenses to drive to Iowa meant that Carolyn didn't gain much financially. That was the only time she entered an exhibition. Although this idea didn't work too well for Carolyn, it might work for you, particularly if the exhibition you enter is close to home.

Carolyn's next marketing effort was to call on all the needlework shops in her area, and on one of these calls she met a sales representative who eventually took her line and sold it like crazy. After a while, though, this woman's husband moved and she didn't want to start a new territory, so Carolyn lost the best salesperson she's ever had. She found another one who likes her work but, says Carolyn, "He has a different attitude. He keeps saying, 'Can't you do something for $16?' And he takes my authentic Indian sashes — which come with a history explaining what they are—and sells them as *bellpulls*. That hurts! My God, I'm so out of touch. First of all, I've never understood why people make bellpulls when they don't pull bells, and you can be sure the Indians never designed them or used them."

The above represents a point of view, of course. Carolyn realizes she's out of touch with the craft needlework market, and certainly out of touch with some of the representatives who are currently selling for her. Her line is expensive, more art than craft, and Carolyn has found that once a shop buys one of her designs they will not buy the same design again. They want a new piece to exhibit. Since Carolyn at present has only 12 designs in her line, her sales are somewhat limited. It takes a lot of time to develop each new item.

It also takes time to create the samples that are necessary to sell any kind of kit. Remember that sales representatives will have to have samples to show to buyers, and even more important, salesmen must have made-up samples to sell to shops who will be carrying the kits. Even if you sell your own line, samples are a must. A shop must be able to show the customer what the finished product will look like. They don't have time to make up kits themselves, so they will want to buy a finished sample, at a good price.

When Lois Moyer was faced with the matter of having to have dozens of samples sewed, she found that labor rates in her area were too high, and eventually she had to find sources out of the country to do this work for her. Be sure to include the cost of samples in your overall pricing structure, or you may not realize the profit you expect.

What other advice do these women have to offer budding kit manufacturers? Lois says to plan in advance, but be flexible enough to react quickly when you haven't. "And never accept no for an answer. There is always an alternative. Accept advice, but don't let others make your decisions." I know Margaret Thompson and Betty Christy would second that suggestion, and Margaret also urges beginners to start small and plan wisely. Betty says to grow slowly. "That way you can keep things under control, and that's very important to the overall success of any business."

Exhibiting at the HIA Show

If you have a line of kits that can be wholesaled, then you should consider exhibiting at the annual Hobby Industry Association (HIA) trade show, which would enable you to introduce your kits to craft supply shops all over the country. While the thought of exhibiting in this show (open only to members of HIA) may seem a bit frightening at first, it's not all that difficult to participate.

Betty Christy, homemaker and businesswoman, talked to me about the HIA show and its advantages to the small manufacturer. You will recall that Betty and her partner, Doris Tracy, own Tree Toys, Inc., a manufacturer of quilling kits and supplies. Betty explained that it is not expensive to participate in this show when you enter the *Division Area Display* section, a special area apart from the booths occupied by large commercial craft suppliers. Exhibitors in the Division Area Display can purchase six feet of table space for about $150. The show runs four days. Everything is provided for the exhibitor who only has to bring his wares for display.

In Betty and Doris's case, this means samples of all their kits, books, and supplies, plus a large supply of fliers and price sheets for distribution to interested buyers. (They suggest that first-time exhibitors take at least 500 copies of printed material for hand-out, adding that it is probably best not to leave these materials on the table with your samples. People tend to take anything that's free,

125

Tree Toys Order Blank

Checks payable to:
TREE TOYS, P.O. Box 492, Hinsdale, Illinois 60521

Phones: (312) 323-6505
or (312) 325-4043

PRICE LIST & ORDER BLANK

QUILLING
and
PAPER SNIPPING DESIGNS

Quan.	Item No.	Description	Unit Price	Cost
	Q100	"Introducing Quilling" booklet (12 pages)	$ 1.50	
	Q200	"Christmas Quilling" booklet (12 pages)	1.50	
		QUILLING: PAPER ART FOR EVERYONE (cloth)	10.00	
		QUILLING: PAPER ART FOR EVERYONE (paperback)	4.95	
		"Quilling Miniature Dimensional Flowers" booklet	2.00	
		"Sculptured Quilling" booklet (16 pages)	2.00	

Single color Quilling papers

	white	Q408 - blue	Q414 - apple green	
	red	Q409 - brown	Q415 - clay pot	
	pink	Q410 - black	Q416 - antique white	
	hot pink	Q411 - lavender	Q417 - colonial blue	
	orange	Q412 - purple	Q418 - gray	.69
	yellow	Q413 - gold	Q419 - pale yellow	
	green			

Description	Unit Price
...nt - 1/8 inch	
...nt - 1/16 inch	
...ge paper	.75
...d Color Pack - 19 colors, 5 strips each	.75
...rian Jewels (pk. 12)	1.00
...ustrian Jewels (pk. 12)	1.50
...e cards (pkg. of 6)	.40
...Paper Fluter	.40
...and Flower Tool	.50
...ower Stem Wires (3" long)	5.00
...Miniature Dimensional Flowers" package	1.25
...booklet, papers, stem wires & tool)	.50
...g Quilling" package (incl. booklet & papers)	4.75
... Quilling" package (incl. booklet & papers)	4.75
... Quilling" package (incl. booklet & papers)	5.75
... Quilling" package (incl. booklet & papers)	5.75

KITS IN MINIATURE

...r Shop	Q708 - Flower Shop	Q715 - Drive-In
... Shop	Q709 - Flower Stand	Q716 - Pink Poodle
...ept.	Q710 - Schoolhouse	Q717 - Saloon each 3.00
...se	Q711 - Tenement	
...read House	Q712 - Depot	Q719 - Santa's Shop
	Q713 - Cafe	Q720 - Valentine House
	Q714 - Shell Shop	

Description	Unit Price
...r (3 sheets 8" x 10")	
...de, white on reverse	
...pping Designs)	1.25
...a (Paper Snipping Designs)	1.50
...Scenes (Paper Snipping)	1.50
...lor (Paper Snipping)	1.50
	1.75
...es	1.50
...g Spirits of '76	1.50
	1.50
	1.50
	1.50
	1.50
	1.50
	1.50

...rates		Total
...3rd		Ill. Res. add 5% tax
...postage		Postage
...e total		Amount Enclosed

...e _____ Zip _____

June 1978

Lo Lo Bags Order Blank

PRICE LIST — ORDER BLANK (Effective Jan. 1, 1978)

Date Order Rec'd _____ DO NOT WRITE BELOW

Cust Order No _____ Order No _____

Invoice No _____

SOLD TO

Cust Dept No _____ Invoice Date _____

Vendor No _____ ALL ITEMS SHIPPED FOB DES PLAINES, ILLINOIS

SHIP TO

Requested _____ Date Shipped _____

Ship Date _____ No. of Cartons _____

Weight _____

Carrier _____

A Stitch 'n Sew Craft Kit

Lo Lo BAGS

700 Northwest Highway
Des Plaines, Illinois 60016
PHONE: (312) 824-5996

SALESMAN: _____

TERMS: _____

Style Number	Description	Color	Retail Suggested	Quantity Ordered Unit	Doz.	Your Cost Unit	Doz.	Finished Models for Display Price Each	Qty. Ord.	Cost
		PINCUSHION SEWING KITS (Includes Stuffing)						$ 7.00		
PC-520	Slo as a Turtle*	Green Calico Print	$ 4.98					$ 7.00		
PC-521	Spry as a Hen*	Brown Calico Print	$ 4.98					$ 7.00		
PC-522	Pretty as a Flower*	Red Calico Print	$ 4.98							
		TOOTH FAIRY POCKETED PILLOW KITS (Includes Stuffing)						$ 4.00		
TF-430	Patchwork Counter	Red/Blue/Yel/Grn	$ 4.49					$ 4.00		
TF-431	My Lost Tooth	Blue Denim/Red	$ 4.49					$ 4.00		
TF-432	Til the Dawn	Gingham Checks/Wht.	$ 4.49							
		SLEEPY SUSIE KIT						$ 6.50		
D/200	Sleepy Susie and Her Sleeping Bag	Asstd. Patch Prints	$ 5.98							
		LONNIE THE LION'S COORDINATED COLLECTION KITS						$ 7.98		
LDS/640	Diaper Stacker/ Laundry Bag	Brt. Yel/Calico	$ 7.98					$ 7.98		
LSB/641	Shoe Bag/ Utility Bag	Brt. Yel/Calico	$ 7.98					$18.98		
LQS/642	2 piece Quilt/Pillow set Quilt top and back (Batting Included)	Brt. Yel/Rd/Calico	$18.98					$ 4.98		
LPO/643	Crib Pillow ONLY (Stuffing Included)	Brt. Yel/Rd/Calico	$ 4.98					$ 3.98		
LKC/644	Door Knob Cover (Stuffing Included)	Brt. Yel/Calico	$ 3.98					$ 6.98		
								$ 7.98		
B/100	Peter Patter	Blue						$ 7.98		
B/100	Peter Patter	Green						$ 8.98		
		QUILTED TENNIS ACCESSORY KITS						$ 8.98		
TCV/301	Racket Cover and Visor Set	Red/Blue	$ 6.98					$ 6.98		
TB/302	Matching Tote Bag	Red/Blue	$ 6.98					$14.98		
TPS/313	3-Piece set of Above Items	Red/Blue	$14.98							

PRE-PACKED ASSORTMENT No. 7801
(INCLUDES THE FOLLOWING KITS and SAMPLES)

	QUANTITY	SUGG. RETAIL	FINISHED SAMPLES FOR DISPLAY
1 Pincushion Sewing Kits (includes stuffing)	1 doz. total	5-pc./520 5-pc./521 2-pc./522	$59.76	1-pc./521
2 Tooth Fairy Pillow Kits (includes stuffing)	1 doz. total	2-TF/430 5-TF/431 5-TF/432	$53.88	1-TF/430
3 Sleepy Susie/Sleeping Bag	3-total	3-D/200	$17.94	1-D/200
4 Shoe Bag/Utility Bag	1 doz. total	3-G/100 3-E/100 2-F/100 2-B/100 2-FG/101	$95.76	1-G/100 1-E/100

TOTAL SUGGESTED RETAIL—$227.34

YOUR COST $ _____   Total Assortment $ _____

Total Samples $ _____

*Handmade samples of Pincushion Sewing Kits include all accessories (embroidery scissors, tape measure, 10 spools of thread).

Total Kits	$
Total Samples	$
Total Assortment	$
Sub Total	$
Frt. Charges	$
Total Invoice	$

Samples of order blanks used by Lo Lo Bags and Tree Toys. Although one form has been typeset and the other typed on an IBM typewriter, both are professional in appearance, and easy to understand and use.

and distributing printed materials in this manner can get expensive. Hand out your literature only to those who stop by and express an interest in your line.)

Like all other exhibitors in the show, Betty and Doris send a supply of "press kits" to the HIA press room. Various members of the press who attend the show can then take the materials of interest and use them to write their articles and stories. Betty says they usually distribute at least 50 sets of promotional materials, and a great deal of free publicity is realized as a result.

I told Betty she made the whole thing sound so simple. "It is easy," she replied, "especially if you like trade shows and like dealing with the public. But I do want to mention one thing. You cannot sell adequately sitting down. We go through the pros and cons of this at every show. People want a chair to sit on. Well, sure, after four days you're tired, and I mean TIRED. Sometimes you're almost sick. But if you're sitting down and you have somebody coming by to look at your products, you're not going to sell to that person. You need to be at eye level with him," (Betty's advice echoes some of what you read earlier in the craft fair chapter. No one can do a good job selling if she's sitting down, reading books, or "star gazing."

When I asked Betty what other advice she would give to beginning manufacturers, she brought up the matter of catalogs and price sheets. "Never include the price of an item in your catalog or on your fly sheets," she warned. "We did that the first time and it was a mistake. If you're going to deal on both the retail and wholesale level, and work with distributors, you will have different pricing arrangements for each. Print your prices on separate sheets and include them with your catalog or descriptive fly sheets."

Tree Toys' advertising literature contains printed black and white pictures with complete descriptions of each item. In the beginning, Betty says they used fly sheets, then went to a catalog, and are now back to fly sheets again. "They have proved more practical, less expensive, and bring in just as many orders as a catalog. You can eliminate fly sheets, change them easier, and they don't have to be stapled."

Incidentally, color coding also plays an important role in Tree Toys' printed materials. Retail price sheets and order forms are printed in yellow; wholesale, in green. Betty also suggests the use of code numbers for each picture used in your advertising materials, with a different number series for each type of item. For example, Tree Toys' new paper snipping designs are numbered P101, P102, etc., and their quilling kits are numbered Q101, Q102, and so on.

Perhaps I should emphasize here that Tree Toys' gets all of its business from two forms of advertising: exhibition in the annual HIA trade show, and classified advertisements that run regularly in several craft magazines. A short classified ad ("Quilling—Instruction booklets, kits, and supplies") brings in a steady stream of inquiries that usually lead to orders for the company. Customers who order once generally order again because Tree Toys' products and service are excellent. "We have always stressed quality control rather than quantity control," says Betty, who adds that it is *not* necessary to run expensive display advertisements in this type of business.

This, and the fact that Tree Toys does not have a minimum-order policy probably accounts for a large part of their success. Because Betty once had a retail shop of her own, she realizes better than most how difficult it can sometimes be to meet the minimum quantity requirements of certain manufacturers, so Tree Toys makes it easy for their smaller customers. As a result, they get a lot of business from craft shops who can't meet the requirements of their larger competitors. (Keep this point in mind concerning your own business).

Now let me give you a few tips I picked up from talking to two other women who have exhibited in previous HIA shows, both of whom shall remain anonymous.

The first one, the same Mrs. X you met earlier, took just one kit to the show and went unprepared at that. She was so eager to get going that she made a fatal mistake: She snowed her idea before it was actually ready to be sold, and competitors were no doubt there like vultures, "lifting" her idea as soon as they saw it. It was a good one. With their experience and money, they could easily have put her product on the market under another name before Mrs. X got her first order. For all I know, that's exactly what happened.

The second woman, who went to the show with two good craft kits, said she went for experience and got at least $5000 worth. Even though she didn't sell much, she discovered that her product was of interest to the mass manufacturers, and thus, the mass market. "I learned that I should concentrate on selling to the mass merchandisers — Venture, Lee Wards, etc. This is actually cheaper for me as they take only a 10 percent discount, whereas wholesale distributors would need 30 to 35 percent."

This woman gave me the following advice about exhibiting in a trade show: "Get your act together and when you're ready to go, HIT BIG. You've got one year's run before the big manufacturers will steal your idea. If you show an item before you're ready to produce, you've had it."

This woman believes that big manufacturers, who already have all the outlets and contacts and avenues to sucess, constantly prey on small manufacturers like her. But she doesn't let this bother her. "Already I know that two manufacturers are working on the same kit idea I took to the show, but by the time they get it on the market, I will have had time to make my killing and will be out with yet another new idea. You gotta take your chances; if you hide your product under the bed, no one will ever see it. You must leave yourself vulnerable at times in order to get into the position where you need to be."

128 *Patents and Manufacturing Pitfalls*

Many people who get a good idea think immediately, "I'd better get it patented." But what they don't think about is the time and cost involved in the patent process. It can take up to a couple of years and a couple of thousand dollars to do the job, and you'd better be sure your product or idea is worth the effort before you go this route. True, it might take less time and money, but there are no guarantees either way. One designer brought up a good point against patents: You can sit with a patent for 50 years, but what good is it if the idea doesn't sell?

What is a patent, exactly? It's a "grant issued by the United States Government giving an inventor the right to exclude all others from making, using, or selling his invention within the United States, its territories and possessions," according to a booklet issued by the Patent Office. Patents are good for 17 years, except for ornamental design patents, which are granted for shorter terms. Anyone has the right to use an invention covered in an expired patent so long as he does not use features covered in other unexpired patents in doing so. A patent may be granted to anyone who invents or discovers a new and useful process, machine, manufacture, or composition of matter, or any new and useful improvement thereof. Any new, original, and ornamental design for an article of manufacture can also be patented. (Additional information is available in a booklet titled "General Information Concerning Patents," available from the Superintendent of Documents in Washington. See resource chapter.)

Some people who invent products and ideas prefer to go to market without a patent. A good example of this is the lady who designed a crocodile sleeping bag and presented the idea to a reputable manufacturer who liked the idea. She made something like $25,000 for that design and later sold several other ideas as well. The manufacturer who bought her original idea owns the design and name, but she is protected by a contract that says she originated the idea and will receive a 5 percent royalty as a result.*

Once you go on the market with an unpatented idea or product, no one else can patent a similar idea; however, they can place on the market a product similar to yours. (This is when one begins to understand what competition really is. Just think of all the similar products on the market and you'll know what I mean.)

"If you've really invented something fantastic, your first job is to get it patented," says Linda Markuly Szilvasy, an artist who developed a

* From an article in *Family Circle* magazine, November 1970, p. 38.

special craft finish that she currently manufactures and markets herself. Linda's favorite canvas is an eggshell, and in a letter she told me about the "complicated, expensive mess" she found herself in when she set out to get her product patented and marketed.

"This all started when I wanted something, knowing there had to be something to give real strength to my egg shells," she wrote. "I use heavy gold-plated findings and do oil paintings on egg shells, and I wanted them to last and be considered works of art. When I found nothing on the market that would satisfy my needs, I began to experiment and eventually developed my secret process. I was immediately warned by others in the field to find a lawyer or the 'big guys' would steal it.''

Linda's product is called Diamond Hardener Finish. It is a three-part finish that was created to toughen and beautify egg shells and make them less likely to chip in the cutting process, but the product turned out to have other craft uses as well. Its no-odor and china-like qualities make it excellent for use on all craft materials. Linda knew she really had something here, so naturally she wanted to patent it. Her advice to others interested in getting a patent follows:

"The first thing to do is get a lawyer that specializes in this," she says. "It will generally run around $1000 for a patent, if it is granted. Sometimes a judge will rule it a thing that does not deserve to be patented, and you will still pay the lawyer's fee. Also, more than once, an inventor has applied for a patent only to discover someone else has already applied for one on the same thing.''

You can make a patent search without a lawyer, by the way. A search room is maintained in Washington, D.C., for the benefit of the public in searching and examining United States patents, and by searching here you can determine, before filing an application, whether your idea has already been patented. Lawyers are generally used for this job, however, because there are over three hundred different patent classifications with thousands of subclassifications in each class.

Be wary of organizations that promise to help you patent and market your invention or idea. I had planned to recommend a certain company in this book, a well-known "invention-developer" whose name has been mentioned with great respect in dozens of books and articles. Then I happened to hear on television that this company, and one other as well, had been investigated and convicted by the Federal Trade Commission for misrepresentation of certain facts. It was reported that only three inventors out of 30,000 actually made any money from the inventions patented by these firms, and the newscaster suggested that individuals should avoid these firms and others like them. Either file a patent application yourself or use a qualified patent attorney.

Linda ran into problems in getting her product patented, but they were small in comparison to the ones she encountered in trying to get her hardener/finish manufactured and packaged. Here's some additional advice she wanted me to share with you:

"Be very careful if you select someone to be your agent — someone between the manufacturer and you who is responsible for marketing and advertising your product. This is usually done for a percentage (a large one) but if you do not want to be involved with the actual business and are content to accept a small royalty for your product, it is ideal. Talk to someone who uses the agent and be assured he is reliable. Experience has shown me that if a lousy agent does not hold up his end of the three-way contract, all you can do is sue, and that can cost thousands. A contract, I have learned, almost boils down to nothing more than merely having the right to sue.

"Keep in mind, when setting up such contracts with an agent or company, that you may find they do a shabby job later on, and you may have absolutely nothing to say about it if no control is written into the contract, such as specific amounts to be spent on advertising, etc. It's tough.

"As a woman, the first problem you will run into is getting funding. The Small Business Administration will grant loans if you really have everything down as far as facts and figures and can convince them of your management skills. Going to a bank can be futile, however, unless you have collateral or want to use family assets.

129

"Put much time into researching prices — custom-made boxes, bottles, labels, printing, etc. These varied by hundreds of dollars in their estimates (which you must request in writing and with samples when applicable). More times than I like to remember I took someone's word on the phone only to find the price was much higher when I was ready to buy. Get the name of the person with whom you are speaking (if by phone) and keep good records of all conversations while researching. Get guarantees of shipment times. How much heartache I have gone through because some essential thing was late. Always have contingency plans."

Linda remarked at this point in her letter that she eventually lost all her trust and naivete in dealing with people, and no longer takes anyone's word on anything. Check everything twice and get everything in writing, she warns, and this is good advice no matter *what* you are doing.

Because Linda's product was a chemical one, she realized the importance of having her business incorporated (which protects family assets in the case of a lawsuit). Interestingly, Linda found lawyers' fees for incorporation varied as much as $200. Because of the nature of her product, liability insurance was also necessary, and this really created a nightmare for her.

"If you are putting out some type of chemical product you will be lucky if you can get product liability insurance. It can run as much as 10 percent of the retail value of what you have produced or stored in inventory. The forms one has to fill out to get product liability insurance are formidable — very long — and they want to know such things as who does the packaging (they wouldn't be too impressed with a backyard-type operation); how long it has been sold, etc. I have been told that most large chains will not touch a product unless you can furnish them with a certificate of insurance proving that your product is covered.

"Do check carefully with a lawyer about your labels," adds Linda. "First remember that no matter how explicit your warnings are, you are still liable for someone getting hurt with your product,

no matter how stupid a thing they do with it." (Or, in the words of Helena Rubinstein: "If there is a wrong way to use this product, somebody will find it.") Linda continues: "I had all my labels printed ($$$) before checking, only to find they were illegal because my complete address was not on each one. More labels had to be printed ($$$). Also, some products must get a special number from the Food and Drug Administration (a lawyer can advise if you have such a product). This number must be printed on the labels."

As you can see by now, a good legal adviser is worth his weight in gold and, according to Linda, will charge darn near that much. Marketing experts are also a great help, she says. "They can get your product on the market, serve as adviser (charging an hourly fee), or set up contracts and work for a percentage. If consulted in advance, they can give you much valuable information as to exactly what the market is like, and help you set up pricing formulas for distributor's prices and wholesale and retail."

Linda says she cannot stress enough the importance of doing comprehensive research before you begin, because once you have invested in something you are committed, and the costs can really get out of hand if you have not done enough beforehand research. Take packaging, for example.

A chemist told Linda to use the wrong lid liner. It dissolved and she had to pay for double packaging of one element and replace kits already sent out. This cost her over a thousand dollars. "Who can you trust?" she asks, then suggests this rule of thumb for others to follow: "Check with several authorities, then experiment and test everything yourself." Linda has also learned to have all elements checked before having them packaged, since a packaging company is not responsible for checking to see that what they have been sent to package is what you think they have received. "I also learned that little gem the hard way ($$$)," moans Linda.

"As far as instruction sheets go," she adds, "I am beginning to feel they should be written for a third-grade level. You cannot believe how easily people can get confused, or how little they understand. Assume they start with absolutely no knowledge of the type of product you are selling or of techniques involved in its use, and write your instructions accordingly."

Linda has come to the conclusion that there is an awful amount of work and money involved in a venture such as hers, but realizes that other women like her may someday take a similar plunge into the manufacturing business. She says she's glad if her experience and advice help someone in the future, adding, "I now know why executives tend to have ulcers. I also know why I was told it takes a couple of years to 'work out the bugs' and show a profit. Some never do. A very high percentage of new businesses go under in a year. I am very fortunate to have a very understanding and considerate husband. That can be as helpful and necessary as a good lawyer."

POSTSCRIPT: Shortly before this book went to press, Linda called to say that her more than five years' work was going down the drain, simply because her husband, an army chaplain, is being transferred to Germany for three years. There is no way she can continue her manufacturing business while in Germany, so her choice is either to sell to someone else or to cease manufacturing. Because of the uniqueness of her product, Linda did not feel the chances of finding a buyer were very good. She has tried to accept the inevitable end of her business philosophically. "I learned a lot," she says with a sigh in her voice. "At least if I ever want to try something like this again, I'll know exactly what to expect. I learned to do all kinds of things I never knew I could do. While it's terribly frustrating to have to give up a business I've worked so hard for, there's nothing I can do about it. My husband does come first after all."

Artist's depiction of Lyndall Toothman and her dog, Flintlock, at work at a country crafts fair. Lyndall's specialty is spinning dog hair, and her services as a demonstrator are in great demand by various tourist attractions in America that feature old-time crafts. She spends a lot of time on the road each year, and travels from job to job in a bright yellow van that symbolizes her sunny outlook on life.

❧11❧

Profit From Specialized Know-How

If you like to talk to the public while demonstrating your art or craft, you may have a promising career as a crafts lecturer or demonstrator, a field that is often overlooked, even by professionals. The best thing about lecturing or demonstrating is that you do not necessarily need a product to sell. But, since the primary purpose of a lecture or demonstration is to educate and entertain, you do need some special qualities not found in everyone. To succeed in this field, you must know how to sell yourself and be able to generate enthusiasm among your listeners. You don't have to be a comedian, but a sense of humor is a tremendous asset when trying to keep the attention of a crowd. The element of surprise is also important, and, of course, a thorough knowledge of your particular art or craft is essential.

A remarkable woman from Williamsburg, West Virginia, incorporates all of the above as she demonstrates the craft of hand spinning.

Portrait of a Successful Crafts Demonstrator

Lyndall Toothman was a teacher of both hand spinning and weaving for several years. Now in her 60's, she is a dynamic and ageless woman who has made quite a name for herself as a demonstrating craftsman, and her services are in great demand by various tourist attractions in America that feature old-time crafts. Why? Because she is by no means an ordinary spinner nor, for that matter, an ordinary woman. In fact, a lot of people have been after Lyndall to write a book about her life and experiences, but she's not too interested in that. The fact that she's lived it is enough, in her estimation, although she admits with a grin that her life has certainly not been boring. (Twice married, she is now single again and firmly resolved to remain that way for the rest of her life.)

Single, yes; but Lyndall is neither lonely nor alone. When she isn't traveling with her granddaughter, Lee, also a demonstrating spinner, she still has her dog for company, and he's no ordinary dog, either. Flintlock is a fluffy grey keeshond who now accompanies Lyndall as she travels about the country in her bright yellow van, and he also shares the spotlight with her as she demonstrates her skill in spinning dog hair.

Yes, *dog hair*. That's her specialty — her gimmick — and it seldom fails to command attention. To date she has spun the fur of more than 90 different breeds of dogs, as well as cats, llamas, bison, camels, horses, wolves, lions, and every other fur-bearing creature she can get hold of. She has even spun human hair successfully. You can imagine how much all this gives her to talk about, and talk she does. As adept at telling a good story as she is at spinning a fine yarn on her old Saxony

133

wheel, she delights in answering the many questions asked by a curious crowd, and generally embellishes her answers with bits of country wit and wisdom. She is always a surprise to those who stop to watch her work, and a diamond in the rough to those who are privileged to know her as a friend.

There she sits, gently rocking in her favorite chair, spinning away with all the casualness of a shoplifter about to make his move, looking not at what she's doing, but at the gathering crowd instead. (She's sizing them up, that's what she's doing.) She wears wire-rimmed spectacles and a white crocheted cap atop her head, and no one would suspect that this lovely old woman in a pink Colonial dress and white apron — this cute "little granny" — actually prefers blue jeans to dresses, and is a strong and energetic worker who, after the age of 60, designed and built her own log cabin practically singlehandedly. Bystanders are seldom prepared, either, for Lyndall's sharp wit and ready sense of humor, which comes into play the moment anyone speaks to her.

"What's that you're spinning?" someone in the crowd will ask.

"This is dog hair," she replies firmly, with a strong emphasis on the last two words that make them sound like "dawg hair."

"Nah," another will argue, "you're kidding."

"No, I'm not," Lyndall will say as she points to her green display board hanging nearby. It is literally covered with photographs of animals, mostly dogs, and stapled to each picture is a small hank of yarn. Lyndall explains that this is yarn she has spun from the animal's fur. She speaks in a high-pitched, raspy voice that is perfectly suited to her character of "Granny," and just as the crowd is really beginning to believe everything she's telling them, she sets them up for a fall with a line like this: "There's only one kind of dog hair I've been unable to spin so far," she says with great seriousness, and after a slight pause for effect, she adds, "and that's the Mexican hairless."

She chuckles pleasantly with her audience, who now realizes what a delightful entertainer she is. And a good spinner, too. A few people move

closer for a better look at her hands, which have never stopped moving for a minute. By this time, of course, she has completely captured the attention of everyone within earshot, and is ready and waiting for the two questions most frequently asked along about now: "Do you kill the dog?" and "Does your foot get tired?".

"No, my foot doesn't get tired," she assures them, "and I don't kill the dog, for heaven's sake! He's sleeping right over there." Then she explains how one simply washes and brushes a dog to get its fur, and several ladies may sigh with relief to learn she doesn't practice cruelty to animals. Soon, someone will inquire about the furry garments hanging on the tree or wall behind her, and she will tell them it's a coat, or a shawl, or a poncho she has made by weaving or knitting the yarn spun from various kinds of dog hair.

"How long did it take to make that coat?" another may ask, and she will answer with a twinkle in her eye, "Oh, — I'm not sure. All I know is, the dog wore it one year and I wore it the next." The crowd roars with laughter — they love her! When she tells people, "Yes, you can wash and dry the coat in the machine," some woman is bound to look at her incredulously and say (as I did years ago) "But won't it shrink or something?" "Of course not," Lyndall answers snappily, "does your dog shrink when you leave him out in the rain?"

Occasionally someone will make a remark that annoys Lyndall, in which case she's apt to spit out a reply that leaves him at a complete loss for words, like she did to the fellow who came up to her recently and said, critically, "That's not the way my grandmother used to spin." She looked at him for a moment and then said with subtle sarcasm, "Well, then, your grandmother just wasn't a good spinner."

In an interview with Lyndall recently, I asked her if she sold her work. "No," she said, "I don't. I give most of it away." Actually, she spins dog hair on a 50-50 basis. That is, if you give her a sack of dog brushings, she will spin the yarn and keep half of what she has spun as her payment for spinning. If someone insists on keeping all the handspun yarn, Lyndall may charge them about $20 a

134

pound to spin it. (And this is poor payment indeed, considering it takes about an hour to spin two ounces. You can see how little money there is to be made in spinning yarn for a living.) After Lyndall has a good supply of yarn on hand, she will use it to make a weaving, or perhaps crochet or knit a hat, purse, sweater, or poncho. Then, in all probability, she will give it to someone who has done her a favor or been kind to her in some special way. Since she is well paid for demonstrating at fairs and shows, she can spin and weave for the sheer love of it when she gets home, and that's the way she thinks it ought to be.

Lyndall says she has the best of two worlds, for she travels and demonstrates her craft in the summer, then retreats to her quiet mountain hideaway in the winter — the home she designed herself — an eight-sided log cabin she calls her "Appalachian Hogan." Here she can watch the morning mist rise from the valley below, enjoy nature at its fullest every day, and spin and weave to her heart's content.

It's true that not everyone has the special ability it takes to be both an engaging entertainer and a skilled artisan or craftsman, but Lyndall's demonstrations are always an inspiration to young and old alike, and a reminder that there are more ways than one to demonstrate a craft and make money from one's special talents.

Lecturing for Pleasure and Profit

If Lyndall's type of demonstrating is not your "cup of tea," perhaps you can identify with Alice Leeds, a designer-craftsman from Jackson Heights, New York. She does soft sculpture and is always researching new concepts with the ultimate goal of integrating them into her work. Although she is involved with gallery shows and exhibitions, selling is not her primary motive for working. Last year she began working with cyanotype, or blueprint photography, and soon became so involved in the unlimited range of this process that she began lecturing extensively on the subject at schools, craft seminars, and adult education classes.

How did she get started? "I was invited to show some quilts at a quilter's convention," she told me, "and I volunteered to lecture on the cyanotype process. The talk was a gigantic success and, through word of mouth, I got other speaking engagements." Alice generally charges $35 for her talks, and her primary problem is that, if anything, she is forced to discourage publicity because she just doesn't have the time, what with her craft work and, in her words, "a super-delightful, albeit demanding almost-two-year-old." For now, blueprint photography on fabric is merely a hobby for Alice, and lecturing about it just a sideline interest. But who knows where this interest will lead her in the future? (And who knows where your special new interest may already be leading you?)

Lecturing about your craft can be profitable in itself, but when lecturing is used as a means to an end (that is, selling the things you make) it can mean even greater dividends for you. Do you remember Ginnie Wise, the farm homemaker I discussed in Chapter 5? She has a shop in her home, and in order to bring new customers into her shop, she invites garden clubs, church groups, hobby and craft organizations, and farm women's clubs to hold their regular meetings in her home shop. Then, after their business meeting is concluded, Ginnie presents her own program, offers some coffee and cookies, and invites them to browse in her gift shop. Ginnie's program is basically a talk about the historic area along the Sandusky River and a "show-and-tell" session in which she explains her craft.

At first Ginnie made no charge for her program, but now she asks that there be at least fifteen people in attendance or there will be a fee. (This eliminates the smaller clubs who are more interested in a free program than anything else, and also helps the individual clubs to urge better member attendance.) Ginnie thinks this method of advertising her shop would be more effective if she weren't situated "so far off the beaten track"; nevertheless she has always been able to create a lot of enthusiasm in people who later come back just to shop. Perhaps Ginnie's original approach to lecturing would work even better for the shop you now have in your home (or are thinking of starting when you finish this book).

135

If you think you'd enjoy lecturing, but don't know what to talk about, consider this suggestion from Margo Daws Pontius, a cornshuckery artisan who has given over 500 lectures and 80 all-day workshops to date. "Supplement your talk with poems that fit in with the theme, or pleasing stories of the era your craft originated in," says Margo. "Or, add music to create an unusual mood, or try unusual lighting techniques. I have tried all of these with tremendous results. An audience loves someone with imagination, so don't be afraid to give them a chance."

How To Become a Successful Lecturer

It's time now for some specifics on how you can become a successful lecturer-demonstrator, and where better to learn the tricks of the trade than from an expert like Margo? Through lecturing to audiences in three states, ranging from children to "golden-agers," she has shown thousands of people how to make cornshuck dolls and taught them to appreciate our great American heritage in crafts. In her 18 years of researching cornshuckery, she has found the history of this craft as fascinating as the actual making of the dolls, and this has naturally provided her with wonderful material for her lectures.

In turn, Margo has provided me with some wonderful material for this book, but before I share with you her tips on how to become a terrific lecturer, I must tell you how she has cleverly managed to solve her special source-of-supply problem.

When I first became acquainted with Margo, I never gave a second thought as to where she got her cornshucks, figuring she got them from the cornfield, like everyone else. But she doesn't. In fact, Margo is a city gal from Neenah, Wisconsin, who didn't even know a farmer at the time she began her craft, so she naturally had to resort to using sweet corn from the grocery store. With time and experimentation, she eventually worked out a good method for drying and storing the shucks and has been using Wisconsin sweet corn for her craft ever since.

Now this fact in itself may not be surprising, but the quantity of corn consumed in the Pontius household is a bit startling. In order to keep Margo supplied with sufficient shucks, she, her husband, Alan, and their three teenagers, Bob, Jim, and Ann, somehow manage to gnaw their way through *eighty dozen ears of corn a year!* That's almost 200 ears apiece, and if that isn't the world's record, it is at least a noteworthy statistic. It was certainly enough in 1976 to capture the attention of the Wisconsin State Committee who asked Margo to represent Wisconsin during the Bicentennial by sending a series of her colonial dolls to the White House. Understandably, Margo is quite proud of the personal letter she received from President Ford as a result, and says it hangs over her ironing board to inspire her to greater things.

Margo's dolls have also been featured on the cover of craft magazines and in the Sunday supplements of leading newspapers, exhibited in various art galleries, and publicized on television — all because she is not only a good craftsman, but also a craftsman who toots her own horn through the medium of lecturing.

136

I've emphasized Margo's accomplishments to show you the kinds of things that can happen to people who bring their talents out into the open where everyone can see them. I'm sure you've heard that old expression about hiding your light under a bushel, and Margo is a perfect example of a person who not only turned the basket over, but filled it with corn. In the beginning she says she was neither an authority nor a daring individual, but now she is both, and she thinks the nicest part of lecturing is to inspire someone else to say, "I'd like to try that." Here, then, are her tips on how to become a terrific lecturer:

1. BE AN AUTHORITY. Know your craft and its background, and all the techniques.

2. BE DARING. Many artists do excellent work, but usually in established patterns set before them. If you do your craft similarly to someone else, then display it differently, but do be unique.

3. BE ON A BUDGET. Figure the costs of your displays and the continual upkeep. Make sure your lecture fee covers the important extras, such as having your hair done or your suit cleaned, or car mileage.

4. DEVELOP ENTHUSIASM. If it is not a natural asset, it can be developed. If you truly love your art, just let the "glow" out for others to see.

5. KEEP UP TO DATE. Work the latest topics of the day into your lecture and displays, such as ecology, big hats, or patriotism, as the case may be.

6. INSPIRE YOUR AUDIENCE. When they go home, perhaps they will try your art, or perhaps they will want to buy yours, or both. It all depends on you.

Margo thinks the most important key to your success as a lecturer may lie in this one word: responsibility. "A dynamic word," she says, "and one that can make or break you." Here are some additional points she emphasizes:

1. CONFIRM ALL DETAILS, such as the date, time, place, where in the building you are to lecture, audio facilities available, table or space requirements, and the fee for your lecture.

2. KEEP CAREFUL RECORDS OF EACH LECTURE. You'll need them for tax purposes.

3. BE PROMPT. Don't let yourself "get lost." Obtain a map of the area if necessary, and make advance arrangements about the door you are to use to unload your displays.

4. KEEP UP YOUR DISPLAYS, replacing backdrops and mats when they need it. Always check beforehand to make sure everything you need is still there and in good condition.

5. REMEMBER THE WEATHER. It's your worst enemy. If the roads are bad, allow extra time to arrive safely. In wet weather, ensure the safe arrival of your displays by placing them inside extra large plastic bags.

6. BE CAREFUL ABOUT YOUR APPEARANCE. People will react to you according to how you appear to them. If some disaster strikes you and there is nothing further you can do to improve on your appearance, let the audience know in a humorous way and then proceed from there.

7. OTHER RESPONSIBILITIES. Always be courteous to your program chairman, and stay awhile after your lecture to give people the opportunity to come up and take a closer look and ask questions before you pack things away. If this is a good time for you to sell your art, then by all means do so.

137

The Elements of a Good Display

You will notice Margo's frequent mention of displays in the foregoing paragraphs. This, to her, is the most important part of any lecture, and I must agree that when crafts are concerned, it is vital for success. "How often have you gone to hear a lecture,'' Margo points out, ''only to come away with an unclear picture of what the person was trying to say? If only a display had been used so one could visualize it as well as listen to the words. So often we can *see* an idea even when we can't understand what we hear.''

When you make your display, Margo suggests you keep the following things in mind:

1. KEEP IT SIMPLE. Eliminate everything unnecessary to the message.

2. MAKE IT INTERESTING AND ATTRACTIVE. Use colored mats and tagboards to create a setting, and then add anything that will contribute to the theme of your program.

3. GIVE IT A DEFINITE MESSAGE OR THEME. For example, you might lecture on your art through one or more seasons, a certain era, or a place in history. Or, use folklore, nationality, ecology, nature, or even song titles to provide a theme.

138

One of the displays used by Margo Daws Pontius. Simple, yet obviously well planned, it stresses one of the points Margo makes in her lecture: with cornshuckery, anything is possible.

4. KEEP THE SIZE WITHIN REASON. You will naturally be limited on size as to your means of transportation in getting displays to the lecture site. (Margo says the 13 x 18 in. mats are excellent when accompanied by a 21 x 28 in. tagboard. These backdrops can also be fastened to cemetery wreath tri-pods, which are lightweight, collapsible, and readily available.)

5. DON'T OVERDO. Once you start making displays, the ideas never seem to stop, and if you're not careful you can make too many. Then your lecture becomes too long and you will lose your audience. They can absorb only so much.

6. USE PSYCHOLOGY. Not only must a lecturer understand how to get the attention of his listeners, but he must design his displays with their needs and interests in mind, appealing to the entire audience, whether they are men, women, or children.

7. CHECK THE FINISHED DISPLAY for position, eye level, balance, and originality. To really see it, take a snapshot of it.

8. A FINAL TIP. If you set up your displays ahead of time, your audience will be able to anticipate your lecture. Instead, try setting them up while you talk. This works very well if you keep your displays simple.

Where To Lecture, and Why

Assuming you have worked up a good lecture, how do you get that first, all-important lecturing date? There are literally hundreds of clubs, groups, and associations who need unusual programs to present to their members, to say nothing of elementary or high schools who are looking for something different and interesting to stimulate their students. Contact them and see what happens. Your local Chamber of Commerce or PTA is also a good place to start, and a thorough reading of your newspapers will probably turn up the names of several garden clubs, church groups, or art/craft associations that might make likely prospects for you. As for getting future dates, Margo thinks the trick is to give your first lecture in such a well-prepared way that word of mouth will take it from there. In the beginning she was asked to give one lecture, and within three months was asked to give forty more.

Professional lecturers such as Margo might be interested to learn of the Lecture and Demonstration Service offered by the American Society of Artists, Inc., in Chicago. This is a national membership organization that is concerned about artists, their ambitions, talents, and problems. It offers several benefits to members, one of which is the lecture-demonstration service. Qualified members will be listed in a bulletin issued by the organization and distributed to various groups interested in hiring lecturers and demonstrators.

Lecturing or demonstrating one's craft is a craft in itself, and not suited to everyone. But, if you have a flair for promoting your own business and have just a touch of "hambone" in your personality, lecturing or demonstrating could prove to be a perfect way for you to increase sales in your shop, gain new students for your craft classes, or help you sell a line of finished crafts, supplies, or books. A good lecture to the right audience could also boost the number of custom-design orders you get each year, promote the new book you've just written, increase the sales of any kit or tool you may have designed, or stimulate interest in a special service you may offer in the community. In cases like this, it may be profitable to give your lectures free of charge, provided, of course, that you are able to advertise your products, publications, or services during or after your talk.

Remember, too, that your lecture could encourage people to visit the local shop or gallery where your work is currently for sale, as well as provide an excellent way to enlarge the size of your mailing list. By providing cards for interested people to fill out with their name and address, you can build a good mailing list for that brochure or catalog you plan to issue in the future.

In short, lectures offer tremendous possibilities for meeting new customers, and perhaps you ought to consider what lecturing might do for you.

Teaching Techniques and Ideas

If you have an excellent working knowledge of your particular art or craft, and a desire to share that knowledge with others, you may find teaching a rewarding and profitable experience. The topic of teaching crafts in one's home was discussed briefly in Chapter 5, but now I'd like to give you more information about teaching in general, and tell you what you need to know before starting a class or workshop of your own.

Let me begin by emphasizing, in the order of their importance, the five qualities needed to be a good teacher, according to Virginia Harvey, noted textile craftsman, teacher, and author:

1. Organization
2. The ability to clearly explain processes, theories, etc.
3. A good strong voice
4. Patience
5. A sense of humor

Virginia also offers the following suggestions for teaching and making arrangements for a class. First, the information to be given each day should be planned carefully. Second, good visual aids and large-scale demonstration materials are very necessary in teaching manual skills to large classes. Third, since people learn in many different ways, explanations should be repeated several times, each time saying it in a different way.

Finally, when making arrangements for a class, remember to include a careful explanation of the material to be covered, as well as what will *not* be covered. This will be useful during your negotiations for the class, and should also be given to the students who sign up for lessons.

Virginia also recommends that a simple contract be signed with the sponsoring group, and says a deposit is advisable. This deposit should be nonreturnable after a certain date so schedules can be finalized without fear of cancellation at the last moment. It is also a good idea to exclude from class everyone who is not officially enrolled. (This neatly eliminates children and pets, which occasionally cause embarrassing situations for both students and teacher.)

Information on teaching, such as that offered by Virginia Harvey, is doubly appreciated when one considers that there is so little published material for the nonprofessional teacher, yet so many nonprofessionals currently entering the teaching field. The people at Carma Press in St. Paul, Minnestota, are trying to change that, however, with the introduction of a new series of books written especially for the nonprofessional teacher of adults. They have recently published a spiral-bound handbook for teaching adults titled *"Yes, You Can Teach!"* Written by Florence Nelson, it stresses how to use professional teaching techniques, solve common in-class problems, encourage students, construct and use teaching materials, and find teaching jobs. (For more information about this book and Carma Press, see resource section. NOTE: At this time, the publishers welcome contact from anyone who is interested in writing for them on an outright-payment basis. Subject matter need not be related to arts and crafts, so long as it applies to the teaching of adults. Query first.)

When someone asked me recently, "Who teaches the teacher how to teach?" and "How does the lady next door know the woman up the block can teach?" I found myself on the doorstep of this conclusion: There are basically two kinds of teachers in the crafts field today — those who are professionally trained, and those who are not. (My husband puts it more simply: Those who are good and those who are bad.) But this doesn't imply that teachers with college degrees are good, and those without them bad. In fact, some of the best teachers in the craft field today have never received any kind of formal training, which leads me to believe that, in the end, the most important thing about teaching is whether a student can learn something from the teacher. Many people believe the best way to judge a teacher (of any kind) is by his or her following. Where crafts teachers are concerned, if the students are producing usable, well-finished products, then the teacher must be getting the message across.

A beginning teacher who has never taught a class before will probably learn more than the students, so perhaps it is the students themselves who are teaching most of today's craft teachers how to teach. And, if the woman up the block can teach the lady next door how to use a particular skill she didn't know she had, so much the better. But, a word of caution here: It is one thing to learn something about a new art or craft for your own enjoyment, and quite another to begin teaching others what you know when you are not confident of your own ability. It is unprofessional to pass along to students information that is inaccurate or techniques that are improper, so if you really want to be a good teacher, it is best to know your art or craft thoroughly before you take on a class.

Ah, you protest, what if this just isn't possible? What if you live in an isolated area where there are no teachers, and you know a little but not a lot about what you are doing? Or, what if you have rediscovered an old art or craft technique no one else knows about, but wants to learn? Maybe the only way you can become an expert at what you do is to start teaching others what you do know, so everyone can learn in the process. That's exactly what happened to Pat Virch, who is now considered one of the nation's leading rosemalers.

A self-taught teacher and lecturer since 1963, Pat is also largely self-taught in the art of rosemaling, and her success story is both interesting and unusual. Perhaps, eventually, it will encourage you to share your knowledge with others through the medium of teaching, even though you may feel less than qualified to teach right now. Says Pat, "Be honest and admit you will share only what you know, and still have plenty to learn."

How One Teacher Learned To Teach

Pat Virch maintains a studio in her Marquette, Michigan, home for classes and workshops, and conducts an annual rosemaling seminar there each summer. She began as a "Sunday painter" and eventually became interested in decorative painting. Her career in rosemaling actually began the day someone passed her a plateful of cookies at a homemaker's meeting. On the plate under the cookies was the first example of Norwegian rosemaling she had ever seen, and she fell in love with it.

Evenutally she took a couple of courses in the art, but just as she was getting serious about it she had to move. Although no one in her new area was giving lessons, or even doing rosemaling, Pat continued to study and research the art, particularly in the Norwegian American Museum in Decorah, Iowa, which houses the largest collection of Norwegian rosemaling in America.

One day Pat met a woman who gave her some unusual and practical advice. She said that the only way Pat was going to find other people interested in what she was doing was to start teaching. "But, I'm no teacher," Pat protested, "and I'm still learning the art itself." But her friend argued: "If you really want to find someone to paint with, you'll have to teach them how first." This logic worked on Pat, simply because she is the kind of person who needs to show others what she is doing, and enjoys sharing the pleasure she derives from painting.

141

Even though she felt extremely inadequate as a teacher, she nonetheless found the courage to offer rosemaling lessons. She began by copying down all the notes she had taken as a student, and digging out all the patterns her own teachers had used. She mixed the colors the way she had been shown, told her new students to purchase quality brushes, and proceeded to give them all the good advice she could. Before long, she was not only an excellent rosemaler, but a good teacher as well.

It was at this point that Pat actually began to climb her "ladder of success." She explains: "I guess I would have continued to work in my basement just being a rosemaler and teaching others, and having a few patterns printed for my students, if I hadn't read a certain article in a brand new crafts magazine.

That magazine was *Creative Crafts,* and it prompted Pat to write the editor and tell her what she was doing, which was developing the Norwegian art of rosemaling. The editor, Sybil Harp, was delighted to hear from a new craftsperson, and asked Pat to write an article for a future issue. When Pat told Sybil she didn't know how to write a magazine article, Sybil replied with the encouragement and suggestions needed. By emulating other articles in the magazine, and having some pictures taken, Pat was able to write a fine two-part article that was soon published in *Creative Crafts.*

Then Pat started getting mail in response to the article, and eventually so many people asked for copies of it that she asked the publisher for permission to reprint it for distribution. This was not possible, however, since the magazine owned the copyright on it. Therefore, in answer to an obvious need for information on rosemaling, Pat decided to write her first how-to book, and ended up publishing and distributing it herself (Chapter 13).

One thing naturally led to another, and soon Pat had gained national attention as a rosemaler. By now she was creating her own designs based on traditional patterns and had issued two portfolios of designs with colored prints, which are now carried by four major book dealers in Norway. Her husband, Niron, was becoming more and more interested in what she was doing, and since they are both of Norwegian descent and extremely interested in their heritage, the Virches made trips to Norway in 1970 and 1973 to photograph and research all the old pieces of rosemaling, further deepening their interest in this art form.

Pat started giving workshops in order to promote her book, and before long decided she wanted to travel to other areas. But she did have a husband and four children to think about. Remembering those days, Pat says, "I want to say right now that there is no way any woman can get this involved with a business out of her basement unless she's got complete cooperation and support from her husband. So I'm going to give this word of advice: To be completely dedicated to something like this, you have to have no personal obligations and ties anyplace else."

Pat asked her husband about doing workshops and he gave his approval, although he did feel she was on an ego trip and wasn't charging enough. After two weeks on the road teaching workshops in several cities out of state, Pat came home feeling like an expert, but decided that this sort of thing couldn't continue. In the end, it was decided that she could make more money advertising and promoting her book in magazines, instead of traveling, and she began running national workshops in her studio instead. (Incidentally, Pat's workshops are unusual, as national workshops go. "People bring their whole families," says Pat, "and when the course is finished, we entertain all the families with a pot luck supper, going up to our cabin on the lake. It has been a charming experience not just for me, but for my family too.")

Pat is indeed fortunate to have a husband who understands and appreciates what she is doing. In fact, since learning woodworking, Niron has become interested in making Norwegian style pieces for his wife to decorate. Although his craft began as a hobby, it now appears that, upon retirement, Niron will be doing woodworking on a full-time basis. "Then," says Pat, "the two of us will be traveling together when I have requests to teach. Niron is becoming so skilled in carving the decorative scrolls that in time he'll probably do some teaching himself."

I asked Pat for some guidelines on what a beginning teacher should charge, and she told me that, in the beginning, she charged $1 per session, and asked students to pay as they came. Occasionally this didn't work well, however, so she started giving 8 lessons for $10, payable at the first lesson. Then, if someone didn't show up midway through the course, she did not lose as a result. A good tip, she says, is this: Make sure you are worth a lot more than what you charge, and you will never have disappointed people.

Actually, Pat says that what she does is not teaching as such, but more like sharing. However, her more than 300 students might argue that point. Recently, she wrote her second rosemaling book and received a special Medal of Honor from the Norwegian American Museum in Iowa. (There are only 13 such medal holders in the U.S.)

Rosemaling has surely gained new popularity in the United States and abroad because of the efforts of Pat Virch, once just a busy homemaker with a new hobby. And to think it all started with a plateful of cookies. Don't you agree this story is good food for thought?

How Teachers Can Attract Students

The best way to get students is simply to publicize yourself. Don't wait for students to find you; go out and find them instead. They are eager to be found and ready to learn, and they will be forever grateful to anyone who will teach them what they want to know.

Try to get a write-up in your local paper, join local art or craft organizations, and speak to them (lecture) if given the chance. Plan an exhibit of your work and see if you can display it in a bank or library near your home. If there is an art or crafts gallery or crafts supply store near you, contact the owners and tell them what you can do. If they aren't holding classes already, they may be interested in starting them.

Are craft classes important to the success of a craft supply shop? "Absolutely!" says Marti Fleischer, owner of the Craft Cottage in Oak Ridge, Tennessee. "But only if taught by competent teachers under good working conditions, and if paid for by the students. Teachers are not hard to find. They don't have to have a degree in education to teach crafts. Anyone who has spent several years devoting a good bit of time to a craft is competent providing they have studied the background, read about the subject, and created original designs. It helps, too, if they have taken some classes themselves."

If your local high school or community college offers adult education courses, contact the school's registrar to see if there is any interest in a class such as you offer. Contact the extension center of your state university, nearby recreational centers, and the recreational department of your park district. If your supermarket or laundry has a bulletin board, by all means tack up a clever poster and see what happens. A simple classified ad in the paper or a regional craft magazine or newsletter might bring surprising results. By reading some of the many craft and needlework journals being published today, you will probably discover other opportunities to obtain free publicity as a teacher.

Once you've lined up some likely teaching prospects, give some thought to your presentation. Letters of inquiry to anyone should include your qualifications as a teacher and an outline of the course you are offering. If contacting prospects in person, take along samples of your best work as well.

Let's go back to the library for a moment. One woman I know got started teaching by simply offering the library a special exhibition designed to give the public a better understanding of arts and crafts in general. It drew so much interest that the library eventually hired the woman to give a series of general craft classes, which ran for two hours one day a week for a period of six weeks. The library paid for all the supplies and offered the teacher a flat salary. She was also allowed to sell her line of art/craft supplies in the class, which nicely supplemented her income. Perhaps this idea will work for you, too.

How One Teacher Became an Author

Now I'd like to tell you an interesting story that will give encouragement and ideas to beginning and professional teachers alike. It's about a

143

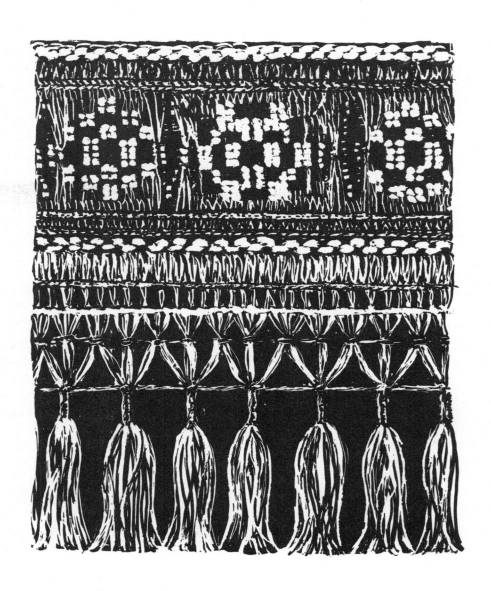

A taaniko weaving design, adapted from a flyer
used by Joyce Ronald Smith.

woman who started her first class by putting a sign in the butcher shop window, of all places.

A funny thing happened to Joyce Ronald Smith on the way to New Zealand with her husband one year. In one of the books she had taken with her, she "discovered" the ancient lost craft of Maori handweaving, or *taaniko,* a little-known process devised by the Maori of New Zealand in about the 14th or 15th century. Here was an intriguing craft that required neither tools nor loom. With a simple twisting movement of the hands and wrists, Joyce found she could manipulate fibers into a woven product.

Before the boat docked, she had not only taught herself the basic techniques of this lost art, but had actually created her first project — a belt that she wore down the gangplank in the hopes it would serve as a conversation piece to learn more from the people. It didn't, however, and when she asked a local taxi driver where she could find examples of taaniko, he didn't know what she was talking about. In fact, the only Maori handweavings Joyce could find at first were exhibited in a museum. Later, while traveling with her husband, Lane, a painter, she found a small village where the people at least knew something about the craft, even if they no longer practiced it.

Joyce says in the book she later wrote: "This method of weaving so ingeniously devised by the Maori, seemed to be begging me to release it from the past, experiment with it, and realize its vast potential."* Thus inspired, Joyce soon began to produce weavings with the kind of frenzy that attacks all creative people in the midst of a new discovery. She made rugs, wall hangings, jewelry, lamp shades, and belts, and in time more and more people began dropping by the cottage to see Lane's paintings and her weavings. One day someone asked her if she would consider giving lessons, and she thought, "Why not?" That's when she put up that sign in the butcher shop window. And the people came, Maori and non-Maori alike, to practice the ancient lost art of taaniko. And just like Pat Virch, Joyce learned from her students,

each of whom had a new weaving variation to show her.

When the Smiths' visas expired and they had to leave New Zealand, they returned to their home in Providence, Rhode Island, with Joyce all fired up with the idea of reviving this craft in America. Toward that end she wrote her first book, *Taaniko — Maori Hand Weaving,* which was published in 1975.

Some people think that when you write a book you achieve instant fame and fortune. Unfortunately, that's not true. Joyce's publisher did arrange for an appearance on national television, which brought in some fan mail, but no invitations for workshops or classes. This was a disappointment, of course, because Joyce had been a full- time teacher of art and design since 1960, and she believed teaching to be the most logical way for her to spread the word about taaniko weaving.

Thus you can see that even professional teachers have to work to find students. In a letter Joyce told me, "None of my workshops came to me as a result of my book or the television interview. I have had to make an effort to solicit all teaching and workshops. My first workshops were conducted by putting posters in congested shopping areas and by running an ad in the newspaper. Later I felt it better to affiliate with the educational programs of established institutions such as museums, colleges, craft organizations, etc. My going rate for private lessons is equal to what the local music teachers charge. For group lessons, the salary is determined by whatever institution I am teaching for. I make an effort to get $25 an hour. For day workshops, I charge $100 plus expenses."

Incidentally, Joyce often uses lecturing as a means of attracting students. "I have given many lectures about taaniko and New Zeland using slides," she says. "Many groups have signed up for the lecture first and this produced enough interest for them to request a workshop at a later date."

Thanks to Joyce, Maori handweaving is alive and well, certainly in Rhode Island, where she has numerous students, and probably in other scattered areas of the country as well because of her

*From *Taaniko — Maori Hand Weaving,* by Joyce Ronald Smith. © 1975 by Vineyard Books, Inc. Used by permission of Charles Scribner's Sons.

book. And I can't help but wonder if Joyce didn't leave behind in New Zealand an enthusiastic person like herself who is trying to rekindle interest in this craft among the Maori people themselves. Perhaps someday this type of weaving will attract wide attention among America's fiber craftspeople, but until then Joyce plans to stay busy teaching, exhibiting, and selling taaniko. In a recent letter she told me she is also currently exploring the possibilities of another little-known textile technique native to Peru. Do you suppose she's going to revive yet another lost craft for us? Let's hope so.

You may never revive a lost art or craft, or write a book about it, or appear on national television, but then again, you just might. Of all the successful people you've read about so far in this book, few ever imagined where their special interests and know-how would lead them. Teaching is just one more option open to a talented person who is interested in earning extra money, and the fact that it can be pursued either in or out of one's home makes it all the more appealing to some. While formal training is always helpful, it is seldom required in the field of arts and crafts where craftsmanship and experience are far more important. What is required, however, is the sincere desire to share your knowledge with others, and as a teacher you should certainly strive to carry on the great tradition of teaching that Albert Einstein so neatly summarized with this remark:

It is the supreme art of the teacher to awaken joy in creative expression and knowledge.

Do that, and you'll be a great teacher.

12

Publicity, Advertising And Promotional Materials

One evening, after a long day of writing, I decided to watch television for relaxation and tuned in on that great old classic, "A Star is Born," with James Mason and Judy Garland. With crafts still on my mind, it wasn't difficult to relate some of the lines in the movie to the crafts business, such as: "Star quality" is the "little something extra" one has; "Talent isn't enough," and, "A career can sometimes rest on a trifle."

"Star quality," as you can imagine, is that elusive "something extra" that makes entertainers like Judy Garland stand out from all other entertainers in the world. In order for you to stand out from all other artisans, you must have a little "star quality" of your own. But having that elusive "something extra" will not insure financial success; or, as James Mason put it so aptly, "Talent isn't enough."

There are many talented craftspeople in America who are creating work that literally sparkles with star quality, but few of them advertise their wares or seek free publicity. It's as though they believe there is some kind of magic telegraph that will transmit their message to the world and bring buyers to their door. These people have not yet learned how far a bit of advertising or free publicity can go. To them, it is merely a trifle not worth bothering about; yet, it could mean the difference between success and failure.

If your success in crafts is going to "rest on a trifle," at least make sure that trifle isn't a lack of publicity, because there's plenty to be had. Says Joan P. Acord, executive secretary of United Maine Craftsmen, "I think that if I could make one point to people beginning to sell their craft (assuming, of course, that they are technically competent) it would be to urge them to take advantage of the many kinds of publicity they can get free. Only a very small percentage of craftspeople, including many so-called professionals, realize the importance of this."

Joan is right. But where does one *find* all those golden opportunities for free publicity? Let's begin with newspapers.

Getting Newspaper Publicity

Since local newspapers are always in need of good news and feature stories to fill their pages, they can be a gold mine of free publicity for enterprising businesspeople. Study the various sections of the paper and determine which one is most appropriate for your particular news — the women's pages, travel, arts, entertainment, business, etc. Then send a news release to the editor of that particular section, or perhaps to someone who writes a regular column for that section of the paper.

EXAMPLE: For a long while, Marilyn Heise, editor of the *Working Craftsman,* wrote a weekly crafts column for the Sunday features section of

147

Free publicity is available to everyone. Use the media to your advantage whenever possible.

the *Chicago Sun-Times*. The purpose of her column was to inform and educate, and she was always looking for good material on, and photos of, craftspeople, new supplies, equipment, and services of interest to the public. Surely there are writers like Marilyn in thousands of cities all over the country, ready and waiting to hear from people like you, eager to give space to newsworthy items. Your job is to find them.

What kind of news is truly newsworthy? Some of the following topics might be of interest to an editor, and could even lead to a feature article on you if you come up with a well-written letter or press release:

- A special demonstration of your art or craft at an annual festival or fair

- A one-man or one-woman show of work at a local shop or gallery, or a special exhibit in a bank, library or shop window

- New classes you may be starting, or your availability to lecture on a topic of interest to women's clubs or civic organizations, etc.

- The activities of your local crafts guild, and your involvement with it

- The opening of your new shop or business

- The availability of some special service or unusual catalog free to the public

- An art or craft you do that is so old it's historically interesting, or so new that few people know about it yet

- A product you've created that is new or of special interest to a particular group of people — homemakers, sports fans, gardeners, collectors, etc.

- A new book, directory, or manual you may have written

- A new craft or hobby kit you've created, a new tool you've invented, or a new use for an old tool and how it relates to the work you do

- A major prize or award you've received

- The idea you just thought of that I forgot.

Okay. Now you know what you want to publicize. But you just can't say that you are opening a business, giving classes, or exhibiting in a show. You have to give the editor a reason for using your publicity, because giving you free advertising space is *not* his purpose. There must be something about your news that will compel the editor to pass it along to his readers. It might help if you could tie your news into the activities of a charitable organization, a benevolent group, a prominent local citizen, a particular season, or a national holiday. Or perhaps what you are doing is an indication of a new trend, or something no one else has done before. Maybe it reflects favorably on your community or benefits a certain group of people — children, working wives, senior citizens, etc.

Ask yourself what there is about your news that warrants attention, then emphasize these points in your press release. Put yourself in the editor's place and ask: "Why should I print this story?"

Preparing a Press Release

A press release, or news release as it is sometimes called, must immediately capture the editor's attention or it will be promptly filed in the wastebasket. Authors Claudia Jessup and Genie Chipps offer this good advice: "Keep your release *brief* and *concise*. In the first paragraph, include the who, what, where, when, and how. Stress your major points, and back them up with facts. Then pep up the release with colorful descriptions, and round it out with minor details."*

Remember that your release is not an advertisement, merely an announcement of news. Use simple English. Short sentences. Short paragraphs. Give no sales pitches, but do include all necessary facts and information. Type your release on plain white paper, size 8½ x 11 in. (or use your letterhead) and allow wide margins (1½ in.) on both sides. Double space it and keep it to one page if at all possible. In the upper left-hand corner, type

* From *The Woman's Guide To Starting a Business,* by Claudia Jessup and Genie Chipps © 1976 by Claudia Jessup and Genie Chipps. Used by permission of Holt, Rinehart and Winston.

your name, address, and telephone number. Down a few lines and over to the right, type the date, and just below it two lines, type "FOR IMMEDIATE RELEASE" (or give a specific date of release if this is important). Then, down a few more lines and in the center of the page, type your heading.

EXAMPLES:

NEW CRAFT SHOP OPENS
IN OAKDALE

CRAFTSWOMAN DISCOVERS
NEW USE FOR OLD TOOL

NEW CRAFT CLASSES
BENEFIT SENIOR CITIZENS

RUG HOOKING
TO BE DEMONSTRATED
AT ANNUAL FESTIVAL

The most important information should come at the beginning of your release since editors will usually cut from the bottom up if it is too long to use. Thus, your opening paragraph might be tailored after the following example, which illustrates the five W's of journalism:

A special demonstration of hand spinning (WHAT) will be presented by Sally Jones (WHO) at Ye Old Yarn Shoppe, 13 Oak Lane, Anytown (WHERE), on Saturday, August 24 from 10 a.m. to 6 p.m. (WHEN). The shop, which sells yarn, supplies, and equipment for fiber workers, hopes to create renewed interest in the art of spinning (WHY). Classes in both spinning and weaving will be offered this fall.

Now, if you want as much free publicity as possible, send your announcement to several papers. But if you are trying to get a feature article written, send the release and a special cover letter to a particular editor. In your letter explain (briefly) why you think the article would interest the paper's readers and give some colorful background information not included in the release. Indicate your willingness to supply additional information should it be of interest, and advise if you can write the article yourself. Enclose a photograph if you have a good one — an 8 x 10 or 5 x 7 glossy black and white print. (Snapshots or Polaroids are of no use to a newspaper.) Add cardboard to your envelope so the photograph won't

149

Ye Old Yarn Shoppe
13 Oak Street
Wilmette, IL 60091

(312) 723-4962

July 16, 1978

ART OF HANDSPINNING TO BE DEMONSTRATED LOCALLY

A special demonstration of hand spinning will be presented by Sally Jones at Ye Old Yarn Shoppe, 13 Oak Street, Wilmette, on Saturday, August 6, from 10 to 4.

The shop, which sells yarns, supplies, and equipment for fiber workers, expects the demonstration to create additional interest in the art of spinning, a craft that is now enjoyed by thousands of people throughout the country. Beginning and intermediate classes in both spinning and weaving will be offered by the shop this fall, and reservations for them can be made on Saturday, or by calling the shop prior to August 31.

Sally Jones, a local, professional craftswoman, has demonstrated the art of spinning at numerous festivals and shows throughout the country, and won several awards for the garments she has created from her handspun yarn. She will be teaching both the beginning and intermediate spinning classes at the shop this fall.

150

Sample of a typed press release, shown in reduced size. It was prepared on plain white paper, size 8½ x 11 in., but a letterhead could have been used in its place.

be bent in mailing, and also enclose a self-addressed, stamped envelope if you want it returned. Photographs are expensive, true; but they can often make the difference between a feature article and a brief announcement of your news.

How does free newspaper publicity compare with paid advertising in a newspaper? Marti Fleischer has an answer to that question. She is the owner of the Craft Cottage in Oak Ridge, Tennessee, a craft supply shop, and here's how she recalls her grand opening: "I had placed several ads in the paper before the date and a few people came by the first day. Early in the morning the store was bustling because I had arranged for the mayor to come for the ribbon-cutting ceremonies and all his dignitaries followed. Sales were pitiful, however.

"About this time the local newspaper decided to run a series on arts and crafts and gift shops in the area. (We have a Friday night tabloid section that features movies, TV, what's happening in town, etc.) Well, I couldn't believe it when I saw it — a photograph and feature story about my shop on page one — continued with two more pictures on another page. After that, sales really picked up. That's the kind of windfall you need and can't afford to pay advertising rates for."

Conclusion? "Publicity is still more valuable than advertising, especially if it carries a photograph," says Marti. "Most newspapers are willing to carry newsworthy stories as long as the shopowner doesn't make a habit of it."

The same goes for craftspeople. Only don't wait for a lucky bolt of publicity to streak down from the heavens as Marti did. Make your own luck and generate your own publicity by writing your own newsworthy announcement and sending it to the paper when you need publicity the most — at the *beginning* of any new endeavor.

Radio and Television Appearances

Although competition for air time is intense, there are opportunities for craftspeople to receive free publicity on radio or television shows, particularly local ones. Radio "talk" shows might like to interview the author of a new crafts book, or talk with anyone who has information and ideas their listeners could put to use. Children's television shows sometimes feature a craftsman who demonstrates a particular skill, and other morning and afternoon radio and television programs may have a host-guest format that features interesting personalities of one kind or another.

If you think you are doing something that could be discussed or demonstrated on radio or television, write or telephone the program director and explain why your appearance might interest listeners or viewers. Obviously, it is important to study the format of a show before trying to get on the air, and once on the air you would want to be able to speak or demonstrate your craft with confidence. Much of the advice already given in the chapter on lecturing could be applied to any radio or television appearance you might make.

Magazine Publicity

People who think of newspapers or radio first when trying to get free publicity, especially craftspeople, often tend to overlook the golden opportunities awaiting them in magazines. Prior to 1970 there were only a few publications being issued especially for needleworkers or craftspeople. Today there are dozens of them, as you can see from the resource chapter. A steadily growing number of magazines, newspapers, bulletins, newsletters, and directories are being published on a frequency that varies from monthly to annually. What you must remember is that each of these publications has an editor — a person who is always on the lookout for interesting articles, photographs, press releases, and informative letters from readers.

To reap the harvest of publicity available through magazines, however, you do have to read them, and be alert to the possibilities. The more you read, the "luckier" you will probably become, because you will "just happen" to discover interesting opportunities for free publicity each time you read a periodical. There isn't an editor alive who isn't looking for fresh and imaginative article material for his or her publication, and readers are often requested to send articles or at least contribute article ideas. Someone always seems to be starting another registry, writing another book, or compiling another directory. And most magazines have new products sections or special columns that mention or review new books, manuals, directories, catalogs, and brochures, as well as a page or two for letters from readers (which often include complete addresses). Let's go back now and discuss each of these possibilities in more detail.

Again, I must stress the importance of reading. If you are serious about making money from your crafts or needlework — or, at the very least, making a name for yourself in your field — you should be reading all publications relating to your field of interest, as well as one or more trade papers and several consumer magazines. Together, these publications will keep you abreast of what's happening in the world you're interested in, and alert you to new trends and the changing interests of consumers.

You may protest that there isn't time for this much reading, but I say you can always find time to read if you are hungry for information and ideas. If you can't afford to subscribe to everything you should be reading, check your library for copies of some of the publications. Or, if you have several friends with interests similar to yours, perhaps you could each buy one or two subscriptions, then pass the issues around. Beg or borrow them, but by all means read them. At the very least, buy samples of all publications that seem important to you, then subscribe to as many as you can afford. If you are making any money from your crafts, you cannot invest it more wisely than this. As one woman told me, "When cutting corners, I don't think it pays to make craft publications a victim. A good craft paper is an invaluable source of information."

Publicity through feature articles: Craft and needlework publications, unlike consumer magazines, have very little money (sometimes none) to pay for articles. Thus it is often difficult for an editor to find feature article material for each issue. As a former magazine editor, I probably appreciate this fact more than most people. For five years I had to dig up stories for *Artisan Crafts* magazine. Few people ever came to me asking to have a story written about them or their

craft, and, from corresponding with other editors, I find this is more often the rule than the exception. Perhaps most craftspeople are just too bashful to bring their work to the attention of an editor, or they are too busy, or perhaps they think that very little will actually come of such publicity anyway, particularly in a magazine of limited circulation.

Don't make this mistake yourself. If a publication has only a thousand readers — even a hundred — it's not too small when it means free publicity for you or your work. If only one reader responds to your article in a positive way, you can receive immeasurable benefit. For instance, once we did a story on a particular artisan, and another editor (from a major publication) picked up on the story. She did a feature on this person and thereby gave her national publicity of the kind she couldn't have purchased at any price. I'm sure this sort of thing happened far more than I know since only a few readers ever took the time to let me know what our publicity did for them.

Which brings up a point. When an editor does something nice for you, remember to say thanks. You might need that person again sometime.

If you are capable of writing an article about your craft, telling its history, describing your special technique, or exloring various other angles, you could certainly benefit from writing for one or more of the craft or needlework magazines. Since editors of various consumer magazines often read the craft and needlework journals to get inspiration for the craft and needlework sections of their own publications, your story could easily catch the eye of someone special and lead to additional exposure for you and your products (to say nothing of additional sales). If you can't write what you believe to be an acceptable magazine article, but do have a craft or technique that you feel would be of interest to an editor, simply write a detailed letter explaining this. Often, this is all that is required to get the publicity pendulum swinging your way.

Publicity through letters to the editor: Occasionally a letter to an editor will end up being quoted in his column, but usually it ends up in the letters section of the magazine. By reading various magazines, large and small alike, you will note that many people manage to get free publicity for themselves, their products, or their businesses, simply by writing an informative letter. Magazines such as *Creative Crafts* and *Decorating & Craft Ideas* often have several pages of such letters. Most provide an answer to a question posed by some reader in an earlier issue, and in some cases the editor will decide to include the sender's address, particularly when it is believed that it will benefit the magazine's readers.

The availability of "free plugs": Study the new products section of various magazines — craft and consumer alike — to see the type of item usually given space. Mostly it will be new tools, kits, unusual materials, or hard-to-find craft or needlework supplies. Handmade items are seldom featured unless they come in kit form or illustrate the use of specific materials that are for sale. Occasionally, however, a craftsperson can get free publicity by offering to send his catalog or brochure to interested readers. If you believe you have something to offer that is suitable for mention in a particular magazine, simply prepare a press release and send it to the editor. Your release will probably be considerably edited if and when it appears in any magazine, but this kind of mention, however small, is worth seeking since it draws a very good response from readers.

There's a method to this kind of madness, of course. The editor knows that if you receive a good response to your "free plug" (and you only get one of them), you'll be more likely to send a paid advertisement in the future. Note, however, that some consumer magazines seldom give free plugs. Editorial mentions are often given only to their advertisers.

Other Opportunities for Publicity

Directories: Directories offer a tremendous opportunity for publicity, but the only way to learn about them is to read craft marketing publications. Listings are often free because the people compiling the directory expect to make money from advertisers or from the sale of the directory itself. An example is *The Marietta College Crafts Directory,* published in 1976. It contains the names and addresses of 5000 artists and craftspeople, as well

as 1000 crafts organizations. At this writing, the first edition is still available, and Marietta College hopes to publish updated editions in the future. Catalogs such as *The Goodfellow Catalog of Wonderful Things* also fall into the category of directories offering free advertising to selected craftspeople who are listed without charge.

Registries: Several slide registries have been established recently, and I suspect this is a trend that will continue in the future as more people seek to bridge the gap between buyers and sellers of art work, crafts, and photography. Only professionals will benefit from inclusion in such registries, however, since they serve such users or buyers as government agencies, museum curators, educators, researchers, designers, dealers, architects, interior decorators, and others. EXAMPLES: The slide registry of the California Craft Museum, designed to function as a visual resource center for crafts in the West; the National Slide Registry of American Artists and Craftsmen in Washington, D.C., a bridge between artists and Washington-based federal agencies; and the slide library of North American Fiber Artists and Craftspeople, established by *Fiberarts*. If you are trying to reach the type of audience mentioned above, read art and craft periodicals to learn about other slide registries which may be started in the future.

Books: Hundreds of new craft books have been published in recent years, and thousands of craftspeople have had photographs of their work included in them. It has become common practice for craft writers to send news releases to art and craft editors when they begin a new book, because they are looking for information and photographs for inclusion. Watch for such announcements and follow up on them when you are producing the type of work that is needed by an author. Although you will receive no monetary gain from inclusion in such a book, it will do wonders for your ego.

Following Leads

Time out. I have a bit of advice to pass on concerning the subject of following up on leads

153

once you read about them. Let me illustrate my point with a brief story.

Recently my husband sent press releases to several craft magazines inviting contact from certain people. He was searching for demonstrating craftsmen with considerable product to sell, for possible participation in a large international crafts show he was producing at the time. His press release clearly stipulated that interested craftsmen were to send complete information about themselves and their craft, and enclose a photograph of their work if at all possible.

He received perhaps thirty letters. Most were hastily scribbled notes which simply said, "Send me more information about your show." Instead of sending Harry the information he had requested, they were asking him for more details. He didn't have any printed literature to send, nor the time to give a personal reply. (Or the desire to do so, considering that his needs had been made clear in the press release.) Two or three people sent exactly what had been requested, and one of them ended up in the show. She not only sold a considerable amount of her work, but also received a lot of free publicity as a result of being in the show.

Moral: When you come across an interesting opportunity, follow up on it with everything you've got. If a press release asks for complete information, send it. If it asks for a resume, be sure to send an account of your background and qualifications. If it says to send photographs, don't send slides, and vice versa. If it says "mail inquiries only," don't telephone. And so on. Although you may sometimes follow through with your best and receive nothing for your effort, at other times your professional approach — and compliance with instructions — will bring an opportunity right to your doorstep.

154

Advertising

If you have a product to advertise and sell by mail, your thoughts will probably turn immediately to a beautiful, big ad in a prestigious magazine. But that beautiful ad will cost a big price, and may not pay for itself in orders received. Before spending a lot of money on a display ad, you would be wise to explore your market by first placing several inexpensive classified ads. If you receive a good response from a classified ad, this may indicate that an even greater response might be received from a display ad in the same publication.

The primary difference between classified and display advertising, besides cost, is its appearance and placement in a publication. Display ads are scattered throughout the editorial pages of a publication, while classified ads are grouped in the back under various category headings. Often, a classified ad will pull better for you than a display ad for the simple reason that such ads are read by people who are looking for something in particular. If your ad happens to be there when someone happens to be looking for what you offer, you'll get a response from that person.

Placing a classified ad: It is important to demonstrate with words exactly how your proposition, or product, will benefit the reader. Since you are going to be charged for each word used in your ad (including your address), don't waste them. Be clear and concise. Use a telegraphic system of writing and omit unnecessary verbs and adjectives. Abbreviations are okay, as are incomplete sentences. Before sending your ad to a magazine, study all the ads in the classified pages to make sure your product fits in with the type of merchandise being advertised by others. Emulate the style of ads you think are best, and remember that magazine ads generally have to be placed two or three months before the month of publication.

When advertising in more than one publication at a time, you should "key" your ads in order to determine which one is bringing in the most inquiries. To key an ad means to write your address in a special way so you can tell by the way the envelope is addressed exactly which magazine prompted the response. EXAMPLES: When using your name, you might say "Mary Smith" in one ad, "M. Smith" in another, or "Mrs. J. Smith" in still another. Or, you might write "Box 281" in one address, and "P.O. Box 281" in another. Or add a department number, such as "Dept. M," or place initials after your business name, such as

"Artisan Crafts/CC." (NOTE: When changing your street address or post office box number, check with the post office beforehand to make sure this will not affect the delivery of your mail.)

Which publications should you consider for an ad? Check the resource chapter for the addresses of several publications that might be good for you, and if you can't find copies of these magazines on the newsstand, ask for a sample copy when you request advertising rates.

To find out whether classified ads for handcrafts and needlework actually bring in many orders, I selected half a dozen ads from as many magazines and wrote the advertisers, explaining my purpose. I offered each person a mention in this book in exchange for a little information. Surprisingly, only one person answered my letter, proving once again that most craftspeople do not follow up on opportunities for free publicity. Here's the ad I selected from *Aunt Jane's Sewing Circle:*

FOR SALE: Beautiful handmade quilts and other things. List, 25 cents.

That ad was placed by Mrs. Elbert Baker of Centerville, Tennessee, and when I wrote to her, I asked the following questions:

1. Do you often advertise your quilts for sale, and do your ads result in many orders?

2. Do you have difficulty selling your quilts?

3. Do you consider yourself a beginning, or experienced, seller?

4. Do you make quilts for the money, or just because you love to make them?

Mrs. Baker replied: 'I realized not long ago the difference between myself and a beginner (although I'm not a professional), when the beginner thought she would get an order from every price list she mailed. My ads result in my mailing several lists to all parts of the U.S.A. and some other countries. I usually average one order for each eight or ten lists mailed. Most are for quilts, and, except for one baby quilt that was the wrong color, I've never had to take any back. Most people locally make their own quilts, so most of mine

are sold by mail. So far, I've never gotten far enough ahead of demand to have any extra for craft shows. I make quilts and all other crafts because I love doing that type of work. For the last few years, I have advertised quilts and other things in several of the Tower Press magazines, and last year I made over $2000 as a result."

Note that Mrs. Baker says she averages one order for each eight or ten price lists mailed out. An order response of 10 percent is quite good for a price list mailing, but response might be even greater with a colorful brochure or catalog. Before advertising the availability of a free brochure or catalog, however, be sure to calculate the cost of each piece you will be mailing, and decide if you can afford to give it away. If a price list or brochure costs you 10 cents to print, and another 15 cents to mail (and postage keeps increasing, of course), every ten you mail will cost you $2.50. When this cost is measured against the dollar amount of any order you might expect to receive, you may decide (as Mrs. Baker apparently did) that it is unwise to offer advertising material free of charge. Some advertisers charge a nominal amount of 25 cents to 50 cents for price lists, brochures or catalogs, while others offer them free but ask instead for a stamp or addressed, stamped envelope (usually abbreviated in ads as "S.A.S.E." or simply "SASE"). Although both methods may tend to cut down the number of responses received from an ad, you may find you have simply eliminated a lot of "curiosity-seekers" who wouldn't have ordered anyway. Some people are natural born catalog collectors, and craftspeople, in particular, seem to enjoy sending away for anything that's free since it might give them a good idea they can use.

Display advertising: If you think a display ad will produce good results for you, remember that it isn't easy to write effective advertising copy. If you can't afford to hire an advertising copywriter, however, you'll have to do it yourself. Study many ads beforehand to learn style and techniques, and check your library for books on how to write effective copy.

In preparing a display ad, marketing expert Merle Dowd suggests you think of it as a small

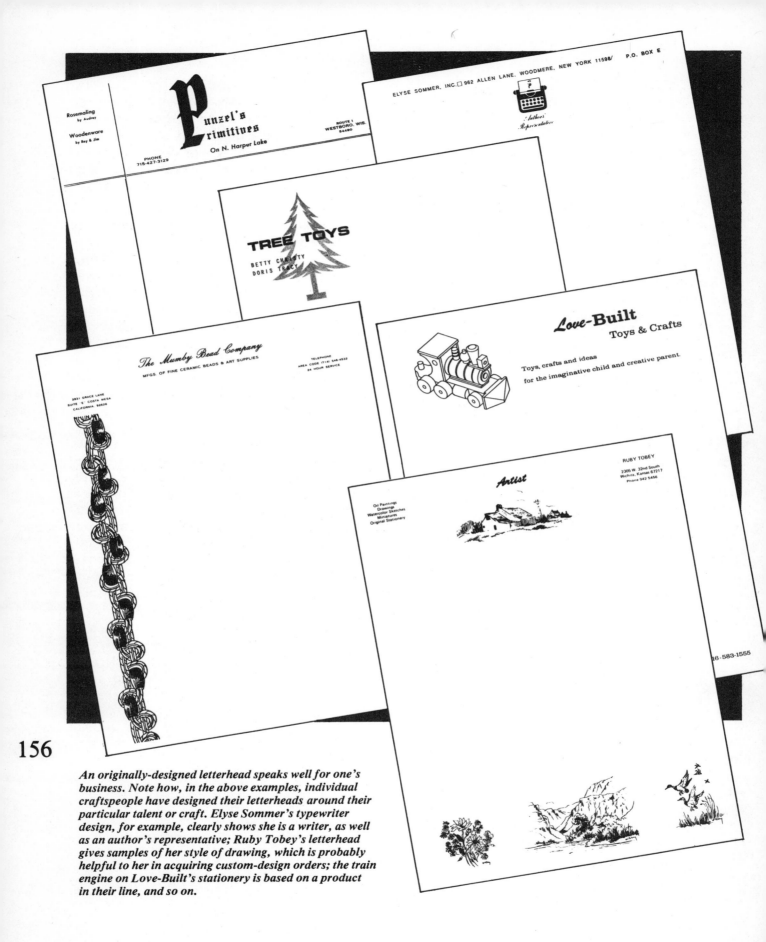

156

An originally-designed letterhead speaks well for one's business. Note how, in the above examples, individual craftspeople have designed their letterheads around their particular talent or craft. Elyse Sommer's typewriter design, for example, clearly shows she is a writer, as well as an author's representative; Ruby Tobey's letterhead gives samples of her style of drawing, which is probably helpful to her in acquiring custom-design orders; the train engine on Love-Built's stationery is based on a product in their line, and so on.

billboard. "While long-copy ads pull mail orders," he says, "you should aim for quick impact with small display ads. Include a benefit or a big promise in the headline along with your name if you can work it in. A reader must see your ad before he or she can react to your message." * Mr. Dowd also stresses the use of an eye-catching logo or symbol that will attract attention and build your identification from ad to ad. If you can write the copy for your ad, and plan its general layout, the magazine's advertising department can take it from there and do the necessary typesetting and "paste-up" for you. The charge for this is usually quite reasonable.

Good ad copy is necessary to pull orders, but even perfect ads won't pull if they are placed in the wrong publications. Once again I must advise you to study the ads in a number of magazines before deciding which is best for your product. In addition to exploring all the craft and needlework magazines, also study special interest journals such as *Early American Life,* and regional magazines such as *Yankee,* which often carry interesting ads for handcrafts. Your library will have other publications of possible interest to you.

If you decide to place more than one display ad at a time, be sure to "key" your ads accordingly. If an ad features a coupon, you can key it by simply placing a code number or letter somewhere on the coupon itself.

Free Advertising: If you can't afford much money for paid advertisements, do take advantage of all the opportunities for free publicity already discussed. And don't forget that word-of-mouth advertising is often the craftsman's best friend. Remember, too, the value of notices placed on public bulletin boards in grocery stores, laundromats, churches, colleges, etc. If you have something to sell, don't be bashful about putting up an eye-catching notice of your own.

The Promotional Materials You Need

In spite of the fact that advertising is an integral part of business, few craftspeople do much

* From *How To Earn More Money from Your Crafts,* by Merle E. Dowd. © 1976 by Merle E. Dowd and used with permission.

of it. Instead, they promote themselves and their work largely through the use of a good letterhead, calling card, brochure, or "hang tag" on their work. Since you will need one or more of these things to do business, a discussion of each follows, along with information on how to design them yourself and prepare your own camera-ready artwork for a printer. (NOTE: The need for price lists or handbills was discussed earlier.)

Letterheads: A well-designed letterhead is important to any business, and, because it says so much about the sender, it should be designed with care. Contrary to popular belief, it is not necessary to spend a small fortune to get quality stationery and envelopes, nor do these items have to be ordered in great quantity. Today there are many printers who offer quality printing from camera-ready copy and who will print as few as 100 copies of anything. "Instant printers" (those who use inexpensive paper masters) can sometimes give you a good printing job for less than $5 a hundred, with price breaks at higher quantity levels. If your artwork has a lot of solid black in it, however, the printer may suggest that you have a metal plate made to assure quality of printing throughout the entire run. This will add a few dollars to your printing bill, but it is well worth it. (NOTE: Although you can always order a minimum amount of stationery, envelopes must be purchased by the box. Number 10 envelopes, the ones used by most businesses, come 500 to a box. 9 x 12 in. envelopes come packaged 250 to a box.)

Calling Cards: An important tool for any seller, calling cards are readily available from any printer, or they can be ordered by mail from companies such as The Stationery House Inc. or Vermont Business Forms. Vermont Business Forms has done many cards for craftspeople, and it welcomes your inquiry and encourages the use of your own artwork which can be adapted for a card.

157

Brochures: Brochures, like stationery, can be designed by you and printed by any printer. If you keep them simple, print in one color only, and don't have a lot of complicated cuts or folds, cost can be kept to a minimum. But here's one word of advice from Audrey Punzel: "Don't put the price of your various items on the brochure itself. Instead, print that information as an insert. Retail shops may want to show customers what you offer, but don't want your prices showing. Also, when you have to change your prices you can save on the expense of a new brochure by just ordering a new price insert.'' Audrey points out that it doesn't make a customer happy to see old prices crossed out and new ones written in.

Hang tags: A hang tag not only adds a professional touch to your products, but is an important promotional tool as well since it carries your message home with the buyer. For this reason, many craftsmen consider hang tags an important form of publicity and advertising. They can be as easily designed and printed as stationery and calling cards. Once printed, you can punch holes in them and add the ties. (This might be far less expensive than purchasing them ready-made. You'll have to do some investigating here.)

A tag should carry information that indicates who made the item, how and why it was made, and, in some cases, how it should be cared for. What you put on your tag will depend on who you are and what you do. The weaver who spins and dyes her own wool would certainly want this fact mentioned on her tag. The potter who digs his own clay would use that as a selling point. The toymaker who uses lead-free paint, the needleworker who uses only the finest yarns, the rosemaler whose designs are completely authentic — all would use such information to their advantage on a tag. Anything that makes you or your work unique is information that belongs not only on a tag, but on other promotional materials as well. (Also see Chapter 15 for other tags required by law, particularly on items of clothing.)

Decorative stickers and labels: While not necessary, these always add a touch of professionalism to craft merchandise, and may be ordered in quantity for less than you might think. Bucher Brothers Company in Ohio, for example, offers ''Mini Stickers'' in gold and silver — 1000 for less than $20. They are listed in the resource chapter with others who can supply such items.

Photo stamps: Another item you might find useful for publicity or advertising purposes is the photo stamp, available from Miles Kimball Company, Oshkosh, Wisconsin. If you have a good black and white (or colored) snapshot of you or certain objects you want to sell, this company will reproduce your photograph on a sheet of gummed stamps that can be used in many different ways. Sizes range from ¾ x 1 in. to 1 x 1½ in., and prices are most reasonable. Your photo will be returned undamaged with your order. This company will send you its catalog on request. (NOTE: When sending colored snapshots for reproduction as black and white stamps, be advised that red, to the eye of the camera, is the same as black, and light blue will show up as white.)

Designing Promotional Materials

When trying to design your own letterhead, brochure, calling card, etc., never use a design or picture you have clipped from a magazine or newspaper because it may be protected by copyright. If you cannot draw, you might create unusual artwork by using ideas found in the *Dover Pictorial Archive* books (which, as you will recall from Chapter 4, are a source for thousands of copyright-free designs and patterns). A drawing or design can be used in conjunction with typesetting ordered from a printer, or transfer lettering that you can easily do yourself.

''Transfer lettering,'' a product available in art stores, is a transparent sheet that has specially printed, pressure-sensitive letters on the back. You simply place the sheet so that a letter is positioned where you want it, then rub the letter with a rubbing stick to transfer it to your ''mechanical,'' the piece of artwork you will give to your printer. If your final artwork is too large or too small, it can easily be reduced or enlarged by the printer to fit the size stationery and envelopes you wish to use.

When designing a letterhead or brochure, keep in mind that standard sizes will be less expensive than special sizes. Every cut or fold the printer has to make will cost you extra. It is always wise to check on the size and availability of certain papers and card stocks before spending hours on a design for a certain piece of printing.

If you don't feel you can prepare your own artwork, perhaps an artist friend can design it for you, using your original ideas as a guideline. If

Scherenschnitte
by
ARLENE FRANCE

BY APPOINTMENT
345 N. BROAD ST.   LITITZ, PA. 17543

THE VILLAGE SMITHY

204 Hulbert Hollow Road
Spencer, NY 14883

(607) 589-6166

A. Atkins

MINIATURE
Things wrought of iron
by forge, hammer,
and anvil

The Patchwork Company

1211 Wilmette Avenue
Wilmette, Illinois 60091
(312) 256-5335

QUILTING SUPPLIES
AND CLASSES
HANDMADE GIFTS
AND QUILTS

HOURS: MON. - SAT.
10 - 4

Evelyn Mendes   Maryan Bagg

Bill Reed Woodcarver

Mineral Wells
West Virginia

Phone:
304-422-6288

• TESTIMONIALS • CERTIFICATES • SCROLLS •

George W. St. Georges
Calligraphy • Lettering
Engraving • Illuminating

MEMORABLE WRITINGS

◆ 7 Victoria Lane, South Hadley, Mass. 01075

• LETTERHEADS • INVITATIONS • LOGOTYPES •

PLATYPUS
Box 396
Planetarium Station
New York, N. Y. 10024

Many craftspeople design their own calling cards today, and here are several examples from the author's collection (shown in slightly reduced size). Interesting effects can be achieved by the use of colored ink or card stock, and cards can be any size or shape desired. The card for Ayn's Shuttle Shop, for example, is a rectangular card folded in half. On the side you do not see, Ayn has listed the various items she weaves for her shop.

Ayn's Shuttle Shop
Box 1207
Oak Bluffs, Mass.
02557

Wesley House Waterfront

SHOP HOURS - MON. thru SAT.
9:30 A.M. to 9:00 P.M.

159

you don't have a cooperative friend, you might write to George W. St. Georges, who specializes in calligraphy, or Alice Bidwell, who did many of the illustrations in this book. (See "Special Services" in the resource chapter). George and Alice enjoy working with craftspeople and, because of their skill and experience, can work from the sketchiest of ideas. Send a letter indicating your needs, and ask for an estimate on the job you would like done. Read ads in craft journals for the names of other artists who offer similar services.

Preparing Camera-Ready Artwork For a Printer

The most important thing to remember when preparing camera-ready artwork is that the final print job will be only as good as your artwork, or "copy." The printer will photograph that copy to make a plate, or "master," and anything your eyes can see, the camera lens will also see — only better. Therefore, remove all smudges and excesses of glue, and cover up unwanted lines or errors with a "white-out" solution available in office supply stores. Many pieces of paper can be pasted on a sheet of white paper or poster board (use rubber cement for best results) and the edges of these papers will all disappear into the background if they are white and thin enough not to cast a shadow when a light is shined on it. (If you can see a shadow, so can the camera, and this would show up on your printing as a dark line.)

For best results, your artwork should be black on white paper, regardless of the color you want printed, and, unless you understand how to use a reduction/enlargement scale, your artwork should also be the same size as you want your finished copy to be. You can work with colored materials, of course, but don't forget that red to the camera is the same as black; red letters on a black background would reproduce as a solid black mass. Light blue or yellow will not show up at all, which is good, because it means you can use a light blue or yellow pencil to make the necessary guidelines on your artwork, and they do not have to be erased or covered up before sending it to the printer. India ink is not required for artwork; you can achieve excellent results using a fine point black felt tip pen or Rolling Writer (a new kind of pen with a liquid ball point that gives an even line when writing).

To save money on typesetting, use the transfer lettering sheets mentioned earlier, or just use a typewriter. Excellent results can be obtained with a typewriter that has a carbon ribbon, such as an IBM. If you must use a regular typewriter and cloth ribbon, however, be sure your ribbon is new and your type bars are perfectly clean.

It is always wise to get quotes from more than one printer when you need to have something printed, and you should ask to see samples of the printer's work. Also ask for prices on different quantities since the difference in price between 100 copies and 500, for example, may be negligible. (An even better price will usually be obtained at the 1000 mark.)

If you do not live near a printer, you can easily do business with one by mail. One I can recommend very highly is the Fay Printing Center in Springfield, Missouri. This company printed our quarterly magazine and all other materials for several years, and their work is of excellent quality. Although they do not have a brochure to send to interested customers, Alice Clark at this company said she would be happy to send any of my readers their "instant printing" price list, or give a quotation on special printing needs. If you will give Alice a clear idea of what you want, specify quantity desired, and indicate any price limitations you might have, she will suggest the kind of paper or stock to use and tell you just what you must send her in order for her to take care of your order.

If you would like additional tips and guidelines on preparing camera-ready copy and working with a printer, send for a copy of the reprint, "Printing for the Craftsman," which is available from *Artisan Crafts*.

13

Writing And Self-Publishing

"If you are creative enough to produce original craft projects that others would like to copy, and if you are well enough organized verbally to write technical procedures in a lucid, detailed manner, then perhaps you should consider writing craft articles," says Sybil Harp, editor of *Creative Crafts* magazine. "If you've worked in one medium and have developed a number of ideas and techniques in that medium, you may even be able to write a book. While there is only a handful of people in the craft field who have made a full living from writing articles and books, many have found it an excellent way to supplement their incomes while enjoying the special prestige that comes from being a published author."

There is no one I know better qualified to give advice to aspiring craft writers than Sybil Harp, who has helped foster the writing careers of many craftspeople since *Creative Crafts* began. Pat Virch is one of those people. (You will recall reading about her in Chapter 11.) When she was just getting started in rosemaling, she sent a letter to *Creative Crafts* describing her work and received a reply from Sybil, who asked for an article on the subject. When Pat said she didn't know how to write a magazine article, Sybil sent back a letter of encouragement, as she has done with so many other craftspeople since that day. Pat followed her lead and, emulating the style of other

articles in the magazine, wrote an excellent two-part article that led directly to her first book on rosemaling.

Advice for Beginning Craft Writers

Always one to give help and advice when needed, Sybil responded warmly to my request for information, and offered the following guidelines for would-be craft writers: "There are certain characteristics required of craft writers. Being a good craftsman is not enough, and simply being a good writer is never enough. Both abilities are required. This does not mean that one must be a highly polished, professional writer; it simply means that the ability to express oneself verbally is essential to the writing of a craft article or book.

"While this may seem self-evident, it is surprising how many proficient craftsmen lack this ability. My own explanation for this is that craftsmen are basically visual people who conceive ideas visually and who learn techniques with their eyes and their hands, rather than through words as verbally-oriented people do. Craftsmen who are highly visual may be able to master a technique and teach it to others through demonstration, but when they have to explain a process verbally, they often are at a loss. Frequently, too, craftsmen who are very adept will assume knowledge on the part

161

of the reader that simply isn't there, and as a result will leave great gaps in writing instructions.

"By the same token, writers unfamiliar with crafts will often assume that writing up a crafts project is the same as reporting on anything else. The truth is that very seldom is a noncraftsman able to capture enough of the feel of a technique to write good, usable instructions. Usually articles prepared by professional writers who are not craftsmen are much too sketchy in the instructions and tend to have overtones of the personality profile. Noncraftsmen writers fail to understand that the readers of craft magazines and books are looking primarily for ideas and for detailed technical information."

Ideas and detailed technical information. That's what all craft magazine editors want. And note that "detailed" does not mean "wordy." Editors have to wade daily through what they call their "slush pile" of manuscripts, and wordy articles on overworked craft topics won't interest them. Clearly and concisely written articles, however, are going to excite them a lot, particularly when the writer is explaining new craft techniques and offering well-designed items readers will enjoy making. When such articles are accompanied by sharply focused photographs or crisp line drawings, it can really make an editor's day.

Beginning writers often prepare an article and send it to an editor without first studying the magazine to see if such articles are even being published. Others will take the time to study the contents of several issues before querying the editor to find out if there is some interest in their idea. Unknown writers are usually asked to write articles "on speculation," which means there is no obligation on the editor's part to buy unless the finished article meets with his approval. The craftsperson with good ideas and the ability to explain techniques clearly will have few problems here, however, since his articles will probably be accepted with gratitude — and nice checks.

If you have decided to try your hand at writing how-to craft articles for magazines, here's what you should do before you start writing: Obtain and read copies of several different craft magazines to gain a basic understanding of the kind of articles needed by each editor, and the type of audience served by each magazine. Sybil Harp is just one craft editor who will be interested in hearing from competent writer-craftsmen. You met several others in an earlier chapter when I discussed the sale of original designs to magazines.

In addition to magazines specializing in crafts or needlework, you might explore a few consumer publications as well, since many are currently seeking craft articles. (You can study this market thoroughly by obtaining a copy of *Writer's Market,* an annual directory published by Writer's Digest. It lists the editorial needs of hundreds of magazine editors and is the "bible" of all serious writers.)

Regardless of whether you are writing how-to articles for a craft magazine or a consumer publication, do not assume knowledge on the part of the reader. People only use how-to-do-it instructions because they want to make the item described. If they already knew how to do your craft project, they wouldn't need you to tell them how, so don't let them down by omitting any step in the process, no matter how simple it seems to you as a skilled craftsperson. Beginners in crafts can become confused very easily, and they need to be led step-by-step through the complete process.

Perhaps the biggest hurdle you will have to overcome as a crafts writer is the need for photographs or line drawings. How-to articles must be illustrated, and it will probably prove too expensive to hire someone to take pictures or do line drawings for you. If you plan to do a lot of writing, you ought to think about buying a good camera and learning how to use it correctly. The more you can do for yourself, the more money you can make as a crafts writer.

Loretta Holz, long-time contributor to *Creative Crafts* and author of *How To Sell Your Arts and Crafts,* agrees: "Develop as many talents as possible," she suggests. "That is, learn not only how to do crafts, but how to do them creatively. Learn to take good black-and-white photographs and color slides, and if possible, learn to develop and print them yourself. Learn to do clear line drawings, and very important, learn to type. The more you can do for yourself, the better."

162

Writing a Crafts Book

Some craftspeople drift into writing as naturally as a duck takes to water. Once they have established themselves as craft writers and learned the ins and outs of writing instructions, taking photographs, doing drawings, etc., they may go on to write a book. That's exactly what happened to Loretta. But her kind of success doesn't happen overnight. As she points out, "It takes time to develop competence in doing all of these tasks, but it's all part of being a competent crafts writer."

It takes effort to become a good writer, and, according to Dona Meilach, "There is only one way to have written a craft book: with difficulty, determination, and slavish attention to detail. If you are willing to expend this effort, your toes may begin to curl over the threshold of the publishing world."* Dona, author of more than 35 craft books, gained experience as a writer by doing children's books, writing for magazines, and teaching writing classes. By the early 60's she and a friend became interested in doing a book on collage since none existed at the time, and after that

book was published, her pen never seemed to stop.

Those who are seriously interested in writing and self-publishing will find the book, *Career Opportunities in Crafts,* inspiring reading. It explores the opportunities in all fields of crafts and includes an interesting chapter on crafts publishing that gives specifics on how to write for periodicals and deal with book publishers, what to expect in the way of contracts and royalties, etc. It is here that author Elyse Sommer stresses the importance of the five "C's" when writing. Be *correct, constructive, clear, concise,* and *compelling,* she says. "A gift for turning a clever phrase certainly won't hurt a crafts book, but the real must ingredient is not extraordinary writing talent but enthusiasm for and knowledge of your subject and the ability to organize material into a cohesive and easily comprehensible whole." *

Elyse did not start out to be a crafts writer, but journalism has always been her vocational interest. She worked her way though college by writing confession stories, and her first published book was an anthology called *Childbirth.* Her first

* From the article, "So You Want To Write A Craft Book," in the *Goodfellow Catalog of Wonderful Things.* © 1977 by Christopher Weills.

* From *Career Opportunities in Crafts* by Elyse Sommer. © 1977 by Elyse Sommer. Used by permission of Crown Publishers, Inc.

163

craft book, on decoupage, began as a series of articles for *Creative Crafts,* and the response from readers was so good she prepared a book outline and presented the idea to a publisher. Several books followed thereafter.

While Elyse does not plan to give up her work as an author and author's agent in the commercial or trade book world, she has recently launched into her own self-publishing venture. *The Annotated Directory of Self-Published Textile Books* contains some 40 collector-oriented reviews, designed to promote these ventures in this as-yet-untapped market. To provide others with the basics involved in this and other self-published efforts, she has also published a very concise little history of *The Making of the Annotated Directory.* Since both self-published and commercially published books are very much dependent on the author's ability and willingness to sell and distribute as well as write them, any of Elyse's books can be ordered directly from her. In fact, most authors promote and sell their own books, as you will note from the resource chapter.

Craftsmen who teach or lecture often find that a book is the most natural thing in the world for them to do. Remember Joyce Ronald Smith, teacher of taaniko, and Margo Daws Pontius, cornshuckery artisan (Chapter 11)? Both illustrate my point. Recently Margo wrote to tell me she had just written her first book, titled *American Cornshuckery in Action.* Because she has already written several articles on her craft, a book was simply the logical thing to do at this point. (Incidentally, Margo's children wanted her to title her book "What My Mother Does in the Cornfield," but she decided making the best seller's list wasn't all that important.)

164 Roberta Raffelli of La Canada, California, explains how books can evolve as a result of doing craft work: "I have been interested in and participated in crafts since I was in high school," Roberta writes, "but it was not until the late 1950's that I decided I would like to do something with crafts for profit. I have always liked to do different things in crafts, be creative — not just do what someone else is doing — so I started working on a line of animals made from styrofoam,

chenille bumps, and chenille stems. I made a whole line, including a pink elephant, camels, cats, poodles, rabbits, etc., and then did my first book for Hazel Pearson Handicrafts (book division now Craft Course Publishers). After this there were several more how-to books for them, such as *Magic with Tin Cans,* a book using craft sticks, and a couple on decoupage. Next I designed a nativity scene with large draped figures. These figures were unique inasmuch as they had ceramic heads, hands, and feet, for which I had molds made. I then traveled the country for about a year teaching these figures at ceramic shops as a representative of Fiesta Colors."

Roberta, who went on to teach 18th Century decoupage and later wrote a book on Early American crafts, says the only way to get started in this business is "to love it enough to sacrifice for it. You must get acquainted with people in the business, swap ideas about what you are doing, and follow up on every lead that comes along and looks interesting to you. It's your perseverance as well as your talent that leads you to success."

Getting Your Book Published

Finding a publisher for a crafts book may require great patience. Some authors submit proposals or complete manuscripts to more than a dozen publishers before they find one who wants it. A friend of mine recently wrote saying her book has already been sent to seven publishers, and so far, no interest. In cases like this, it would be difficult not to get discouraged, but one must remember that a publisher's refusal to take on a book often has nothing to do with how good or bad it is. More likely, it is simply because it isn't the kind of book the publisher is looking for right now. An incredible number of craft titles have been released in recent years and publishers are much more selective now than they were a few years ago.

Of course, publishers have been known to make bad judgments from time to time, as Dr. Seymour Isenberg can tell you. When he and his wife, Anita, wrote their first book, *How To Work in Stained Glass* (Chilton), it got turned down by about twenty publishers, all of whom claimed there wouldn't be enough interest in the subject. "And now," says Dr. Isenberg, "the book has taken on a life of its own and become a real classic. When we were at the last Stained Glass Association meeting, many of the younger members told us they owed it all to our book." Humorously, he added, "I don't know if they were being complimentary or querulous, however."

The Isenbergs, who have written two other books on stained glass in recent years, also run the Stained Glass Club and publish a magazine called *Glass Workshop.* A friendly and informal publication, it is issued "four times a year at erratic intervals," according to the good doctor, who always serves his lessons in the art of stained glass with a generous dollop of humor.

How can you find publishers most likely to be interested in your book? Study other books similar to yours and note who has published them. Large companies such as Chilton Book Company, Van Nostrand Reinhold, Charles Scribner's Sons, Watson Guptil, and Simon and Schuster are among those who have published many craft titles in recent years. But only the most professional manuscripts will be of interest to big publishers like these whose first question is apt to be: What does your book offer that is not already available in other books we have published?

How do you find out what books have already been published by a certain publisher? The resource chapter of this book lists the names and addresses of several well-known publishers, most of whom offer book catalogs. A study of them will tell you a lot about what they might be interested in publishing. If you cannot get a catalog, you can learn more about the needs of publishers by studying the *Writer's Market* directory, whose listings on all major book publishers explain the type of books handled by each and the kind of work currently of interest to them. Information about publishers will also be found in the *Literary Market Place,* a directory available in libraries.

You don't have to write a whole book before you start looking for a publisher, by the way. In fact, it's better to find a publisher first and write later. To get a publisher's attention, however, you will have to present a good proposal that includes:

1. A table of contents and an outline of the entire book, with a brief description of the contents of each chapter.

2. One or two sample chapters that illustrate your writing ability, the scope of your knowledge on the subject, and the overall feel of the finished book.

3. A few examples of the types of photographs, drawings, or artwork you will use to illustrate the book.

4. A time schedule indicating when you would plan to deliver the finished manuscript.

5. Information about your background and credits as a writer/craftsman.

6. A few reasons why you think your book is needed, who would be most apt to buy it, and why — in other words, a sales pitch. If you are prepared to help market your book through lecturing, teaching, writing for craft magazines, etc., be sure to mention it. Publishers are interested in making money on the books they publish and if you can help promote or sell your own book, this could be a deciding factor in their decision to publish or not.

Specific information on submitting manuscripts to publishers can be found in books about writing available in your library. Basically, manuscripts should be typed on one side of a page only, double spaced, with wide margins on sides, top, and bottom. Pages should be numbered consecutively throughout the entire manuscript and never stapled together. The original copy should be mailed (flat) to the attention of the publisher's Craft Book Editor, and you should retain a carbon copy for yourself. Include with your manuscript a stamped, self-addressed envelope or sufficient postage for its return.

Unknown or inexperienced writers may stand a better chance of being published by someone like Craft Course Publishers, whose emphasis is on inexpensive 8½ x 11 in. paperbacks that are distributed nationally through hobby and craft shops,

165

rather than book stores. These books, usually 24 pages in length, are how-to manuals, printed in color and illustrated with many photographs or drawings. In a letter, Richard A. Merton, vice president of this company said, "We always encourage people to contact us if they have either a single project or a complete manuscript on a certain type of craft. It facilitates our decision if they include a photo, several samples, and instructions for the particular projects that they send." (This company does not work on a royalty basis, but purchases the right to publish the instructions, photos, or projects that are submitted to them.)

Several craftspeople have been published by Mangelsen and Sons, Inc., which also encourages contact from artists and craftspeople who have good ideas for books. Like Craft Course Publishers, this company's books are sold in hobby and craft shops throughout the country and they are printed in a similar format and price range. According to Mike Jeffries, publications manager, Mangelsen's is also interested in purchasing individual craft ideas for publication as a craft card. He says the best method for submitting manuscripts or ideas is an outline form along with either completed samples or color photos. This company offers interested readers a sheet entitled "Are Your Ideas Lyin' Idle" that gives more information on crafts of interest to Mangelsen's and also tells how to submit a manuscript to their attention. Mangelsen purchases manuscripts on both a royalty and a downpayment basis, based on the value of the book to them and the amount of work that has gone into the manuscript. Says Mr. Jeffries, "Our downpayment and royalties paid are the highest in the craft industry. We currently have over 75 book titles and are very interested in any new, exciting book manuscripts on almost any craft idea."

Mr. Jeffries noted that two of their most popular titles last year sold over 100,000 copies, and that the emphasis now is away from macrame books and into areas such as weaving and new ideas in established craft lines.

All authors dream of writing a best-selling book, even craft writers like me. But it is unrealistic to dream of getting rich from the sale of one book, or even a dozen. Books make money, sure, but few writers ever get rich from them. As one author told me. "You ask if authors make money? The ones we hear about make a great deal of it, but I would hate to have to depend on writing for a living. I'm making money at this point, but not enough to support myself, much less a family. Still — I wouldn't do anything else. Money only has to do with writing when you need it to eat or buy some clothes, as far as I'm concerned."

What could you reasonably expect in the way of payment for a craft book? It may vary from as little as $500 for the outright purchase of a book idea to several thousand dollars in royalties over a period of many years. Royalties may vary from 5 to 10 percent depending on the publisher and the type of books released each year, but generally, 10 percent of the book's retail price is paid to the author as a royalty on hard-cover copies; 7½ percent on paperbacks. Some craft books released by major publishers sell fewer than 5000 copies while others achieve sales of 100,000 or more.

Something many craft authors complain about is the fact that their publishers do not continue to promote their books after the first year or so. Understandably, publishers will always have new books to promote, and they cannot continue to wage a sales campaign forever on every book they release. For this reason, it is sometimes more profitable to work with a publisher who specializes in mail-order book selling, or at least one who will be willing to advertise and promote your book for several years to come.

Or, you might think about publishing your own book. It really isn't that difficult.

Publishing Your Own Book

I know dozens of craftspeople who have become publishers in recent years, and the exciting variety of publications they've issued boggles the mind. Everything from little booklets, patterns, designs, and calendars, to newsletters, magazines, directories, and books have been published by individuals with no previous experience in this field. Some craftspeople become publishers because they can't find anyone interested in their book, but others simply enjoy the challenge of doing everything themselves and like the idea of getting all the profit.

The book you publish yourself may not get into bookstores, but if it is one that appeals to craft shop owners or lends itself to mail-order selling, it could continue to yield a good profit for you for many years to come. And if you happen to teach or lecture, just think of all the extra sales you might make.

When Pat Virch wrote her first book, *Traditional Rosemaling*, she decided to publish it herself, and found a good printer who put it all together for her. She had 2500 copies printed, and her husband loaned her $5000 to pay for the printing and advertising. Fifty pages in length, the book was advertised for $3 and sold out within six months. "I had enough money then to pay for another printing," she recalls, "so we got brave and printed 5000 copies this time. Believe it or not, that second printing sold in less than a year and we went on from there and have been reprinting the book ever since. At last count we had sold more than 30,000 copies."

In 1976, Pat wrote a second book on rosemaling, and followed it up in 1977 with a third one titled *Decorative Tinware*. She figures she spends around $3000 a year on advertising, and sells about half her books at retail, with the rest being wholesaled to shops. She admits it was a little frightening at first when she realized she had to promote her own book, but she met the challenge just as she did when she was faced with the problem of learning how to teach.

Before you get the idea that publishing and selling your own book is as easy as I've just made it sound, let me point out that self-publishing has its pitfalls and problems like everything else. As with selling handcrafts, having the best product is useless unless you also have a market for it, so the most important question to consider before trying to publish your own book is: Will it sell? Do you really have something of interest to write about, and are there people who will want to buy your book? (You will have to do some market research to find out. Refer back to Chapter 2.)

Assuming you have answered yes to both questions, then it's time to think about what it will cost to publish your own book. Since its cost will be directly related to the number of pages and copies you will have printed, you have to sit down and do some figuring and planning. First, determine the size of your book. Will it be a mini-booklet, something a little larger, or an 8½ x 11 in. paperback? Paper can be cut to any size, of course, but it will always be less expensive to use stock sizes, such as 8½ x 11 in. or 11 x 17 in. sheets (which would fold to an 8½ x 11 in. book). Actual sizes would be a bit less than this, of course, since the printer would trim the edges after the books were put together.

Once you have determined the size of your book, get some paper in the proper size and make a "dummy" book, numbering the pages and planning what you might put on each page. For example, imagine a 12-page booklet, plus cover, printed to size 5½ x 8½ in. Take four sheets of paper size 8½ x 11 in., fold them in half, and put them together in book form. The outside sheet would be your cover (and you will need to talk to your printer about "cover stock" — something a bit heavier than what will be used in the inside of your book). Then, number the remaining three sheets (now folded in half) pages one through twelve. Now open up the pages and flatten them out and note how the numbers lay: Pages 1 and 12 are on the same sheet of paper with pages 2 and 11 on the back. Pages 3 and 10 are together, with pages 4 and 9 on the back; 5 and 8 are together, with 6 and 7 on the back. You'll soon understand the importance of this page sequence.

The book you publish yourself does not have to be a drab job in black and white. Paper comes in many interesting colors, and the addition of even one color to your book would add considerably to its appeal if this is important to its sale. Black ink on white paper is the least expensive, of course, but brown ink on ivory stock, for example, might cost only a little extra. (Discuss the possibilities with your printer.) You can also print black ink on white paper and have another color on a few pages throughout the book. This would involve additionl negatives, plates, and another run through the press for each page with color,

167

which will add to your printing costs, but it may also add to your eventual profit if books are to be sold through bookstores or craft shops. Color adds life and helps sell a product.

Now, back to your dummy book and the way the pages are numbered. In order to save money on your printing bill, you should try to place photographs and color on the same sheets of paper, since this will mean that fewer negatives, plates, and printing runs would be required. That is, plan to have photographs and your extra color on any two pages that are on the same sheet of paper in your dummy book. Always prepare a dummy book for anything you plan to print, and when you take your finished camera-ready copy to the printer, present it to him in the same way. (Type on one side only, and paper clip the pages together.)

The least expensive method of putting a book together is to have it "saddle stitched" or stapled, and this can be done even for thick books of 80 pages or more. Spiral-bound books are especially nice for certain types of books that may be used as reference guides since they will lie flat when opened, but this adds considerably to your costs. Even more expensive is the "perfect bound" method, where pages are glued to a flat spine.

Remember that there will always be an initial charge for plates and negatives, which will be the same regardless of how many books you print. Sometimes the difference between printing 1000 and 2500 copies of a book (or anything else, for that matter) will be surprisingly small for this reason. Be sure to get printing estimates for several quantities before deciding how many to print, and keep in mind that it may be wise to pay a little more for your first printing and see if the book is going to sell, rather than to try to save money by printing an extra thousand copies you may have to store under the bed for years. Be sure to tell the printer to save the negatives, since they can be used again if you decide to reprint. (In fact, it might be best to take them with you, since many printers will automatically destroy them after a period of one year.)

You can save a lot of money by putting your own camera-ready copy together, and you've already read about how to do this in an earlier chapter. Typesetting is *not* necessary in a *self-published book*. It may seem more professional to you, but since you are likely to be selling your book by mail in the first place, no one is going to know whether it is typeset or typed unless you tell them, and they aren't going to care one way or the other so long as the book contains the information they want to receive. Rent an IBM typewriter or hire a typist to prepare your manuscript for a printer. It will be much less expensive.

Naturally you will want to copyright your book, and this was discussed in an earlier chapter. Simply write the Copyright Office and request a copyright claim form for a book (Class TX). Place the proper copyright notice on your work before it is printed; then when it is finished, complete the form, enclose your check, and send two copies of the book to the Copyright Office. That's all there is to it. Later you will receive a copy of the form, stamped with the official seal of the Copyright Office.

Promoting and Selling Your Book

Here are some tips on how to let the world know you've published something worth reading:

1. Prepare a press release and send it, along with a review copy of your book, to every magazine that carries reviews on books similar to yours. The resource section of this book includes a fine list of publications to consider. Not everyone will review your book, but many will, especially the craft journals.

2. If your book is one that craft or hobby shops might like to carry, be sure to send a review copy to the journals serving such shops, and advertise it as well in magazines such as *Profitable Craft Merchandising,* which is read by the majority of craft retailers throughout the country. Remember that you will have to give retailers a discount of from 30 to 50 percent off the cover price of your book.

3. The largest book wholesaler in the world, Baker and Taylor Company, might be interested in your book. They publish a

168

monthly Journal for Academic Libraries, and each issue contains a bibliographic listing of recently published titles. Write them for additional information.

4. It would be wise to investigate the advantages of membership in COSMEP, the Committee of Small Magazine Editors and Publishers, since they publish a very helpful newsletter. Through COSMEP you would be able to obtain lists of distribution outlets; libraries, book reviewers, and others interested in reviewing releases; plus helpful booklets for publishers.

5. I'm sure you already know you will have to advertise, advertise, advertise! Read the publicity and advertising chapter again for additional ideas.

Getting your book distributed can be difficult, but I picked up a few good tips on this topic from Dianne Dolowich, one of the three women who compiled and published *The CraftsPeople Directory — 1978,* which was discussed earlier. "We got distribution in several ways," Dianne explained. "We began by calling and sending sample copies to the bookstores that were most important to us. Also the New York Public Library. Persistence and a willingness to bargain are important here. Kroch's and Brentano's turned us down originally because the book has no spine, but they now carry it in seven of their outlets."

Dianne said the process of distribution eventually became very taxing, so they turned the job over to a major distributor in their area, although they continue to send fliers and stop in at bookstores to push the book. "Distributors take a big chunk of the price," she warns, "but they do some advertising and pushing for you. Any bookstore owner will tell you the major distributors in your area, and there is a yearly publication that lists all the bookstores in the country, their specialties, buyers' names, etc."

Periodical Publishing

I've been talking only about book publishing up till now, but I wonder if you're aware of the fact that individual craftspeople are behind many of the fine craft and needlework periodicals being published today? It would be hard to guess, considering the professional quality of most of these publications, and I thought you might enjoy having a peek behind the scenes of one of these journals, *Interweave,* a quarterly weaving magazine published by homemaker Linda Ligon of Loveland, Colorado. If you are thinking about starting a "little newsletter" or a quarterly craft or needlework publication of any kind, the following story will be enlightening, to say the least.

"It's been over two years now since I started the magazine (laying groundwork, that is) and my feelings are overwhelmingly positive," says Linda, whose idea of doing the magazine grew out of her need to have a challenging job at home. She was also dissatisfied with the periodical literature available for weavers at the time. "I started it when I found myself at home with a new baby (my other kids were 6 and 8 at the time). Day was very ill for a time after his birth, and there was no way I could think of going back to my job teaching high school English. Straight housewifing is not for me, nor production weaving. And I don't have the art background to feel like I can go around weaving museum pieces or brilliant commissions."

Linda had her teacher's retirement fund money, about $1700, to start with. She used it to buy a couple of cameras, a used keyboard for phototypesetting, and to pay her first printer's bill. She scrounged mailing lists from guilds and from one friendly mail-order supplier. "The magazine has been in the black from the beginning," she says, "but then I haven't had to support the family with it. I've only just started to think about paying myself anything."

Except for some experience on her high school newspaper, Linda has no background in journalism, so how did she learn to be a publisher? "I got all the magazines off the newsstands that I thought were well done," she told me, "and *studied* them. Tried to figure out what it was about the writing, design, format, that made them appealing. And I found a sympathetic printer (his bid wasn't the lowest, but he didn't ask me who my boss was, either). And I asked lots of questions."

Linda's subscriber's list has grown slowly but

169

steadily, and as of mid-1977 it totaled more than 1600 subscribers, an impressive figure for a craft magazine so young. An additional 800 to 1000 magazines are dispersed in other ways, she notes. "While these are really modest figures, the growth has been steady enough that I'm optimistic about the magazine's achieving financial viability, not just hand-to-mouth existence."

When talking about the benefits of her business, Linda includes confidence and a growing sense of self-esteem. She's grown and learned a lot, too. "I'm more independent and assertive than I ever dreamed of being," she says. "I've learned a lot (not enough, though) about layout and design, about printing presses, selling ads, coping with the post office, bookkeeping, etc. The magazine also provides me with an excuse to go around meeting really neat people. I'm basically a pretty introverted sort, and it has really opened new worlds for me to have to go out and talk to people."

Problems? Of course. As you might suspect, Linda doesn't have enough time for her craft, and doesn't see an immediate solution for that. "If I'm ever to the point that I can afford full-time help," she dreams, "things might even out a little and I won't be a month behind on the mail and I can weave. However, much of the problem is of my own making. I'm a Brownie leader, a 4-H leader, parent-teacher council member, etc. Those things are important to me, too, so I make some deliberate choices about my time that I could change if I chose to. My family has been extremely supportive. The older kids have helped prepare mailings, my husband is always a sympathic ear, and has given good advice on occasion. And they're all very nice to me during my quarterly frenzy."

170   The Ligons live on a little acreage and have a big garden, chickens, ducks, goats, pigs, and so forth. Her husband, an electrical engineer, "goes around building solar collectors and other strange things in his spare time," says Linda, "so our life has always been chaotic, and that fits right in with publishing a magazine in your dining room."

Linda started her business just about the way she quit smoking. Just said, "I will do it" and never gave herself a chance to say, "Yeah, but..." She adds, "People, and dependent women in particular, need to be told about the possibilities that exist for them. I regret that I was 32 years old before it occurred to me I could do anything besides be a teacher. But no one ever told me."

That's one of the purposes of this book. To tell you what your possibilities are and to guide you along your road of discovery. Linda's story leaves one with a good feeling about self-publishing, doesn't it? But it wouldn't be fair of me to let you believe that all craft publishers live happily ever after, so I'm going to give you another side of the picture. Listen to the words of another homemaker who has been issuing a quarterly craft publication for several years now:

"I keep promising myself one day I will have time for me. Time to sew, do my crafts, teach again, read a book, work in the garden, and a lot of other things. I feel as though I am on a merry-go-round that just never stops, and as it goes round and round, I see posters listing all the things that must be done, and I try to grab one off each time I go round. But as one poster comes down, another takes its place."

Publishing a periodical gets like that after a while. It runs your life because there is always one more deadline to meet, one more job to do, one more new problem to cope with. It's an exciting field, though not for everyone. But at least I've shown you that it *can* be done, even by ordinary people.

Or perhaps I should say *ordinary people who have extraordinary ambitions* and the kind of inner strength it takes to make a special dream come true.

POSTSCRIPT: In a recent letter from Linda, she told me about a second periodical she is now publishing, called *Spin-Off,* a fat annual just for spinners. Linda recently moved from the dining room to her own office in the basement, and although she is currently not one but three months behind in her correspondence, she has me convinced that she's never been more content.

14

All Things Legal And Financial

Most creative people hate the thought of "all things legal and financial," and frankly, that's precisely why this chapter is at the end of my book instead of the beginning. I wasn't too keen about writing it, and I suspect you won't be exactly ecstatic about reading it either, particularly when you discover the number of laws you may unknowingly be breaking as a selling craftsperson or small business owner.

But don't panic just yet. Maybe it's not as bad as you think.

Since I am neither a lawyer nor an accountant, I can only give you some common-sense advice based on my research in the area of law and finance as it applies to artists and craftspeople. Although this chapter in no way constitutes "legal advice," it has been read and approved by a lawyer to insure that it contains no misinformation, and its primary purpose is merely to alert you to some things that could cause legal or financial problems.

Do you need a lawyer? When I asked Attorney Marion Schenk this question she said,

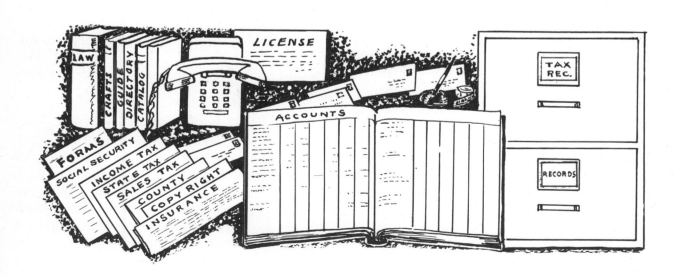

"When you come out of the kitchen, the complexities are such that you cannot do without a lawyer." Marion, an avid needleworker in her spare time, is well aware of the many "complexities" involved in the field of arts and crafts, and she believes everyone should have a laywer as soon as he goes into any kind of business. (You will recall that this opinion has been voiced by others whose businesses have been discussed in this book.)

The hobbyist who is only interested in selling at weekend fairs or through a couple of local craft shows may believe he has no need of a lawyer, and possibly this is true. But just to make sure, it would be wise to ask a lawyer if you need his services. An initial consultation with a lawyer should include a discussion of your particular circumstances and your plans for the future. Find out if there are any legal precautions you should take, and try to determine, in advance, if you might be heading for unforeseen trouble somewhere down the line. Discuss with him some of the points mentioned in this chapter, then decide which things affect you, and what must be done about them.

Looking for a lawyer is like looking for a doctor in that you will want someone you can trust — someone with whom you can establish a special relationship. Perhaps a friend or business acquaintance can recommend a good lawyer or, as Marion Schenk suggests, inquire about a lawyer at your bank since it will probably know most of the attorneys with private practices in your area. "Having a good banking connection is valuable in more ways than one," notes Marion.

Although legal fees are a legitimate business expense and, as such, deductible on your income tax, it would be wise to find out a lawyer's fee before your first meeting since most lawyers charge by the hour and some may be too expensive for you. The initial consultation is one expense, but remember that any work done for you after that first meeting will generally be charged on an hourly basis as well.

If you are just beginning in business and cannot afford a lawyer, you may be eligible to receive free legal service from the Volunteer Lawyers for the Arts (VLA), a New York-based, nonprofit organization with chapters all over the country. In addition to providing legal aid for performing and visual artists and craftspeople, individually or in groups, the VLA also provides a range of educational services, including the issuance of publications concerning taxes, accounting, and insurance. (NOTE: The VLA is also a good place to find an attorney who can be retained on a regular basis, since attorneys associated with the organization are more apt to be sensitive to a craftsman's needs.)

The Legal Structure of Your Business

One of the first things you will have to think about when you start your own business is the legal structure it will assume: individual proprietorship, partnership, or corporation. Most of the people involved in the arts and crafts field find the individual, or sole, proprietorship most suitable for their needs, but craft partnerships and corporations are also formed quite often. As you probably know, you do not need a lawyer to form an individual proprietorship, but it would be folly to enter into a partnership of any kind without legal guidance. (There are two kinds of partnerships — general and limited — see below.) Although one can legally incorporate in most states without an attorney, this practice is not recommended.

Which legal structure is best for you? Only a lawyer could answer that question for you, since many different things must be considered, including: (1) your personal financial situation, (2) your marital status (and, if married, your husband's tax bracket), (3) the scope of your talent, (4) the possibilities for growth of your business, etc. A brief look at the main advantages and disadvantages of each type of legal business structure will alert you to other factors that should be considered.

INDIVIDUAL PROPRIETORSHIP

Advantages: Simplest to form; least complicated to dissolve. You're your own boss here; the business ends automatically when you stop running it. No government approval required to start. Business profits (or losses) taxed as personal income.

Disadvantages: Proprietor is fully liable for all business debts and actions. In event of a lawsuit, one's personal assets (car, home, savings, etc.) are not protected. Also, many one-person businesses fail because there's too much work for one person to do, and not enough money to hire help.

GENERAL PARTNERSHIP
(two or more people).

Advantages: Easy to start; no federal requirements involved. Business profits (or losses) taxed as personal income. Written partnership agreement advised, but not necessary. Business ends with withdrawal of any one of the partners. Each partner shares the work load, contributing work, time, or money in amounts agreed to by all. With more people involved in the business, its chances for success are greater than with a single proprietorship.

Disadvangates: The debts incurred by one partner must be assumed by all other partners. If business fails, creditors can attach each partner's personal income and assets, as in an individual proprietorship. Partnerships between or among friends often end the friendship when disagreements over business policies occur.

LIMITED PARTNERSHIP (two or more people)

Advangages: Liability of one or more partners is limited to the extent of money invested in the business. Profits (or losses) taxed as personal income.

Disadvantages: More complicated to establish; legal contract must be filed with state. Partnership must adhere to laws of the state in which it is organized. Limited partners not permitted to advise in administration of the business — one or more general partners must be designated to run it. (NOTE: General partners often take on limited partners when they need additional cash for their business.)

CORPORATION

Advantages: Owner-shareholders not individually liable for the debts of a corporation, and, in the event of a lawsuit, personal assets are protected. Sole proprietors can form a corporation without losing control of the business, simply by buying majority of stock. Because a corporation is a legal entity unto itself, it does not die with the retirement or death of its officers, and investments may be transferred from one party to another without affecting operation of the company.

Disadvantages: Complex to establish; certification of incorporation must be filed with state in which business is located. Much paperwork involved in running a corporation, requiring legal and accounting services. Higher taxes. (NOTE: Check with a lawyer about Subchapter S Corporations, a corporate structure for new or low-income businesses. When there are ten shareholders or fewer, the Internal Revenue Service will permit each owner-shareholder to report his share of the profits or losses on his personal income tax return, as in a partnership.)

Local and State Licensing And Regulations

Since most small businesses are regulated at the local level, you should check with your city and county to see if you need any kind of permit or occupational license to do business. A *license* is a certificate granted by a government agency that gives one permission to engage in a business, occupation, or activity otherwise unlawful. Only certain businesses need a license to operate. A *permit* is similar to a license, except it is granted by local authorities. Some communities require a permit for almost everything; others require it only for businesses involving food, door-to-door selling, and home shops.

Registering a fictitious, or assumed, business or trade name: When you operate a business under any name other than your own, you are using a "trade name," and it must be registered since trade names cannot be held legally responsible for anything. Thus, if your name happens to be Mary Smith, and you call your business "Knotty But Nice," you would be using an assumed name. On legal documents, and at your bank, it would read, "Mary Smith, d/b/a Knotty But Nice," the "d/b/a" meaning "doing business as."

The registration procedure may vary from state to state, but basically you simply complete special forms given to you by the County Clerk and pay a small registration fee of a few dollars. There is one small hitch, however. In Illinois, California, and probably most other states as well, you must also place a legal ad in a general circulation newspaper in the county and run it three times. The newspaper will then give you a "Publication Certificate," which you in turn will mail to the County Clerk who will file it with your registration form. This makes your business completely legitimate.

In Illinois, it is a Class C Misdemeanor (and punishable accordingly) to operate a business that has not been registered with the County Clerk. In case you've been operating illegally and are shaking in your boots right now, let me ease your mind by telling you that no one goes around checking to see if all small businesses have been registered, and a check would not normally be made unless someone reports you, or otherwise brings your business to the attention of the County Clerk. Anyone who should register a business name, but has not done so to date, should do so now. Since the form you will complete does not ask when you started your business, the County Clerk will assume you've just started it, and there will be no problems.

Zoning laws: You could have problems here. You should find out if your business conforms to local zoning laws by calling your county courthouse. Generally, artists, craftsmen, writers, designers, mail order businesses, etc., have few worries about zoning laws because businesses such as these are usually operated quietly and cause no disturbance in the neighborhood. But if you are thinking about opening a studio or shop in your home that will bring customers to your door on a daily basis, you'd better investigate local zoning laws first. Also read your lease or title papers for information about building restrictions, etc. In many cases, a home studio or shop would be in direct violation of the law, and it might even invalidate your present tenant's or homeowner's insurance policy.

"It is very important to be honest with your insurance agent," advises Marion Schenk. "A simple and inexpensive rider may be all that is required to make your present insurance cover a business in your home and, of course, such cost would be a tax-deductible expense." (NOTE: Also refer to Chapter 5 in which I discussed the legal "grey area" of running a seasonal boutique in your home and inviting the public to attend.)

Most residential areas do not allow business signs, of course, and if this is important to the success of your business, it will be necessary to rent a shop or building elsewhere. In addition, large or unusual equipment, such as a gas-fired kiln, for example, might require a special permit in some areas, and, if it is noisy and disturbing to neighbors, you may not be allowed to operate it in your home or garage. And neighbors will surely complain if you are using anything that causes a strong odor.

The use of hazardous substances or chemicals may also be forbidden in one's home or neighborhood and, again, could invalidate one's insurance policy in the event of an accident involving their use.

Here's a good example of how you can run into zoning and legal problems when you least expect it. Betty Christy of Tree Toys explains: "We were recently given very short notice to get out of our warehouse and had to scurry about looking for a new building. Within 36 hours we had found another warehouse, but we talked to our lawyer first, and our insurance man second. Both of them said, 'Check with the Village because there's a zoning ordinance.' We did, and found that we had to have a fire inspection by someone in the fire department. We had to get three people together at the same time to make the inspection so we could get a temporary permit and move. If the fire department had found us after we moved in, and we hadn't notified them, we would have been in for a fine and trouble."

Resale tax number and collection of sales tax: All states require sales taxes of one kind or another, and in most states there are county and city taxes as well. *If you make anything for sale, or if you buy goods for resale, you are required to register your business with the Department of Revenue in your state.* This is a simple and painless process whereby you will fill out a form in order to receive a special document from the state. It will bear a

174

tax exemption number that is sometimes called a "Retailer's Occupation Tax Registration Number" or, more generally, a "resale tax number." This is a very valuable number, indeed, since it will enable you to buy materials for resale without paying sales tax. (This doesn't mean you can run down to the corner hardware store, buy two dollar's worth of something at retail and avoid the tax, but it does mean you will not have to pay sales tax when you purchase materials for resale at wholesale prices.)

Once you have a resale tax number, you will also have to start collecting sales tax on everything you sell directly to consumers, and file the appropriate reports with the state. Naturally, it is illegal to collect sales tax and retain it as income.

A great many craftspeople ignore the sales tax law and sell their wares at fairs without collecting a cent of tax. Some of them get caught, too. I was at a large craft festival once and saw officials shut down several craft booths for this reason. But failure to collect sales tax and file returns could result in more than just having one's booth closed. According to one authority at the Illinois Department of Revenue, lawbreakers in that state are subject to a penalty of 20 percent over and above any normal tax obligation, and could receive for each offense (meaning each return not filed) from one to six months in prison and a fine of as much as $5000. Other states may have similar penalties for sellers who ignore the sales tax law, so if you're going to sell at craft shows or by mail order, you should apply for your resale tax number as soon as possible.

At one time I was led to believe that the hobbyist who only sells occasionally ("for the fun of it") is not considered to be "in business" and thus does not need to be concerned with the resale tax number. This is not true. It doesn't matter to the state's Department of Revenue whether you are "in business" in the eyes of the Internal Revenue Service or not; all they are concerned with is whether you are selling directly to consumers on the retail level. In a conversation with Steven Davis of the Illinois Department of Revenue, Regulations and Hearings Division, he said that everyone who sells anything to consumers must collect sales tax. "If you hold yourself out as a seller of merchandise," he said, "then you're subject to tax, even if you only sell a couple of times a year."

Mr. Davis added, however, that people who do art or craft work only on commission need not be concerned with a resale tax number since they are considered to be performing a service, rather than making a retail sale. In addition, a tax number is not required for anyone who sells only on consignment, since in this case it is the shop — not the craftsperson — who is responsible for collecting the sales tax.

Craftspeople who sell only at wholesale prices fall into yet another group. Although they do not need to collect sales tax on their wholesale sales to shops, stores, etc., they *do* need a tax exemption certificate from the state in order to buy their raw materials at wholesale without paying sales tax. And, further, they must always be sure to obtain, for their tax files, the resale tax number of any retail shop or store with which they do business. Just as craftspeople must furnish their resale tax number to suppliers when they are buying supplies for resale, so must a craftsman's wholesale customers furnish him with their tax-exempt number when they purchase finished crafts for resale.

In summary, if you are working at your art or craft as a business and selling to consumers on a retail level — such as at a fair or by mail order — you must collect sales tax and file regular reports with the state. "Hobbyists" are not exempt from this law, regardless of how little money they make.

Better not take chances here. It's not that difficult to collect sales tax and file the necessary reports. If your income is low, you may find you only have to file quarterly or annually, instead of monthly as larger businesses do. For additional information, call your state's Sales Tax Bureau, Department of Taxation and Finance.

Income Taxes and Record Keeping

Some craftspeople probably sell their work at craft fairs and do not report cash earnings from sales on their annual income tax reports. I am reminded of one woman who told me she was "secretly selling" at one craft fair each year, and not reporting her income because she just didn't want to take that step from being a hobbyist to being "in business." But she became so worried about what she was doing that she said she was waking up in the middle of the night imagining that IRS agents would soon be knocking at her door. Her fear eventually forced her to "go legal," and I'm sure she is much happier as a result.

I'm not here to preach honesty to anyone, but I should remind readers that intentional tax evasion or falsification of tax returns can lead to severe penalties. If you are going to break the law, then you must also be prepared to pay the penalty. I should also point out that it is sometimes more advantageous to declare one's craft earnings than to try and hide them. There are many legitimate deductions available to the person in business, and it would be wise to explore this area thoroughly with a competent tax-preparer, accountant, or lawyer.

For example, in addition to standard business deductions for materials, labor, supplies, postage, shipping, telephone, advertising, office supplies, etc., you can deduct the amount spent on insurance related to your business, the expenses incurred when using your automobile for business purposes, and the cost of craft memberships, fees, subscriptions, etc. If you buy equipment, machinery, or any special tools, they can be depreciated over a period of years, or written off entirely in some cases. If you use a room in your home exclusively for business, you can deduct expenses for it accordingly, including a certain percentage of your rent or mortgage, plus fuel and electric costs.

A couple of women told me their husbands didn't want them to work because their extra income would put them in a higher tax bracket, but as Marion Schenk says, "With good accounting you can make quite a bit of money before you have to pay tax. And remember that the tax will only apply to the net profit, not the amount the business grosses in any given year." One might remind a husband that in the early years of a business, expenses will often exceed income — at least on paper — thus resulting in a lovely deduction that can decrease one's overall tax liability.

In talking about taxes with the average homemaker who sells her work, the question often arises as to whether she is, indeed, "in business" or working and selling just as a hobby. Either way, how should she handle her income and expenses? The following comment found in the *Los Angeles Times* provides one answer to that question: "The Internal Revenue Service has a clear, totally illogical rule about hobbies: If they cost you money, you can't deduct that; but if they make you money, you must pay income tax on that. Heads they win, tails you lose."

This was confirmed by an official in the Internal Revenue Service (IRS) office in Chicago, who told me that:

1. The IRS defines a hobby as an activity engaged in primarily for pleasure, not for profit.
2. Losses sustained in the pursuit of a hobby are not deductible.
3. If hobby income is under $400, it should be entered on the 1040 form.
4. If income from any hobby activity is over $400, a "Schedule C" must be filed, and one can then deduct related expenses so long as they do not exceed the amount earned from the activity.
5. Making a profit from a hobby does not automatically place one "in business," but the activity will be presumed to have been engaged in for profit if it results in a profit in two out of five consecutive years.

Once you are engaged in an activity for profit, then you are considered to be "in business" in the eyes of the Internal Revenue Service, and as such, are entitled to deduct expenses in excess of income. If you work at your business for five years, however, and never make a profit, the IRS may question your tax report, and you may then have to prove that you are really trying to make a profit, even though you failed. If you have maintained complete records for your business, that will be a strong point in your favor, as will be your expertise in the area of your endeavor.

In the end, the question of whether your art or craft-related activity will qualify as a business for tax purposes is a complex one, but no one factor, such as failure to achieve a profit in at least two out of five years, can be used by the IRS to disallow your deductions, which will certainly help offset income from other sources and, in effect, help underwrite your art or craft.

Tax laws are constantly changing, and to put them into a book such as this would be futile. This is an area you will have to investigate on your own. The Internal Revenue Service offers a number of pamphlets of interest to artists, craftsmen, and small business operators, such as "Tax Information on Operating a Business in Your Home," "Tax Information on Business Expenses and Operating Losses," and a larger publication, "Tax Guide for Small Businesses." These and other publications are listed in the resource chapter, and all are free on request from any IRS office.

Additional tax help is available in publications such as *Changing Times,* which regularly provides its readers with up-to-date information on new tax laws. Most of the craft periodicals also carry special articles on taxes for artists and craftsmen, especially at tax time each year.

The help of a competent tax-preparer can prove invaluable, and will often save you far more in taxes than the amount he will charge for his services, a tax deductible fee, of course. A tax-preparer will tell you whether you must file quarterly tax returns, and can even help you calculate the amount of tax that will be due each quarter. When using his services, however, you will save time and money by going to your meeting well prepared, with all figures neatly arranged. Dumping a sack full of receipts on someone's desk at year's end could prove to be very expensive for you. TIP: Make sure you always check all addition and subtraction on your tax report. Many times I have found simple typographical errors made by our tax-preparer that could be corrected before the IRS computer ejected our return, thus increasing our chances of being audited. Being audited is, to say the least, an inconvenience, even when you have prepared your return honestly. But if you have "fudged" a bit here and there, you're going to find it hard to explain and may be forced to pay penalties or a severe fine. Therefore, always be able to substantiate any deductions you take. This means you will need a good record keeping system.

Record keeping will be easier with the help of "Fear of Filing," an excellent and inexpensive booklet available from the Volunteer Lawyers for the Arts (VLA). This is a beginner's handbook on record keeping and federal taxes written especially for visual artists, writers, dancers, and other performers. The VLA also offers "The Individual Artist: Recordkeeping, Methods of Accounting, Income and Itemized Deductions for Federal Income Tax Purposes." You might also investigate the Dome Simplified Monthly, which is sold in stationery stores. Other tips on record keeping:

1. Get a receipt for everything, even the 50 cents you spend on paper clips.
2. Retain all receipts in orderly fashion, posting all expenses and income regularly to avoid year-end pile-up (and panic).
3. Simplify your record keeping by maintaining accurate, yet uncomplicated books that balance costs against sales.
4. Accounting records should be kept for at least six years after tax returns are filed, according to Price Waterhouse and Company, noted accounting firm. This period will cover the federal income tax statute of limitations and the statutes of various state and local taxing authorities. *

Social Security Taxes

When you make a net profit of $400 or more, you must file a Self-Employment Form along with your regular income tax form, and pay into your personal Social Security account. This could be quite beneficial for some homemakers with previous work experience. A woman's re-entry into the business world as a self-employed worker, and her additional contributions to her Social Security account, could result in increased benefits upon retirement.

177

* From *Profitable Craft Merchandising,* January 1978 issue, p. 20.

The whole topic of Social Security is quite complex, and I do not wish to delve into it here. But I might mention that, after the age of 65, one can currently make as much as $4500 a year without its affecting one's Social Security benefits. For every $2 in earnings over that amount, however, Social Security will withhold $1 in benefits. (When one attains the age of 72, this no longer applies.)

For more information on how working will affect your Social Security benefits, check the white pages of your telephone book for the number of your nearest Social Security office. (Look under "U.S. Government; Health, Education and Welfare, Social Security Administration.") Ask for a booklet called "Your Social Security," and also inquire about the new law that became effective in January, 1979. One change pertains to the way in which "calendar quarters" will be calculated in future; another shortens the length of time a woman must be married in order to collect benefits on her husband's Social Security account.

Individual Retirement Programs

Self-employed people who have not organized their business as a corporation may establish a retirement program and defer income tax payments on this investment until it is claimed upon retirement. One can either start an Individual Retirement Account (IRA) and invest up to 15 percent of his income (or a maximum of $1500 each year) or establish a Keogh Plan, which enables one to deposit up to 15 percent, but no more than $7500 of self-employed income in a given year. In both cases, funds cannot be drawn until the age of $59\frac{1}{2}$ without a severe penalty.

Each of the above plans has its own advantages and drawbacks, and one may be better for you than another, so discuss them thoroughly with your banker, accountant, or lawyer before deciding on one or the other.

15

Other Things You Should Know

Did you ever fix a terrific meal that called for many different ingredients, then found afterwards that you had a lot of things left over, like half a package of frozen spinach, the liquid from a can of mushrooms, a wedge of onion, etc.? If so, maybe you threw them into a pot and made vetegable soup. Well, this chapter is my "pot of soup" or, if you want to get fancy, a "potpourri" of things that just didn't find their way into earlier chapters. The first "ingredient" is a dandy, and enough to spoil your appetite, but it's really important, so don't overlook it.

Hazards in the Arts

"Are the materials you are working with slowly killing you? Or maybe they are just going to make you chronically ill. Scary? I hope so, because many of the materials artists are working with are much more dangerous than is commonly believed." So warns Michael McCann, Ph.D., in his booklet *Health Hazards for Artists.*

Did you know that anything can be toxic in the wrong place, at the wrong time, to the wrong person, and in the wrong amount? This means, in effect, that nearly all materials can be toxic under some conditions. So Says Gail Barazani in *Working Craftsman* magazine, in her column "Protecting Your Health."

And here's a quote from *Hazards in the Arts,*

a newsletter edited by Gail Barazani and funded in part by the National Endowment for the Arts:

> Environmental contaminants, particularly those encountered in the industrial workplace, are creating serious health problems for millions of Americans. Ironically, many of those contaminants are being brought into the home (unintentionally) and into the daily recreational lives of at least one in five of the population in the form of art, craft, and other hobby materials.

Now that I have your attention, I'd like to give you a few examples of what all the fuss is about:

- Aerosol paints, adhesive sprays, fixatives, etc., are very dangerous unless used in such a way as not to breathe the vapors.

- Traditional art materials, like lead paints and pottery glazes, solvents, inks, welding fumes, and wood and plastic dusts from sanding, can also be dangerous.

- Solvents, casting plastics, polyester resins, polyurethane paints, and varnishes constitute "jeopardy materials," and any person using them is taking an unnecessary risk unless he knows the proper precautions.

According to Dr. McCann, toxic substances can enter the body in three ways: by skin contact, through breathing, and through the mouth and digestive system. Many materials can harm the skin directly, causing rashes, burns, and other skin

179

problems. Acute lung diseases result when strongly irritating substances burn the tissues of the air sacs in the lung. Certain fumes are injurious to the kidneys and liver, with effects being cumulative. Symptoms such as weakness, fatigue, palpitations, and pale complexion may be caused by chemical substances that affect the red and white blood cells. Mental problems and nervousness can often be symptoms of physical problems related to chemicals found in art/craft materials: in fact, the entire central nervous system can be affected by certain substances.

An article by Jean Kennedy in the May 1977 issue of *The Crafts Report* urges all craftsmen who are ill to tell their doctors what materials they are using in the workshop, and what is known about them. Request consultation from an internist, neurologist, or occupational health consultant, Ms. Kennedy suggests, because the average doctor may not take complaints seriously.

Those who read the various publications for artists and craftsmen have become well aware of the many hazards to health in the long-range use of certain art/craft materials, but I suspect the general public remains largely unaware of these dangers to date. For that reason, I urge every reader of this book to take steps to educate himself on this topic by ordering one or more of the publications listed in the resource chapter, under "Health Hazards Literature."

In the meantime, steps can be taken to diminish the dangers of any materials you are currently using. Here are a few things you can do:

1. Do not inhale fumes, sprays, or dusts, and take special precautions to ALWAYS HAVE ADEQUATE VENTILATION IN YOUR WORK AREA. Improper ventilation is the major health problem in all the crafts.

2. Be especially careful about personal hygiene. Always wash hands before touching cigarettes or food, and never work with chemical substances in an area normally used for food preparation or eating.

3. Wear gloves when using any liquid other than water, but note that rubber does not work in some solvents; plastic must be substituted.

4. Keep children away from your workshop, since they are much more susceptible to toxic substances than adults.

5. Wear a dust mask when sawing, sculpting, grinding, or carving any material, as minute particles of dust can easily penetrate one's lungs. Also wear a face shield or eye goggles. In cleaning up dust, never sweep. Vacuum instead, or wet-mop, or both.

6. If a manufacturer does not list the chemicals in his product, and will not tell you what it contains when you write for this information, do not use it. This could mean its contents are hazardous to your health.

This whole business of hazards in the arts has become so important that a special Art Hazards Information Center has been opened by the Center for Occupational Hazards, Inc. (COH), as a service to artists, craftspeople, art schools, and teachers. The Center will provide advice on safety precautions and hazards of arts and crafts materials. Other activities of COH include scientific research into the health hazards of arts and crafts materials (including children's art materials), as well as lectures and workshops for artists, teachers, and others on these health hazards and possible precautions. "Art Hazards Newsletter," a regular column appearing in *Art Workers News,* serves to keep readers up to date on new findings in this field, as does the quarterly column in the *Working Craftsman* magazine.

Important Regulations Affecting Craftspeople

"Increased concern about consumer protection, employee safety, and environmental protection has resulted in increased regulatory activity by local, state, and federal governments," says Gerald E. Ely, craft specialist with the Farmer Cooperative Service, Department of Agriculture, Washington, D.C. "Many laws exist which have significance for craftspeople. However, in many cases, craftspeople are either unaware of these laws or poorly informed of the provisions of the laws.''

Following is a brief discussion about several laws and regulations you may not know about and who to contact for additional information about each:

● The Consumer Product Safety Act of 1972: This law protects the public against unreasonable risks of injury associated with consumer products. The Act created The Consumer Products Safety Commission, which has powers to establish and enforce mandatory safety standards for consumer products sold in the United States.

One of the Commission's most active regulatory programs has been in the area of toys and consumer goods designed for children. Anyone who makes toys should strive to meet certain guildelines, in order to meet safety standards. Make sure all toys are: (1) too large to be swallowed; (2) not apt to break easily or leave jagged edges; (3) free of sharp edges or points; (4) not put together with easily exposed pins, wires, or nails; (5) nontoxic, nonflammable, and nonpoisonous.

● The Federal Hazardous Substances Act: This relates primarily to, and prohibits the use of, any substance or mixture that is toxic, corrosive, combustible, an irritant, a strong sensitizer, or any substance that may cause personal injury or illness during handling or use, including "reasonably foreseeable ingestion by children.''

● The Flammable Fabrics Act: This act prohibits the introduction or movement in interstate commerce of articles of wearing apparel and fabrics that are so highly flammable as to be dangerous when worn by individuals, and for other purposes.

(More information about the above three acts is available from The Consumer Products Safety Commission.)

● The Migratory Bird Treaty Act of 1918: This obscure regulation has had considerable impact in fines to at least one craftsperson. It prohibits the sale of feathers of all North American migratory birds. Also, protected under other laws are certain waterfowl and, of course, endangered species. For complete information contact the Department of the Interior.

● The Textile Fiber Products Identification Act: Craftspeople involved with textiles and wearing apparel should be familiar with the labeling requirements of this act. All items made of any textile or fiber (garments, quilts, stuffed toys, rugs, etc.) must have a "securely affixed" label showing (1) the name of the manufacturer or other person marketing the textile fiber product; (2) the generic names and percentages of all fibers in the product in amounts of 5 percent or more, listed in order of predominance by weight. (Examples: "100 percent combed cotton"; "92 percent cotton, 8 percent other fibers.'') More information is available from the Bureau of Consumer Protection.

● NOTE: A separate law, the Wool Products Labeling Act of 1939, is similar to the above, and pertains to all things manufactured of wool.

● Care labeling of textile wearing apparel: Any textile, suede, or leather product in the form of a finished article of wearing apparel, or any textile product in the form of a finished household furnishing, must have a label permanently affixed or attached thereto by the manufacturer of the finished item that clearly discloses instructions for the care and maintenance of such item. This includes all wearing apparel, household furnishings, piece goods, yarn, and rugs.

A label should indicate if any item is to be dry cleaned or washed; if it is to be washed, indicate whether in hot or cold water. Indicate whether bleach may or may not be used, and specify at what heat the item may be ironed. (More information is available from the Federal Trade Commission.)

● Bedding and Upholstered Furniture Law: Are you ready for this one? This is a state law that requires the purchase of a license in order to sell items with a concealed filling. It also requires printed tags attached to the items that bear the manufacturer's registry number. "Concealed filling" items include not just bedding and upholstery, but works of art that resemble a pillow, quilt, or any soft sculpture that can be used for sitting.

181

This particular law is stirring up a storm of protest among craftspeople at this time because it does not distinguish between the large manufacturing company and the craftsperson who sells one pillow or quilt a year. The law is currently being enforced on an arbitrary basis, but if it were to be enforced in every state it would mean that craftspeople would have to purchase a license for each state in which their work is sold. Since licenses are costly, and renewable yearly, few could afford them. Fortunately, Maryland seems to be the only state to date where the law has been enforced against craftspeople, and this happened recently when the Maryland State Health Department recalled pillows, quilts, and other items with an inner filling from several galleries and shops.

Groups of craftsmen are currently working to have this law changed, but until it is changed, craftspeople would be wise *not* to seek information from authorities since that would only draw unnecessary attention to their products. As I understand it, aparently the worst that will happen if your work comes to the attention of authorities is that you will be ordered to cease selling until a license has been purchased. Watch professional craft periodicals for more information on this topic in the future.

● Proper labeling of items containing metals: Anyone who works with gold, silver, platinum, and combinations of these materials should order the brochures available from the National Bureau of Standards.

● Federal Trade Commission trade practice rules: Several booklets are available that define the trade practice rules for all industries. Some of possible interest to the readers of this book are:

1. The Jewelry Industry
2. The Hand Knitting Yarn Industry
3. The Ladies' Handbag Industry
4. Catalog Jewelry and Giftware Industry

NOTE: When an FTC rule has been violated, it is customary for the Federal Trade Commission to order the violator to cease the illegal practice. No penalty is attached to most cease-and-desist orders, but if one violates such an order, he may be fined.

Liability Insurance

All the foregoing talk about rules and regulations leads me neatly to the topic of liability insurance, which has been discussed at length in most of the craft magazines and newsletters. There are three kinds of liability insurance, namely:

1. Personal liability, which protects you as an individual
2. Public liability, which protects you as a business owner
3. Product liability, which protects you in the event one of your craft objects causes injury to the user of the product.

If you have a business in your home, and it brings customers to your door, talk to your insurance broker about your need for public liability insurance. If someone falls off your front step while coming to or from your office, studio, or workshop, and seriously injures himself, you would certainly want to be protected in the event of a lawsuit. If you already have public liablilty insurance as a homeowner, talk to your insurance broker and find out if your present policy would cover a home business.

"Anyone who is involved in production and marketing should already be carrying public liability insurance, and should add product liability as well," notes the *Kentucky Guild Newsletter.* "Product liability is a legal time bomb that could wipe out some craftsmen and retailers, taking not only their businesses but life savings as well," warns *Crafts Business Management,* a monthly for crafts producers and retailers. "Guarding against this situation is an aspect of your business you cannot overlook," adds another publisher.

If a child swallows part of a craft toy, if a fiber wall hanging enflames, if a ceramic casserole cracks and spills its hot contents into the lap of its user, the maker of the product can be held responsible. More than one craftsman has already been sued in similar instances, and, in fact, recent court cases across the country have made product liability coverage nearly essential to every craftsman's protection. Selling through a shop that carries product liability is not the answer to the problem, since if a customer sued a shop, the shop's insurance company would undoubtedly turn around and sue the manufacturing craftsman.

In an article in the *Southern Highland Handicraft Guild* newsletter, Alan Ashe points out that:

> Some of the things which have caused injury and court cases are: lead glazed pottery, flameware, stuffed toys with wire or pins in them, knitted items which are made of yarn or fiber which will burn rapidly, furniture not sturdy enough to hold when a reasonable weight is put on it for support (such as a chair), jewelry that might injure the wearer or another person because of features in its design (sharp points projecting that would cut or injure).

Mr. Ashe adds that the the best way to prevent a lawsuit is to be certain that the items you make have no health hazards and can be safely used.

Michael Scott, in *The Crafts Report,* advises:

> ...make the product as safe as possible, and alert the customer if special precautions have to be taken. If you inform the customer not to put the glassware in a dishwasher and put the precautionary notice in writing, you have generally met your responsibility, even if she cuts two fingers while taking the broken glass out of the dishwasher. But if the glass breaks and spills hot liquid on someone because you were careless in the production of the item, watch out.

Perhaps the advice given in *Crafts Business Management* sums it up best: "...brainstorm your products, and try to make them as idiot-proof as possible."

For more information about product liability insurance, talk to your insurance broker and stay informed by reading publications such as those mentioned above. (NOTE: Product liability insurance is not inexpensive. In fact, many small businesses cannot afford it, and this problem has recently been investigated by the House and Senate Small Business Committees, who introduced legislation to help solve the problem. Your local Small Business Administration should have additional information on this matter in the future.)

Other Insurance

In addition to the liability insurance discussed above, you should investigate other forms of insurance available for artists and craftsmen. For example, as a member of the American Crafts Council, you would be eligible for four different insurance plans being administered by Association and Society Insurance Corporation (ASI):

1. Term life
2. Hospital indemnity
3. Major medical
4. Craftsman's protection coverage.

The first three policies are self-explanatory, but the fourth plan is quite special and requires additional explanation here. It is a broad all-risk policy that offers blanket coverage for all unfinished craft objects, finished craft objects, raw materials and supplies, tools, equipment, and other property usual to the craft, as well as any articles being repaired by the craftsperson.

The coverage is provided both at home and in the studio. One's property is even covered while in transit, on exhibition, at fairs, etc. The policy covers loss or damage, including theft at home and burglary at other locations. Insurance can be purchased in amounts from $5000 to $25,000, and premiums are reasonable.

Write the American Crafts Council for information on how to join the organization and obtain the insurance, or write ASI for brochures and applications on the ACC plans. (NOTE: The insurance company regularly sends a list of insureds to the ACC to confirm their membership in the ACC. Termination of insurance coverage may occur as a result of discontinued membership in the ACC.)

Talk to your regular insurance agent about other insurance needs, and particularly inquire about the coverage provided by your homeowner's policy. Since it is designed to cover a building occupied principally as a dwelling, it could become null and void if the home is used for commercial purposes — such as having a shop or artist's studio in it. In some cases, you may only need the addition of a special rider to cover a business activity in the home.

Also inquire about coverage for your personal possessions. A tenant's or homeowner's policy will only insure normal household furnishings and will probably not cover any of your craft equipment or tools — looms, potter's wheels, kilns, etc. Again, a rider will be required to cover such special items. (Or you will need the special craftsman's protection coverage policy described earlier.)

Finally, if you use your automobile for business purposes, talk to your insurance agent about this. A policy issued for a car normally used only for pleasure or driving to and from work may not provide complete coverage for an accident that occurs during business use of the car, particularly if the insured is to blame for the accident.

NOTE: Remember that all insurance premiums for business purposes will be tax deductible. One more thing: Keep your policies in a safe place, such as a safe deposit box or fireproof container.

Craft Organizations

A recent planning study sponsored by the National Endowment for the Arts revealed that there are approximately 300,000 craftspeople who belong to about 2000 organizations in the United States.

Organizations of craftspeople exist on all levels, of course — local, state, regional, national. While some have full-time staffs and permanent headquarters, others operate through volunteers, and often, in cases like this, an organization's address is likely to change every year as new officers are elected.

Why join an organization? "The environment of an association," says Margaret Boyd in *Working Craftsmen* magazine, "provides an impetus, a thrust into crafts participation that excites the imagination. It aids the craftsperson in gaining a sense of awareness of himself in regard to his craft work — helps him determine where his work stands in terms of talent, originality and quality."

Professionals in all fields recognize the value and importance of association membership, and readers of this book should learn what particular organizations can do for them. Although no one has ever been able to compile a complete list of all the organized craft groups in America (including

ORGANIZATIONS
A HELPING HAND
FOR A CREATIVE HAND
ASSOCIATIONS
COOPERATIVES

184

associations, leagues, guilds, and clubs) an extensive list can be found in *The Goodfellow Catalog of Wonderful Things,* as well as in *Contemporary Crafts Marketplace.* (Both publications may be available through your library.) The resource chapter of this book also contains the addresses of several well-known regional and national organizations, just to whet your appetite.

Many organizations publish a magazine or newsletter that serves to keep members informed of various happenings and opportunities in the craft field, and some offer such special services as marketing help, workshops and educational programs, discounts on books and craft supplies, etc. A few sponsor large, annual craft fairs as well. Some organizations obviously work a lot harder for their members than others, but what some members forget is that they will only get as much out of an organization as they put in.

Cooperative Ventures

Occasionally a group of concerned craftspeople will get together and form a special kind of organization known as a "cooperative." A craft cooperative is a nonprofit business organization — a special tool that craft producers can use in many different ways. People with similar desires, problems, or interests may use a cooperative to improve marketing conditions, purchase supplies, secure needed services, etc. For example, the practical result of a cooperative might be the formation of a central workshop, the opening of a shop or gallery, a materials and equipment buying group, the publication of a crafts catalog or directory, the organization of a large annual fair, and so on.

In correspondence with Dorothy Harris of Haradora Designs in New York City, I learned what it means to be a member of a smoothly working cooperative. Dorothy is one of 23 craftspeople who are members of Artworkspace, a cooperative studio located in a large loft in Manhattan. The co-op was started in 1975 by 10 craftspeople who decided they could find a better working space if they combined forces and split expenses. Once established, their cooperative quickly grew and now includes an interesting blend of craftspeople.

Dorothy, who makes a line of fanciful stuffed animals, shares space with others who do pottery, jewelry, batik, weaving, calligraphy, graphics, soft sculpture, puppetry, painting, fiberwork, and creative framing. Members often hire one another when they need a helping hand to get out a big order, or need a special job done, such as the creation of a brochure.

The studio (5600 square feet) provides sufficient space for each craftsperson to work, store heavy equipment, materials, and craftwork, and even has a special gallery area where work can be shown to potential clients and customers. Members meet once a month to discuss problems that arise in maintaining the cooperative, and each assumes certain responsibilities in its operation. Each member pays a fixed amount each month (approximately $80) that covers rent, utilities, and other operating expenses. Naturally, this amount is a mere fraction of what each individual would have to pay for a private studio, yet Artworkspace provides its members with a business identity most could not otherwise afford. A sharing of equipment such as typewriters, saws, kilns, slide projectors, etc., offers obvious advantages, and because the craftspeople work in a studio with a business telephone number and address, they are taken more seriously by clients, vendors, and others.

"An invaluable advantage of membership in a cooperative like ours," says Dorothy, "is the separation of working and living quarters, especially for those living in small urban apartments. Having space for heavy equipment, storing materials, and work, and not having to worry about ruining furniture and household with one's mess while working is extremely important."

Kay Radcliffe, another member of the co-op who does marbelized art, points out other advantages to membership in Artworkspace: "Members share information about resources, fairs, outlets, galleries, and suppliers, and often refer buyers to each other and suggest sales opportunities. Publicity is easier to obtain as a group, and credit advantages are possible when individual members share with others in ordering supplies in wholesale quantities."

Especially important, adds Dorothy, is the

185

sense of community and support in working with a group such as this. "The loneliness that usually accompanies craft work done at home, in isolation, is relieved by the sense of working within a supportive, stimulating atmosphere where creative ideas are exchanged and encouraged, and similar goals make individual goals fit within the framework of a social unity."

"The combined knowledge of individual members contributes continually to its successful operation," notes Kay. "One member is skilled in bookkeeping, another in legal matters, another in publicity, and so forth, and our combined knowledge about practical matters is necessary to the success of continuing our co-op in an effective manner."

Some cooperatives are formed as a means of increasing sales, but this is not the primary goal of Artworkspace, and Dorothy believes this has contributed to their minimal turnover rate and kept disharmony to a minimum. "Our co-op does not stress sales as a joint venture, but on an individual basis," she explains. "Individual members sell through shows, shops, buyers, fairs, and other outlets. Artworkspace has only one joint sale, and that is our Christmas show. Each member contributes his mailing list, which we use to send out invitations. We get television and newspaper coverage, and find our sales experience successful enough to repeat."

Readers interested in starting a cooperative are referred to a publication issued by the Farmer Cooperative Service (FCS), United States Department of Agriculture, titled "How To Start a Cooperative," and another titled "The Cooperative Approach to Crafts." Many cooperatives have been formed by the FCS to strengthen the economic position of farmers and other rural residents. A formal craft program was established by the FCS in 1971 to assist craft associations, and many craft producers have benefited as a direct result, particularly in the Appalachian region.

A final tip from Dorothy and Kay: "As for others who want to start a co-op, we would say that much of their success will depend upon the good fortune of finding people with mutual goals who can work together compatibly. Fortunately, our incompatibilities have been minimal, and most of our members have been cooperative and responsible in their approach to maintaining the studio. Their combined knowledge contributes continually to the successful operation of Artworkspace."

16

Epilogue

It's time to add the final seasoning to my "pot of soup." Time to take it off the fire, dish it up, and hope everyone likes it. Time to leave you with a few last words of encouragement, a philosophical thought or two, and a couple of reminders about luck and success.

Until now, you may have lacked the courage to get your craft ideas off the ground, but now that you've seen how other people have accomplished their goals, I hope you feel more confident and adventurous, and are ready to capitalize on your creativity.

About that courage I mentioned — Dr. Joyce Brothers recently made a very interesting comment in one of her many lectures to women across the country. She said that the only difference between being a neurotic and a creative artist is *courage,* adding that the creative person is capable of turning adversity to his advantage, whereas a neurotic would wallow in self pity.

No one really knows why some people are more creative than others, but I believe all people are inherently creative, whether they realize it or not. Everyone seems to have his own definition of creativity, like Miriam Fankhauser, who says, "To be creative is to dare to try something new with no manual at your side." (Well, you can cheat a *little.* Your use of *this* manual doesn't mean you're not creative.) Miriam adds, "Don't be afraid to dare

to try. It is essential. And don't be afraid to fail. It is all part of learning and succeeding next time. Only by making mistakes do we learn how to find solutions and come up with something really fine."

Carol Bernier encourages all women to develop their talents, but adds, "Don't expect to succeed at everything. Instead, concentrate on the fields that seem to work out for you. Work hard; don't be nonchalant."

And Ruby Tobey advises, "Keep on keeping on. Keep on working at your chosen art or craft — you will be surprised at how much you improve, and how the new ideas keep coming as you work."

Why do women work so hard at certain things? Money, sure. But many work just for self-fulfillment, as we have seen, and those who work with crafts seem to derive special pleasures and satisfactions that are often difficult to explain. Making things by hand obviously feeds the soul, and although it is nice to please others with the work that has been created, pleasing oneself is really what it's all about.

As Jude Martin writes: "My greatest happiness is sitting on the floor, making a basket or designing a one-of-a-kind crocheted vest, or trying to learn to quilt or make toys. No matter how fragmented life becomes, I can go back to these and restore my perspective and peace of mind. I cannot envision ever leaving crafts; I feel there will always be something I can make for the pleasure of trying an idea.''

As for success, remember that it is a journey, not a destination. (I don't recall who said that, but I like it.) Your attitude toward success is very important, of course. If you think it's impossible to achieve your goal, it probably will be. On the other hand, if you're confident of your ability and convinced you will succeed in time, you probably will. It can never hurt to assume a determined attitude when you set out to do anything, so long as you can accept failure as a possibility. And, even when we occasionally fail, we can justify our failures by simply accepting the fact that through failure we can correct our mistakes.

Or, as Margaret Thompson puts it, ''You may fail, but you will learn something, even if it's your own limitations.'' She adds that ''It's all out there for the taking'' and suggests that you ''take a course at the 'Y,' read a book, buy a kit, get involved.'' In her life, Margaret says, happiness is busy-ness. Successes, great or small, have been a lucky by-product of her trying and failing, then trying once again.

Did I just mention luck? Yep. Luck does play an important role in success, according to Max Gunther, author of *The Luck Factor*. He has some very interesting theories about luck, and here's one that seems especially appropriate now: ''The luckiest people I know haven't lived their lives in a straight line but in a zigzag. You've got to be ready to jump off in a new direction when you see something good.''* Mr. Gunther also believes that people who would ''catch good luck'' are generally those who have taken the trouble to form a great many friendly contacts with other people.

188 Perhaps your luck is going to improve now that you have the opportunity to make some good craft contacts and form some new friendships with creative people like yourself. Don't forget that the addresses of most of the people mentioned in this book are included in the resource chapter for this reason.

* From *The Luck Factor* by Max Gunther. © 1977 by Max Gunther. Used by permission of Macmillan Publishing Company, Inc.

Since *Creative Cash* has concentrated on the topic of selling one's work, it seems only fitting to close on the subject of money. Making money from your needlework and crafts is what I hope you'll soon be doing, of course, but don't get so carried away by the idea of financial success that you lose track of your real goals. As Jude Martin says, ''I have been called a ''soft sculptress,'' when I know that I am a toymaker. Keeping your head on straight about your goals will do much to make them come faster and be more successful.''

Finally, I want to remind you that the happiest years of your life are not necessarily going to be the years in which you make the most money, but rather the years in which you accomplish the things that are most important to you. My wish is that this book will open many new doors of discovery for you — so many, in fact, that it will take you the rest of your life just to explore the possibilities.

I hope someday you'll tell me about your accomplishments.

P.S.

How would you like to be able to communicate not only with me and the craftspeople mentioned in this book, but with many of its readers as well — people like you who are still in the learning/sharing/growing process?

As Creative Cash *went into production, someone suggested that a newsletter should be published as a follow-up to this book; and I, for one, think this is a splendid idea! There is so much to be learned from the shared experiences of others, and because the craft world is in a constant state of change, serious craftspeople always need fresh information, ideas and inspiration.*

So, if you think you would like to subscribe to a newsletter that I would write and edit — with the help of my readers, of course — send a postcard to me in care of Countryside Books, 200 James Street, Barrington, Illinois 60010. Just write ''Creative Cash Newsletter'' and be sure to include your name and address.

Barbara

17

Resources

As Harry S. Truman once said, "The only things worth learning are the things you learn after you know it all." Although you now know a lot about selling crafts, needlework, designs, and know-how, I hope you will continue your crafts education by exploring the many information sources listed in this chapter.

Do understand, however, that this chapter has been included as a service to readers, and is not to be considered an endorsement of those listed herein. Neither author nor publisher will accept responsibility for any unfavorable action or transaction that might occur as a result of the information published in *Creative Cash*.

NOTE: When writing to anyone mentioned in this book, please mention *Creative Cash* in your correspondence. Thank you.

Guide to the Resource Chapter

Section I — Art and Crafts Periodicals

Publications are listed in alphabetical order and include a wide range of magazines, newsletters, newspapers, bulletins, and show listings (or "calendars" as they are sometimes called). All of these periodicals are available by subscription; several will be found on newsstands, but some are available only in certain regions of the country. (See Section II for additional periodicals published by organizations.)

A brief description follows each listing, and will serve as a general guide to the periodical's content and type of reader. For additional information about any publication, request a brochure and inquire about the availability of single copies when this is not mentioned in the listing. (NOTE: Subscription prices have not been given because they will surely increase in the future as production costs continue to rise. Single copy prices, however, have been indicated when known, as a service to both reader and publisher.)

American Artist, 1515 Broadway, New York, NY 10036. Susan E. Meyer, editor. A monthly for professional artists.

American Home Crafts. This magazine, mentioned in Chapter 9, recently ceased publication.

Art Hazards News, Center for Occupational Hazards, 5 Beekman St., New York, NY 10038. Michael McCann, Ph.D., editor. A four-page newsletter published 10 times a year. Contains news of events, articles, and other items about art/craft hazards.

Art Letter, 150 E. 58th St., New York, NY 10022. Lee Rosenbaum, editor. A national monthly newsletter for arts professionals published by *Art in America* magazine. Contains information on grants, opportunities to show and sell, news developments affecting visual artists and craftspeople. Sample, $3.

Artweek, 1305 Franklin St., Oakland, CA 94612, Cecile McCann, editor. A weekly newspaper for West Coast artists, with emphasis on contemporary work. Sample, 75 cents.

Canada Crafts, Page Publications, Ltd., 380 Wellington St. West, Toronto, Ontario M5V 1E3, Canada. Bimonthly edited for the professional craftsman in Canada. Sample, $2.

Canada Quilts, Conroyal Publications, 360 Stewart Dr., Sudbury Ontario P3E 2R8, Canada. Newspaper published five times a year with news, reviews, and patterns for quilters. Sample, $1.

Ceramics Monthly, P.O. Box 12448, Columbus, OH 43212. Features on professional ceramicists, instructional articles, show calendar, etc.

Ceramic World, 429 Boren Ave., N., Seattle, WA 98109. Dale Swant, editor. A monthly devoted to the world of fun in ceramics; ideas, techniques, and special how-to-do-it articles.

Colorado Art Show News, P.O. Box 609, Littleton, CO 80120. Quarterly listing of shows in Colorado and adjacent states.

Craft Range — The Mountain-Plains Craft Journal, 6800 W. Oregon Dr., Denver, CO 80226. Carol Maree Hoffman, editor. Bimonthly magazine covering news in a nine-state area.

Crafts, PJS Publications, Inc., News Plaza, P.O. Box 1790, Peoria, IL 61656. Joyce Bennett, editor. A new monthly for crafts enthusiasts featuring how-to-do-it articles. Magazine is available on newsstands ($1.25), and every project in it uses products and materials readily available in local craft supply stores.

Crafts Business Management. This monthly newsletter, published by a subsidiary of the American Crafts Council, recently ceased publication.

The Crafts Fair Guide, Box 262, Mill Valley, CA 94941. A quarterly listing of West Coast craft shows, with evaluations provided by participating craftspeople. Published by Lee Spiegel. Single issue, $5.

Crafts 'N Things, Clapper Publishing Co., Inc., 14 Main St., Park Ridge, IL 60068. Kay Dougherty, editor. Bimonthly consumer how-to crafts magazine featuring a variety of quality crafts projects.

The Crafts Report, 700 Orange St., Wilmington, DE 19801. (Editorial office: 3632 Ashworth North, Seattle, WA 98103. Michael Scott, editor.) Newsmonthly of marketing, management, and money for crafts professionals. Single copy, $1.25.

Creative Cash Newsletter, Countryside Books, 200 James Street, Barrington, Il 60010. Barbara Brabec, Editor. Write for free brochure and subscription rates.

Creative Crafts, Carstens Publications, Inc., Box 700, Newton, NJ 07860. Sybil C. Harp, editor-in-chief. A bimonthly whose emphasis is on crafts for the serious adult hobbyist, with well-written how-to articles. An excellent source for craft information and supplies. Available on newsstands. $1 single issue.

Decorating & Craft Ideas, Box 2522, Birmingham, AL 35201. Evelyn L. Brannon, editor. Consumer magazine published monthly except January and July. For women whose main interests are crafts, decorating, and sewing. Many how-to projects in each issue.

Design Magazine, 1100 Waterway Blvd., Indianapolis, IN 46206. Bimonthly featuring the ideas and projects of art educators, students, specialized craftspeople, and home hobbyists.

Early American Life, Early American Society, P.O. Box 2534, Boulder, CO 80322. (Editorial office: P.O. Box 1831, Harrisburg, PA 17105; Robert G. Miner, editor.) A bimonthly for people interested in Early American arts, crafts, travel, restoration, and collection.

Enterprising Women, Artemis Enterprises, Inc., 525 W. End Ave., New York, NY 10024. A business monthly offering profiles of women in business, with practical information and guidelines for starting new businesses; a "lifeline" to what other women are doing.

The Feminist Art Journal, 41 Montgomery Place, Brooklyn, NY 11215. Quarterly; nonprofit, with circulation being aided by public funds from the N.Y. Council on the Arts. Emphasis is on what is now being produced by women in the arts, film, literature, poetry, music, and other media. $2, single copy or back issue.

Fiberarts, 50 College St., Asheville, NC 28801. Mara Bishop, editor. Bimonthly dedicated to the needs and interests of the professional, semiprofessional, or would-be professional fiber artist, with emphasis on contemporary weaving, crochet, knitting, basketry, stitchery, fiber sculpture, and clothing. Sample, $1.50 (NOTE: *Fiberarts* maintains a slide library on fiber artists from all over North America.)

Fine Woodworking, Taunton Press, Taunton Lake Rd., Newtown, CT 06470. Paul Roman, editor/publisher. Beautifully printed bimonthly magazine for serious woodworkers; the only one of its kind. Single issue, $2.50.

Glass (Formerly *Glass Art*), 408 S.W. 2nd Ave., Rm. 420, Portland, OR 97204. Albert Lewis, editor/publisher. Edited for professional glass workers and published quarterly.

The Goodfellow Review of Crafts, P.O. Box 4520, Berkeley, CA 94704. Christopher Weills, editor and publisher. A monthly newspaper for craftspeople; with emphasis on good reading and the sharing of vital information. Several unusual columns and articles in each issue, plus special departments, book reviews, etc. Sample, $1.00.

Handweaving with Robert and Roberta, Ayottes' Designery, Center Sandwich, NH 03227. A step-by-step home-study course published quarterly by professional weavers. (Also inquire about their yarn club.)

Hobbies, The Magazine For Collectors, 1006 S. Michigan Ave., Chicago, IL 60605. Monthly. Emphasis is on "collectibles," such as dolls, antiques, stamps, old toys, Americana, etc.

Interweave, 2938 N. County Rd. 13, Loveland, CO 80537. Linda Logon, editor and publisher. A quarterly journal for weavers that began as a regional publication and is now gaining national attention from serious fiber workers. Emphasis is on a sharing of techniques, ideas, and news. (Also see *Spin-Off,* this section.)

Lace Magazine of the World, 2141 W. 29th St., Long Beach, CA 90810. Muriel Perz, editor. Eleven issues per year. Features original, as well as old, out-of-print patterns; plus charts and complete instructions on laces, embroidery, and needlework.

Ladies' Home Journal Needle & Craft, 641 Lexington Ave., New York, NY 10022. Ann B. Bradley, crafts editor. Semi-annual magazine available on newsstands. Features knitting, crochet, sewing, needlepoint, fiber crafts, and a host of other needle and craft ideas.

The Looming Arts, The Pendleton Shop, P.O. Box 233, Jordan Rd., Seconda, AZ 86336. Mary Pendleton, publisher. A bulletin containing supply sources, instructional articles, and patterns, accompanied by swatches and yarn samples.

McCall's Needlework & Crafts Magazine, 230 Park Ave., New York, NY 10017. Margaret Gilman, managing editor. Quarterly, available on newsstands. Features directions, diagrams, and charts for making various craft and needlework projects.

Make It with Leather, P.O. Box 1386, Ft. Worth, TX 76101. Earl F. Warren, editor. Bimonthly. Features how-to-do-it leathercraft articles illustrated with cutting and carving patterns.

The Miniature Magazine, Carstens Publications, Inc., P.O. Box 700, Newton, NJ 07860. A semi-annual magazine for dollhouse lovers and miniaturists, with how-to information on creating and finishing doll houses and miniature rooms.

Mother Earth News, 105 Stoney Mountain Rd., Hendersonville, NC 28739. A bimonthly publication edited by, and for, people interested in alternative energy and lifestyles, ecology, working with their hands, etc. An increasing number of craft-related articles are planned for future issues.

Mother of all News, Spinning Study Group of Long Island, Stony Brook Craft Centre, Christian Ave., Stony Brook, NY 11790. A quarterly newsletter with articles on spinning and dyeing, useful tips, book reviews, and product information.

National Calendar of Indoor/Outdoor Art Fairs and *National Calendar of Open Competitive Art Exhibitions,* available from Henry Niles, 5423 New Haven Ave., Ft. Wayne, IN 46803. These quarterly publications cover the Midwest and East, with some events in the West.

National Carvers Review, Drawer 693, Chicago, IL 60642. Larry Martin, editor and publisher. Published quarterly by and for woodcarvers, with articles, patterns, hints, and information on tools and woods. Single issue, $1.50.

Needlecraft for Today, P.O. Box 10142, Des Moines, IA 50349. A new monthly devoted to the exploration of the needle, fiber, and fabric arts. With full-size patterns and projects for beginner and experienced needlewomen alike.

Needlepoint Bulletin, Home Federal Bldg., Suite 200, 50 S. U.S. 1 and Indiantown Rd., Jupiter, FL 33458. Bimonthly newsletter for both beginner and professional; with patterns, designs, how-to tips. Sample, $2.50.

Needlepoint News, Box 668, Evanston, IL 60204. Carol LaBranche, editor. Bimonthly devoted exclusively to needlepoint, with techniques, designs, news, book reviews, etc.

Nutshell News, P.O. Box 1144, La Jolla, CA 92038. Catherine MacLaren, editor. A highly regarded quarterly for serious devotees of miniatura. Random sample copy, $1.

Quality Crafts Market (formerly *Craft Market News*), 521 5th Ave., Suite 1700, New York, NY 10017. Marvin David, editor/publisher. A monthly that concentrates on providing new market leads for craftspeople, with articles, tips, trends, and news.

Quilter's Newsletter, Box 394, Wheatridge, CO 80033. Bonnie Leman, editor. Monthly needlework magazine that includes good patterns, how-to information, biographical articles, and historical research on the art of quilting.

Regional Art Fair List, Box 136, Rt. 1, Stockholm, WI 54769. Nelson Brown, publisher. Detailed information on several hundred art/craft fairs in Upper Midwest, notably Illinois, Wisconsin, Minnesota, Iowa, and the Dakotas. Quarterly.

The Rug Hooker News & Views, Kennebunkport, ME 04046. Joan Moshimer, editor. Bimonthly with instructional articles on hooking, designing, and hand-dyeing.

Southern Crafts & Art News (S.C.A.N.), c/o Art Scene, Jim Ready, 1025 No. H St., Lake Worth, FL 33460. Monthly magazine with emphasis on show listings and shops/galleries needing crafts.

Spin-Off, Interweave, 2938 N. County Rd. 13, Loveland, CO 80537. Linda Ligon, editor and publisher. First published in 1977, this annual magazine is a review of up-to-date information and special in-depth articles relating to spinning. 1977 edition, $4 plus 50 cents postage.

Stained Glass Round Table, Box 225, Waldwick, NJ 07463. Martha Roy, editor. Bimonthly national newsletter that serves as an information center and forum for exchange of ideas among stained glass artisans. Issues include articles, projects, patterns, calendar of events.

Studio Potter, Box 172, Warner, NH 03278. Semiannual magazine for the serious potter. Also of interest to students and teachers.

Textile Artists' Newsletter, 5533 College Avenue, Oakland, CA 94618. Susan C. Druding, editor. A quarterly review for weavers, spinners, dyers, and other fiber artists.

Tole World, 429 Boren Ave. N., Seattle, WA 98109. Dale and Arlene Swant, editors and publishers. A bimonthly magazine devoted to the fine art of tole and decorative painting.

Tower Press, Inc., P.O. Box 428, Folly Mill Rd., Seabrook, NH 03874. Publishers of *Stitch 'n Sew, Popular Needlework & Crafts, Aunt Jane's Sewing Circle,* and other bimonthly magazines edited for consumers with an interest in arts, crafts, sewing, and hobbies. Available on newsstands.

Treasure Chest and *The Egg Artist's Journal,* 87 Lewis St., Phillipsburg, NJ 08865. Kit Stansbury, editor and publisher. Two quarterlies for people who enjoy egg decorating as a hobby or profession. Sample of either, $1.50.

The Weaver's Journal, P.O. Box 2049, Boulder, CO 80306. Clotilde Barrett, editor and publisher. Quarterly for textile craftsmen, featuring patterns and techniques.

Weaver's Newsletter, P.O. Box 259, Homer, NY 13077. Cyril M. and Ora Hunter Koch, editors. Published nine times a year (September to May) for active weavers, spinners, and fiber artists. Trends, exhibitions, marketing information, book reviews, etc.

Westart, Box 1396, Auburn, CA 95603, Jean Couzens, editor. A semimonthly newspaper for professional artists and craftspeople, with an emphasis on contemporary work.

Woman's Day Needlework & Handicraft Ideas, Fawcett Publications, Inc., Fawcett Bldg., Greenwich, CT 06830. A consumer magazine available on newsstands; features needlepoint, embroidery, handicrafts, knitting, crocheting, and sewing.

The Workbasket, 4251 Pennsylvania, Kansas City, MO 64111. Roma Rice, editor. A monthly devoted exclusively to the homemaking arts, with emphasis on needlecraft and other handwork.

The Working Craftsman, In late 1978, this magazine merged with *The Crafts Report.* Working Craftsmen, Inc. then changed its name to Craft Books, Inc., and now sells art and craft books to individuals, schools and libraries nationwide. Their address remains the same: P.O. Box 42, Northbrook, IL 60062.

Yankee, Dublin, NH 03444. Monthly magazine featuring articles about the New England Region. Includes a ''Forgotten Arts'' series on New England arts, crafts, etc.

NOTE: Other consumer magazines of possible interest to craft-minded readers will be found in the alphabetical listing, Section VII.

Section II — Organizations

Each of the following organizations offers special benefits of membership, and many publish outstanding periodicals for artists and craftsmen. Readers should write to each organization of interest and request a brochure, along with current membership rates. This list of organizations is given merely to whet the appetite of readers; lengthier lists of national, regional, and local organizations will be found in directories such as *The Goodfellow Catalog* and *Contemporary Crafts Marketplace.*

The American Crafts Council (ACC), 22 W. 55th St., New York, NY 10019. A nonprofit, educational, cultural organization serving a national membership. Publishes *Craft Horizons* magazine and many other publications for craftsmen. Request free information about all ACC publications and membership benefits, which include special insurance plans.

American Society of Artists, Inc., 700 N. Michigan, Chicago, IL 60611. A national organization for professional artists.

Canadian Crafts Council, 46 Elgin St., Suite 16, Ottawa K1P 5K6, Canada. Publishes a bimonthly, *Artisan.*

Canadian Guild of Crafts, 29 Prince Arthur Ave., Toronto, Ontario M5R 1B2, Canada. Membership includes the bimonthly *Craft Dimensions Artisanale.*

Center for the History of American Needlework (C.H.A.N.), P.O. Box 8162, Pittsburgh, PA 15217. Main goal is to legitimatize and document the importance of needlework in America. Activities include special needlework shows and exhibitions, publication of booklets, and the building of a resource library that includes books, periodicals, catalogs, patterns, clippings, pamphlets, and many slides, photographs, and items of needlework. (Donations of any of the above are gratefully accepted. See ''Donating Needlework,'' Sec. IV, Part C.) Members receive C.H.A.N.'s quarterly newsletter.

COSMEP (The Committee of Small Magazine Editors and Publishers), P.O. Box 703, San Francisco, CA 94101. Richard Morris, coordinator. *The* international association of small magazines and presses. Membership is open to any press or periodical, including self-publishers, and includes a helpful newsletter.

Counted Thread Society of America, 3305 S. Newport St., Denver, CO 80224. Elizabeth Stears, editor. Society's purpose is to encourage and promote the practice and knowledge of counted-thread embroidery in all its forms. A quarterly magazine is published for members.

Embroiderer's Guild of America, 6 E. 45th St., Room 1501, New York, NY 10017. This is the American offshoot of the Embroiderer's Guild of England, an educational, nonprofit organization that sets and maintains high standards of design, color, and workmanship in all kinds of embroidery and canvas work. Members receive the quarterly magazine, *Needle Arts.*

Erica Wilson's Creative Needlework Society, 717 Madison Ave., New York, NY 10021. Membership includes quarterly publication, *The Creative Needle.*

Foundation for the Community of Artists, 280 Broadway, Suite 412, New York, NY 10007. Nonprofit organization working for the benefit of artists everywhere. Members receive *Art Workers News.*

193

Handweavers Guild of America, Inc., 65 LaSalle Rd., P.O. Box 7-374, W. Hartford, CT 06107. Nonprofit volunteer organization of some 20,000 weavers, spinners, and dyers. Members receive *Shuttle, Spindle & Dyepot* magazine. Organization also publishes annual directories and other publications.

International Guild of Craft Journalists, Authors and Photographers, 3632 Ashworth North, Seattle, WA 98103. A loosely structured organization that works to enhance the professionalism and prestige of people who communicate in the crafts field via the written word. Members receive a press card and a newsletter, published irregularly.

International Wood Collectors' Society. Send self-addressed, stamped envelope to receive an application and brochure from Willard G. Cookman, 3155 Edsel Dr., Trenton, MI 48183. This nonprofit organization was established for the mutual pleasure and benefit of all persons interested in working with wood; members receive a newsletter.

Minnesota Crafts Council, P.O. Box 1182, Minneapolis, MN 55440. Membership includes subscription to *Craft Connection,* a nontechnical tabloid published six times a year and designed to foster a sense of community among Midwestern craftspeople.

National Association of Women Business Owners, 2000 P St., N.W., Washington, DC 20036. Organization's purpose is to encourage women to establish and operate their own businesses; to advise and assist them with reports, newsletters, directories, workshops, seminars, etc. They also offer group benefits for insurance, financing, purchasing, and credit. Women may elect to join the organization or simply subscribe to its newsletter, *Statement.*

National Carvers Museum Foundation, 14960 Woodcarver Rd., P.O. Box 389, Monument, CO 80132. The foundation operates a growing carver's museum and an educational program, plus *The Mallet,* a monthly filled with how-to projects, patterns, information about carvers and their activities, etc.

National Quilting Association, Inc., P.O. Box 62, Greenbelt, MD 20770. Organization has chapters in the U.S. Membership benefits include instruction at meetings, exhibitions, annual juried show, and quarterly publication, *Patchwork Patter.*

194 National Society of Tole & Decorative Painters, Inc., P.O. Box 808, Newton, KS 67114. Aim of this nonprofit organization is to preserve and enrich all forms of decorative painting. They hold an annual convention, and publish an annual directory, as well as a quarterly called *The Decorative Painter.*

National Woodcarvers Association, (NWCA) 7424 Miami Ave., Cincinnati, OH 45243. Membership includes bimonthly magazine for carvers called *Chip Chats.*

Ontario Crafts Council, 346 Dundas St. W., Toronto, Ontario M5T 1G5, Canada. Membership includes bimonthly magazine, *Craftsman.* This organization has also published a directory of Canadian craft guilds and organizations, plus a directory of suppliers for craft materials.

Society of Craft Designers, Box 2176, Newburgh, NY 12550. Membership is open to any individual who develops new products for the consumer craft field, invents new materials, prepares new formulations of consumer materials, or writes for the consumer craft field. Only professionals will be able to afford the society's steep initiation fee.

Southern Highland Handicraft Guild, 15 Reddick Rd., P.O. Box 9145, Asheville, NC 28805. A very special organization. Publishes *Highland Highlights* newsletter; sponsors two craftsmen's fairs annually in Asheville, NC and Gatlinburg, TN; offers two 15-min. color/sound movies for public and private showings. Welcomes as members all who are "Friends of the Crafts."

Stained Glass Association of America, 1125 Wilmington Ave., St. Louis, MO 63111. For professionals. Aim is to promote the finest development of the stained glass craft. Membership includes a quarterly, *Stained Glass.*

The Stained Glass Club, P.O. Box 244, Norwood, NJ 07648. Membership is open to all who enjoy working with stained glass, beginners and professionals alike. Members receive subscription to quarterly *Glass Workshop,* plus discounts on supplies and materials.

Surface Design Association, School of Art, E. Carolina University, Box 2704, Greenville, NC 27834. Group's primary aim is to improve communication among artists, designers, industry, and teachers working in surface design on textiles and related media. Membership includes a newsletter.

United Maine Craftsmen, Dutton Hill Rd., Gray, ME 04039. A nonprofit, educational organization with membership open to all. Publishes an annual membership directory of Maine craftsmen, shops, and supply sources as well as a periodical, *The Craft Tradesman.*

Section III — Trade Magazines

Trade magazines are not meant to be read by consumers, but consumers-turned-craft sellers will find such publications a gold mine of information, and the key to finding necessary supplies and materials. Use your business letterhead to request subscription information about any of the following publications:

Ceramic Scope, Box 48643, Los Angeles, CA 90048. Circulation is limited to dealers, distributors, manufacturers, importers, and teachers in the ceramic hobby field. Published monthly. Issues an annual ''Buyer's Guide'' of enormous value to anyone who needs source-of-supply information.

Gift & Tableware Reporter, 1515 Broadway, New York, NY 10036. A monthly trade publication edited for the needs of active dealers in the gift and tableware market. Publishes an annual directory, *Gift Guide.*

Gifts & Decorative Accessories, 51 Madison Ave., New York, NY 10010. A monthly for retailers. A subscription also brings the annual *Gift and Decorative Accessory Buyer's Guide.* (See Sec. IV.)

Homesewing Trade News, 129 Broadway, Lynbrook, NY 11563. The national newspaper of fashion fabrics, sewing notions, needlework, and sewing machines. Monthly. Subscription includes *Resource Directory.*

National Needlework News, 171 Guadalupe, Sonoma, CA 95476. A trade newspaper edited for needlework buyers (shopowners).

Playthings, 51 Madison Ave., New York, NY 10010. A trade publication serving the hobby industry.

Profitable Craft Merchandising, News Plaza, P.O. Box 1790, Peoria, IL 61656. Published monthly for craft retailers, wholesalers, and manufacturers.

Sew Business, 666 Fifth Ave., New York, NY 10019. Monthly trade magazine for retailers in the home-sewing industry, and an excellent guide to suppliers in the field.

Section IV — Directories/Books/Other Publications

This section is divided into three groups: A. Directories; B. Books; C. Other Publications. *All the publications listed in these three groups can be ordered from a source whose address is listed elsewhere in this chapter.* In parenthesis after each publication's description, the reader will find the seller's name, along with a Roman Numeral that relates to the section where the seller's address will be alphabetically listed. Prices have been included only when it is expected they will not change in the future; no guarantees, however.

A. Directories

The Best Years Catalogue, by Len Biegel (G. P. Putnam's Sons). A source book for older Americans covering 11 areas of concern, from food to creative leisure. Further details available from the author. (Len Biegel, VII)

Contemporary Crafts Marketplace ('77-'78 Edition), compiled by the American Crafts Council. Published biennially. Includes: courses, suppliers, events, reference books, shops/galleries, periodicals, services, audiovisual materials, organizations. ($15.95 ppd. from R.R. Bowker Co., VII)

The CraftsPeople Directory 1978. New regional directory serving artisans in the three-state area of New York, New Jersey, and Connecticut; a consumer's guide that enables buyers to deal directly with craftspeople. ($2.95 plus 60 cents P&H from CraftsPeople Directory, VII)

Craftworker's Market. First published in October 1978, this new annual is aimed at helping craftsmen sell one-of-a-kind designer crafts and handmade production items. (Writer's Digest, VII)

Directory of Suppliers for Craft Materials (in Canada). Listing of Canadian craft retail and wholesale suppliers, divided by medium within each province and region. (Ontario Craft Council, II)

The Gift and Decorative Accessory Buyer's Guide. 27,000 listings of manufacturers, importers, distributors, plus sources for manufacturing and assembling materials, and classifications of trade names, trade shows, industry associations, etc. (Gifts & Dec. Accessories, III).

The Goodfellow Catalog of Wonderful Things, by Christopher Weills. A catalog in the truest sense — there are over 1000 things you can order from it, directly from the craftsmen — this is also a directory of resources, listing organizations, publications, and books. Includes photos of the work of several hundred craftspeople, along with a personal statement of each craftsperson represented. ($7.95 plus 85 cents shipping/handling from Goodfellow Catalog, VII)

HGA Education Directory. A guide to where to study the fiber arts; universities, schools, studios; with articles related to the teaching of fiber arts. ($3 from Handweavers Guild, II)

Handicrafts Supply Directory. A guide to how and where to get all types of hobby arts and handicrafts. ($3 from R.P.H. Mfg. Co., VII)

How To Get All the Free Benefits and Services the U.S. Government Owes People Who Love Sewing, Needlework, Handicrafts and Hobbies. ($1.95 plus 25 cents P&H from Mark Weiss, VII)

The Mail Order Crafts Catalogue by Margaret Boyd (Chilton Book Co.). A listing of nearly 1600 companies, stores, and individuals that sell all types of craft materials via the mail. Listings include availability and cost of catalogs and materials carried. (Chilton Book Co., VII)

Marietta College Crafts Directory, USA, Edition I. Directory of some 5000 artists and craftspeople, plus a thousand crafts organizations. (Marietta College, Attn. Arthur Howard Winer, VII)

National Directory of Valuable Free Things for People Who Are into Sewing, Needlework, Handicrafts and Hobbies. ($1.95 plus 25 cents P&H from Mark Weiss, VII)

National Guide to Craft Supplies by Judith Glassman (Van Nostrand Reinhold). Over 600 wholesale and retail supply stores listed by state and craft. (Check library. No longer available from publisher.)

Suppliers Directory published by the HGA. Listing of some 600 firms specializing in supplies and equipment for weavers, spinners, dyers, and other fiber artisans. (Handweavers Guild, II)

TWC Source Directory, 1978 edition, Includes information sources, new products and catalogs, where to obtain art/craft films, slides, tapes, directories, plus learning opportunities, grants, scholarships, workshops, etc. ($2.95 ppd. from Working Craftsman, I)

Wholesale Arts & Crafts Directory. Lists hundreds of wholesale distributors and manufacturers specializing in arts and craft lines. Regularly updated. ($3 from R.P.H. Mfg. Co., VII)

Writer's Market published annually by Writer's Digest. Lists book and magazine markets, syndicates, contests, and awards; writer's workshops, and agents. (Writer's Digest, VII)

B. Books

Comments have been given only for those books not discussed in the text of *Creative Cash*. (Refer to the index to locate a particular book's mention in the text. For informaion about all books available from any author mentioned, write

that author requesting a price list. Enclose a self-addressed, stamped envelope.)

Again, the names and Roman Numerals in parenthesis are your key to locating the seller's complete address elsewhere in this chapter.

Approaching Design Through Nature, The Quiet Joy, by Grace O. Martin. (Viking Press, VII)

The Art and Craft of Displaying Arts and Crafts by Margaret Bovenkamp. Scheduled for publication by the author in mid-'79. (Bovenkamp, VII)

Career Opportunities in Crafts by Elyse Sommer (Crown). (Sommer, VIII)

The Crafts Business Encyclopedia by Michael Scott (Harcourt Brace Jovanovich). (The Crafts Report, I)

The Craftsman's Survival Manual — Making A Full or Part-Time Living from Your Crafts by George and Nancy Wettlaufer (Prentice-Hall). A very popular book with professional craftsmen and those who aspire to be professionals, by two full-time potters who learned everything the hard way. (Wettlaufer, VIII)

Craftsmen in Business — A Guide to Financial Management & Taxes by H. W. Connaughton. Concise information in easy-to-read format, with emphasis on organizing and managing all financial aspects of a business. (American Crafts Council, II)

The Creative Woman's Getting-It-All-Together-At-Home Book by Jean Ray Laury (Van Nostrand Reinhold). (Laury, VIII)

Design and Sell Toys, Games & Crafts by Filis Frederick (Chilton). Excellent guidebook for anyone interested in creating and marketing a volume item. Includes a great deal of information about the most popular toys of our time, how they were created, and by whom. (Chilton Book Co.. VII)

Dover Pictorial Archive Books. (See ''Design Books'' in ''Other Publications,'' Part C of this section.)

Financing Your Business by Egon W. Loffel. One of a series of books in the Small Business Profits Program. For everyone who owns, operates, or wants to start a small business. (David McKay Co. VII)

How To Create Your Own Designs by Dona Z. Meilach (Doubleday). (Meilach, VIII)

How To Earn More Money from Your Crafts by Merle E. Dowd (Doubleday). A crafts marketing book whose emphasis is on making a profit from crafts. Recommended for both hobbyists and serious craftspeople. (Dowd, VIII)

How To Make Money with Your Crafts by Leta Clark (Wm. Morrow). Women who are seeking personal freedom and a sense of self, and who are trying to earn money from their crafts, will appreciate this marketing book, which is not only informative, but very readable. (William Morrow, VII)

How To Publish, Promote and Sell Your Book (4th Edition) by Joseph V. Goodman. A good guide for the self publisher, it includes addresses of review media, book jobbers, etc. (Adams Press, VII)

How To Sell Your Arts & Crafts — A Marketing Guide for Creative People by Loretta Holz (Chas. Scribner's Sons). A well-researched, detailed manual covering all aspects of arts and crafts marketing, especially suited to beginners. (Holz, VIII)

How To Start and Operate A Mail-Order Business by Simon & Simon (McGraw Hill Book Co., VII)

Opening Your Own Retail Store by Lyn Taetzsch (Henry Regnery Co.). Everything you need to know to survive in the world of small business; how to be successful in retail sales, whatever type of shop you decide to open. (Contemporary Books, VII)

The Woman's Guide To Starting A Business by Claudia Jessup and Genie Chipps. How to turn a bright idea into a profit-making enterprise; includes interviews with women in every field from retailing to maintenance and repair services. (Holt, Rinehart & Winston, VII)

Yes, You Can Teach by Florence Nelson. (Carma Press, VII)

C. Other Publications

This is merely a sampling of the many unusual publications available to craftspeople today. Read the ads in various craft periodicals to find other helpful booklets, catalogs, and reprints. As before, the seller of each publication is indicated in parentheses, and the Roman Numeral tells you in which section of this chapter to look for the seller's complete address.

American Crafts — A Rich Heritage and a Rich Future, Progam Aid 1026, Free. (Farmer Coop Svc., VII)

Catalog of Textile Books (Weaving, spinning, dyeing). 50 cents. (The Unicorn, VII)

Consignment Forms (mentioned in Chapter 7). 50 for $3. (The Unicorn, VII)

The Cooperative Approach to Crafts, Program Aid No. 1001. Free. (Farmer Coop. Svc. VII)

Copyright Pamphlets, free. (Copyright Office, VII)

Craft Magazine Reprints; various topics, 35 cents and up. (Artisan Crafts, VII)

Design Books — a free flyer describes several design books in the Dover Pictorial Archive Series and includes a few sample designs. (Artisan Crafts, VII)

Donating Needlework & Textiles to C.H.A.N. Free brochure, available for a stamped, self-addressed envelope, business size, marked ''Donating.'' For anyone interested in having a special piece of needlework preserved in the Center for the History of Needlework & Textiles. (C.H.A.N., II)

Encouraging American Craftsmen, No. 3600-0010, 45 cents. (Supt. of Documents, VII)

Fear of Filing: A Beginner's Handbook on Recordkeeping and Federal Taxes, For Dancers, Other Performers, Writers, and Visual Artists. ($1.50 plus 50 cents postage from Volunteer Lawyers for the Arts, VII)

Federal Trade Commission Rules & Regulations. Several free pamphlets available, as discussed in text. (FTC, VII)

General Information Concerning Patents, Booklet, 75 cents. (Supt. of Documents, VII)

Grants, Information on. Free. (Nat'l Endowment for the Arts, VII)

The Handcraft Business, Vol. 10 No. 8, from the series, "The Small Business Reporter." Free at any Bank of America community office, or $2 if ordered by mail. (Bank of America, VII)

Health Hazards Literature "Health Hazards in the Arts & Crafts" by Bertram W. Carnow, M.D. ($2.35 ppd. from Hazards in the Arts, VII); "Health Hazards Manual for Artists" by Michael McCann, Ph.D. ($4 ppd from Art Hazards Information Center, VII); "Health Hazards in the Arts & Crafts," free pamphlet (Chicago Lung Assn., VII); "Work Is Dangerous to Your Health," a handbook of health hazards in the workplace, and what you can do about them by Stellman/Daum. (Random House, VII); "Don't Let Your Pottery Poison Someone," magazine reprint with information about lead glazes and how to have pottery tested for lead ($1 from Artisan Crafts, VII); "Protecting Your Health," magazine reprints of Gail Barazani's column. ($1 each from Working Craftsman, I)

How To Get A Patent. (75 cents from Supt. of Documents, VII)

How To Sell to Museum Shops. Marketing booklet. (Quality Crafts Market, I)

How To Start A Cooperative, Educational Circular No. 18. Free. (Farmer Cooperative Svc., VII)

The Individual Artist: Record Keeping, Methods of Accounting, Income and Itemized Deductions for Federal Income Tax. ($1.50 ppd. from Volunteer Lawyers, VII)

Internal Revenue Service Pamphlets: "Tax Information on Operating a Business in Your Home"; "Tax Information on Business Expenses and Operating Losses"; "Tax Guide for Small Businesses." Free (IRS, VII)

Mail Order Enterprises, Vol. 11 No. 7. From the series, "The Small Business Reporter." Free at any Bank of America community office, or $1 if ordered by mail. (Bank of America, VII)

Planning Your Craft Show. A booklet for groups who intend to sponsor craft fairs. (60 cents stamps or coin from United Maine Craftsmen, II)

The Potential of Handicrafts As A Viable Economic Force: An Overview. (65 cents from U.S. Govt. Printing Office, VII)

Printing for the Craftsman. 3-pg. magazine reprint; discusses how to select a printer and prepare camera-ready copy. ($1 from Artisan Crafts, VII)

The Publicity Handbook — A Guide for Publicity Chairmen. (25 cents from Sperry & Hutchinson, VII)

Small Business Administration Pamphlets. A wide range of management and technical publications designed to help owner-managers and prospective owners of small business. Ask for free booklets No. SBA 115A & 115B, plus their "For Sale Booklets." (Much of this information can be applied to crafts businesses.) (SBA, VII)

Threads in Action by Virginia Harvey. Rare fiber periodical no longer in publication, but all issues remain in print and available to all interested in the fiber arts. Macrame artists will find the series especially valuable. (HTH Publishers, VII)

Your Portable Museum. A free catalog describing over 100 slide kits and filmstrips, plus motion films documenting significant exhibitions or crafts. (American Crafts Council, II)

Section V — Special Services

Artworkspace, 5 E. 17th St., 6th floor, New York, NY 10003. A cooperative crafts studio dedicated to offering assistance to nonmembers through its free telephone information service, "A Fair Exchange." Craftspeople may call (212) 691-2821 between 11 a.m. and 6 p.m. weekdays for information about fairs, shows, and block parties throughout the greater New York area.

Alice Allen Bidwell, 90 River Drive, RD 2, Box 107, Titusville, NJ 08560. Will work with craftspeople to create special artwork, illustrations, and design for brochures, flyers, etc. Write for information and estimate.

Bookquick, Inc. (Attn. David Tarbell), 160 Eagle Rock Ave., Box B, Roseland, NJ 07068. Craft books can be ordered at discounts from this company, which handles orders for virtually any of 475,000 titles listed in "Books in Print." Request a free "Bookquick Order Card" for additional information.

Gerald E. Ely, Craft Specialist, Farmer Cooperative Service, U.S. Dept. of Agriculture, Washington, DC 20250.

Provides technical assistance to local state and regional craft associations to develop an orderly marketing system and improve management.

Fay Printing Center, Inc. 1923 S. National, P.O. Box 3373, Springfield, MO 65804. Attn: Alice Clark. This firm offers quality printing services and will be happy to work with *Creative Cash* readers on any printing job, large or small. A free "Quick-Print" price sheet is available upon request, and special quotations will be made on all other jobs.

Stewart W. Goodwin, Photographic Specialty, Box 81, South Ryegate, VT 05069. Offers special photographic services for craftspeople. Mention this book when requesting additional information, and receive a special discount on first order.

George W. St. Georges, 7 Victoria Lane, South Hadley, MA 01075. Specialist in calligraphy, lettering, engrossing, illuminating. Will design letterheads, calling cards, etc. Inquire.

Section VI — Packaging, Printing, and Publicity Aids

Bucher Brothers, 729 Leo St., Dayton, OH 45404. Offers self-adhesive and regular gummed "Mini Stickers" that can be imprinted and used to label craft merchandise.

Creative Packaging Company, 4411 Hollins Rd. N.E., Roanoke, VA 24012. Selection of over 100 hinged-lid plastic boxes. Imprinting available.

Gaylord Specialties Corp., 225 Fifth Ave., Suite 443, New York, NY 10010. Wide range of colorful wrapping supplies and ribbons, plus tote bags and sacks that can be imprinted with your business name. Also carries personalized name seals.

Howard Decorative Packaging, Inc., 7300 N. Lawndale Ave., Skokie, IL 60076. Giftware boxes; pressure-sensitive foil labels in decorative shapes imprinted to your order.

Miles Kimball Co., 41 W. 8th Ave., Oshkosh, WI 54901. Your source for "Photo Stamps." Request free catalog.

Sealed Air Corp., 3800 W. 45th St., Chicago, IL 60632. Has a special line of bags, mailers, and cushioning materials for protection of merchandise during shipment, such as bubble-pack containers and lightweight mailers. Request price list for quantity purchases.

The Stationery House, P.O. Box 1393, Hagerstown, MD 21740. Free catalog of stationery, letterheads, envelopes, business cards, etc.

20th Century Plastics, Inc., 3628 Crenshaw Blvd., Los Angeles, CA 90016. Catalog features vinyl products, including zipper bags that can be imprinted.

United States Box Corp., 1296 McCarter Highway, Newark, NJ 07104. Offers a catalog of stock packaging — folding and set-up boxes, mailing containers, boxes with acetate covers, and air cushion bags and padding.

Vermont Business Forms Co., Business Card Div., RD 4, Montpelier, VT 05602. The craftsman's source for creative business cards. Free brochure on request.

Adams Press, 30 W. Washington St., Chicago, IL 60602

Art Hazards Infomation Center, Center for Occupational Hazards, Inc., 5 Beekman St., New York, NY 10038 (Phone: 212-227-6220)

Artisan Crafts, c/o Countryside Books, 200 James St., Barrington, IL 60010.

Association & Society Insurance Co., 13975 Connecticut Ave., Suite 204, Silver Spring, MD 20906

Ayottes' Designery, Center Sandwich, NH 03227

The Baker & Taylor Co., P.O. Box 4500, 6 Kirby Ave., Somerville, NJ 08876

Bank of America, Dept. 3120, P.O. Box 37000, San Francisco, CA 94137.

Better Homes and Gardens, 1716 Locust St., Des Moines, IA 50336

Len Biegel Associates, 5914 Greentree Rd., Bethesda, MD 20034

Margaret Bovenkamp, 130 E. 8 St. N., Newton, IA 50208

R.R. Bowker Publishing Co., 1180 Ave. of the Americas, New York, NY 10036

Bucilla, 30-20 Thomson Ave., Long Island City, NY 11101

Bureau of Consumer Protection, Div. of Special Statutes, 6th & Pennsylvania Ave., N.W., Washington, DC 20580

Carma Press, Box 12633, St..Paul, MN 55112

Center for Occupational Hazards, Inc., (See ''Art Hazards Information Center,'' above.)

Changing Times, The Kiplinger Service for Families, 1729 H St., N.W., Washington, DC 20006

Chicago Lung Association, 1441 W. Washington, Chicago, IL 60607

Chilton Book Company, Radnor, PA 19089

Consumer Products Safety Commission, Bureau of Compliance, 5401 Westbard Ave., Bethesda, MD 20207

Contemporary Books, Inc. (Formerly Henry Regnery), 180 N. Michigan Ave., Chicago, IL 60601

Copyright Office, Library of Congress, Washington, DC 20550

Craft Course Publishers, P.O. Box 280, Rosemead, CA 91770

CraftsPeople Directory, 905 Grant Place, N. Bellmore, NY 11710

Crown Publishers Inc., One Park Ave., New York, NY 10016

Division of Law Enforcement, U.S. Fish & Wildlife Svc., Dept. of the Interior, Washington, DC 20240

Doubleday & Co., Inc., 245 Park Ave., New York, NY 10017

Dover Publications, 180 Varick St., New York, NY 10014

Family Circle, 488 Madison Ave., New York, NY 10022

Farmer Cooperative Service, U.S. Dept. of Agriculture, 500 12th St. S.W., Washington, DC 20250

Fay Printing Center, Inc., P.O. Box 3373, Springfield, MO 65804

Federal Trade Commission, Div. of Legal & Public Records, Washington, DC 20580

Goodfellow Catalog of Wonderful Things, P.O. Box 4520, Berkeley, CA 94704

Good Housekeeping, 959 Eighth Ave., New York, NY 10019

Hazards in the Arts, Box 110, Rt. 1, Steuben, WI 54657

HTH Publishers, P.O. Box 468, Freeland, WA 98249

Hobby Industry of America, 319 E. 54th St., Elmwood Park, NJ 07407

Holt, Rinehart & Winston, 383 Madison Ave., New York, NY 10017

House Beautiful, 717 Fifth Ave., New York, NY 10022

Internal Revenue Service, Washington, DC 20224

Ladies' Home Journal, 641 Lexington Ave., New York, NY 10022

Lee Wards Creative Crafts, 1200 St. Charles St., Elgin, IL 60120

McGraw Hill Book Co., 1221 Avenue of the Americas, New York, NY 10020

David McKay Co., Inc., 750 3rd Ave., New York, NY 10017

Macmillan Publishing Co., Inc., 866 Third Ave., New York, NY 10022

Mangelsen and Sons, Inc., 8200 ''J'' St., Omaha, NE 68127

Marietta College, Marietta, OH 45750

Miles Kimball Co., 41 W. 8th Ave., Oshkosh, WI 54901

William Morrow and Co., 105 Madison Ave., New York, NY 10016

National Bureau of Standards, Technical Bldg. B167, Standards Development Services Section, Washington, DC 20234

National Endowment for the Arts, Attn: Crafts Coordinator, 806 15th St., N.W., Washington, DC 20506

The National Slide Registry of American Artists and Craftsmen, 806 15th St., N.W., Suite 426, Washington, DC 20005

Open Door Enterprises, Inc., 1201 Comstock St., Santa Clara, CA 95050

Prentice-Hall, Englewood Cliffs, NJ 07632

R.P.H. Mfg. Co., 24 Winter St., Stamford, CT 06905

Random House, Vintage Books Dept., 457 Hohn Rd., Westminster, MD 21157

Charles Scribner's Sons, 597 5th Ave., New York, NY 10017

Simon & Schuster, 1230 Avenue of the Americas, New York, NY 10020

Small Business Administration, Washington, DC 20416

Sperry & Hutchinson Co., Consumer Svcs., Sperry & Hutchinson Bldg., 330 Madison Ave., New York, NY 10017

The Stitchery, Inc., Wellesley Hills, MA 02181

Superintendent of Documents, U.S. Government Printing Office, Washington, DC 20402

The Unicorn, Box 645, Rockville, MD 20851

Van Nostrand Reinhold Co., 135 W. 50th St., New York, NY 10020

The Viking Press, 625 Madison Ave., New York, NY 10022

Volunteer Lawyers for the Arts, 36 W. 44th St., New York, NY 10036

Watson-Guptill, 1515 Broadway, New York, NY 10036

Mark Weiss and Daughters, P.O. Box 402091, Miami Beach, FL 33140

Woman's Day, 1515 Broadway, New York, NY 10036

Writer's Digest, 9933 Alliance Rd., Cincinnati, OH 45242

Section VIII — Individuals Who Contributed to the Text of *Creative Cash*

(NOTE: A few contributors chose not to be listed here.)

Donna Adam, Crafts Incredible, 7217 Mission Rd., Prairie Village, KS 66208

Alfred Atkins, The Village Smithy, 204 Hubert Hollow Rd., Spencer, NY 14883

Pat (Mrs. Elbert) Baker, Rt. 1, Centerville, TN 37033

Carol Ann Bernier, Bernier Studio, Rt. 25, Wentworth Village, NH 03282

Margaret A. Boyd, 3511 Rushing Rd., Augusta, GA 30906

Lassie Bradshaw, c/o Georgia Mountain Arts Products, Inc., Box 67, Tallulah Falls, GA 30573

Judy Bridge, Judy Bridge Originals, 1712 Field Rd., Sarasota, FL 33581

Ayn Chase, Box 1207, Oak Bluffs, Martha's Vineyard, MA 02557

Betty Christy, Tree Toys, P.O. Box 492, Hinsdale, IL 60521

Mark Davis, Sugar Camp, Rt. 2, Rhinelander, WI 54501

Dianne Dolowich, CraftsPeople Directory, 905 Grant Place, N. Bellmore, NY 11710

Joni DeBus, 6215 Palm Ave., Riverside, CA 92506

Merle E. Dowd, 7438 S.E. 40th St., Mercer Island, WA 98040

Miriam K. Fankhauser, House of Pearl, 6525 N. Cr. 15, Rt. 1, Box 218B, Green Springs, OH 44836

Marti Fleischer, 128 Monticello Rd., Oak Ridge, TN 37830

Horman & Maria Foose, 17 W. Spruce St., Fleetwood, PA 19522

Carolyn Handy, Rt. 1, Hanover, IL 61041

Dorothy Harris & Kay Radcliffe, Artworkspace, 5 E. 17th St., 6th Floor, New York, NY 10003

Virginia Harvey, P.O. Box 468, Freeland, WA 98249

Loretta Holz, 97 Grandview Ave., N. Plainfield, NJ 07060

Harry Houpt, P.O. Box 2, Worcester, PA 19490

Bucky King, King Bros. Ranch, Box 371, Buffalo Star Rt., Sheridan, WY 82801

Jean Ray Laury, 25090 Auberry Rd., Clovis, CA 93612

Alice W. Leeds, 34-20 78th St., Jackson Hts., NY 11372

Dave Leitem, 409 New Castle Rd., Butler, PA 16001

Linda Ligon, 2938 N. County Rd. 13, Loveland, CO 80537

Bonny Cook Lowry, The Country Craftsmen, Rt. 1, Box 529, Long Beach, WA 98631

Joan McGovern, The Final Touch, W404 Heather Ridge, Mantua, NJ 08051

Raymond Martell, P.O. Box 107, Little Falls, NJ 07424

Jude Martin, Rt. 7, Box 215, Clinton, TN 37716

Dona Z. Meilach, 2018 Saliente Way, Carlsbad, CA 92008

Evelyn Mendes, The Patchwork Co., 1211 Wilmette Ave., Wilmette, IL 60091

Pamela M. Milroy, Global Designs, 1331 Atkinson Rd., Libertyville, IL 60048

Sandy Mooney, 3422 Beveridge Rd., Flint, MI 48504

Lois Moyer, Lo Lo Bags, 700 Northwest Highway, Des Plaines, IL 60016

Marian H. Mumby, The Mumby Bead Co., P.O.Box 1743, Costa Mesa, CA 92626

Margo Daws Pontius, 224 Berkeley Dr., Neenah, WI 54956

Dale C. Prohaska, Jr., Love-Built Toys & Crafts, 2907 Lake Forest Rd., P.O. Box 5459, Tahoe City, CA 95730

Audrey & Ray Punzel, Punzel's Primitives, Rt. 1 Westboro, WI 54490

Robert Raffelli, 1020 Descanso Drive, La Canada, CA 91011

Bill Reed, 1108 Quincy St., Parkersburg, WV 26101

Carol Reeves, Reeves Knotique, Box 5011 AB, Riverside, CA 92517

Marion Schenk, Attorney at Law, 1931 Bradley Pl., Chicago, IL 60613

Joyce Ronald Smith, 15 Keene St., Providence, RI 02906

Elyse Sommer, P.O. Box E, Woodmere, NY 11598

Connie A. Stano, The Greenfield Needlewomen, P.O. Box 464, Greenfield, IN 46140

Gail Steinberg, Jasmine & Bread, Inc., 219 Xenia St., Yellow Springs, OH 45387

Linda Markuly Szilvasy, c/o Mr. & Mrs. P. Markuly, 2422 Benton, Granite City, IL 62040

Margaret Thompson, Maggie's Mini Mottos, 993 W. Outer Drive, Oak Ridge, TN 37830

Ruby Tobey, 2305 W. 32nd South, Wichita, KS 67217

Lyndall Toothman, Rt. 4, Box 354, Ashland, KY 41101

Pat Virch, 1506 Lynn Ave., Marquette, MI 49855

George & Nancy Wettlaufer, 12 E. Lake St., Skaneateles, NY 13152

Virginia Wise, Wises-on-High Banks, Rt. 3, N. River Rd., Tiffin, OH 44883

Colette Wolff, Platypus, Box 396, Planetarium Station, 200 W. 82nd St., New York, NY 10024

Please mention *Creative Cash* in all your correspondence with those listed in this chapter. Thank you.

Index

207

214

215